Authors' Praise for *Writing Alchemy:*
How to Write Fast and Deep

Writing Alchemy is the Next Best Thing. It will help you create purpose-driven writing, develop a more productive writing practice that makes better use of your time and energy, and take more pleasure from the creative process....You'll find something you can use on every page--and it's fun to read, too! - **Susan Wittig Albert (www.susanalbert.com) memoirist and NYT best-selling author of the China Bayles series and other mysteries**

Deconstruction could easily become the buzz word for anyone writing family stories. It's a user-friendly, step-by-step method of gathering detailed information before the writing begins....It's fun and fast. I'm using it as I write my manuscript "Living with 12 Men." - **Betty Auchard (www.bettyauchard.com) award-winning author of** *Dancing in My Nightgown* **and** *The Home for the Friendless*

Writing Alchemy is one of the most exciting books about writing I have read in a long while....This book is indispensable for not only memoir writers, but writers of fiction as well. *Writing Alchemy* is going on my shelf, right next to Natalie Goldberg's *Writing Down the Bones!* - **Pamela Jane Bell (www.pamelajane.com) author of 13 popular children's books; she's currently writing her memoir**

Deconstruction to the rescue! If you feel your writing is missing some "magic" element, this is the book for you! Using analogies, Matilda Butler and Kendra Bonnett present the left-brained processes of story construction in a right-brain friendly way....And you can begin improving from the very first chapter! - **Robyn Chausse (www.wow-womenonwriting.com) writer and Book Blog Tour Manager for WOW! Women on Writing**

Writing Alchemy is an invaluable resource to aspiring authors. With fresh insights drawn from social science, the guide offers fun and creative new tools for overcoming writer's block. - **Jerramy Fine (www.jerramyfine.com) author of** *Someday My Prince Will Come* **and** *Bright Young Royals*

Writing Alchemy is going to have a permanent home on top of my writing desk and will become well-worn and dog-eared in no time....I know I'll be using *Writing Alchemy* in my future writing projects. - **Linda Hoye (www.lindahoye.com) author of *Two Hearts: An Adoptee's Journey Through Grief to Gratitude***

Readers will be inspired and empowered to create stories that move and resonate, filled with deep and memorable characters who converse in dynamic and organic dialogue. I couldn't wait to finish the book so that I could bring what I learned to my current novel in progress. - **Leslie Gilbert-Lurie (www.bending-towardthesun.com) author of *Bending Toward the Sun***

Writing Alchemy helps you to translate your memories into an artistic construct. It very effectively reminds you that fact is far more fascinating than fiction. Having read *Writing Alchemy*, I now know how to practice memoir writing in my daily emotional life. - **Jid Lee (www.jidlee.com) Associate Professor of English and award-winning author of *To Kill a Tiger***

Oh, if my client X had only read this book first, my job would have been so much easier! (On the other hand, maybe they wouldn't have needed me to rewrite and I'd be out of a job!)....Highly recommended! **- Kim Pearson (www.primary-sources.com) poet, ghostwriter, editor and award-winning author of *Making History***

If you ever wanted your readers to "Be There Now," this is the book for you. *Writing Alchemy*...[is] a handbook to turn the raw materials of our memories into writing gold. - **Janet Grace Riehl (www.riehlife.com) poet and author of *Sightlines: A Poet's Diary* and companion audiobook**

Writing Alchemy is a finely detailed guide to writing skillfully and purposefully....Drawing on research in the social sciences and tested by the authors' own students, *Writing Alchemy* can help memoir writers make their own pasts come alive for their readers. - **Hawley Roddick (www.hawleyroddick.com) novelist and author of *Your Memories: Saving the Stories of Your Life and Work***

Writing Alchemy...is an encyclopedia and workbook for writers of all genres. I wish I had had *Writing Alchemy* right beside me when I started my novel. Now I have to go back and insert all the things I've learned. - **Madeline Sharples (www.madeline40.blogspot. com) poet and author of memoir *Leaving the Hall Light On: A Mother's Memoir of Living with Her Son's Bipolar Disorder and Surviving His Suicide***

The revolutionary ideas in *Writing Alchemy* jumpstart the process through the use of pre-writing exercises that...guide the reader through the secrets behind the alchemy, the craft behind the magic, until your own important life narrative shimmers upon the page. - **Sue William Silverman (www.suewilliamsilverman) poet and award-winning author of two memoirs and *Fearless Confessions: A Writer's Guide to Memoir***

Writing Alchemy is a fresh, dynamic approach to writing...it is anything but a rigid set of rules and guidelines....Once you try it, *Writing Alchemy*'s innovative approach to creative writing will become indispensable to your writing practice. - **Amber Lea Starfire (www.writingthroughlife.com) writing teacher, editor, author of *Week by Week: A Year's Worth of Journaling Prompts & Meditations***

[Butler and Bonnett] show how to assemble a story by first detailing the essential parts...From there, it's a matter of assembling the parts into a narrative. Easy, right? No, but with Butler and Bonnett as guides, the transformation from raw material to memoir may well be magic. - **Susan J. Tweit (www.susanjtweit.com) naturalist and award-winning author of *Walking Nature Home: A Life's Journey***

The deeper you get into *Writing Alchemy* the more sense it makes.... And indeed, they have developed a grand new approach to writing that I intend to try with my own writing classes....a unique writing system that is certainly worth exploring.... - **Maralys Wills (www.maralys.com) award-winning author of 13 books, including *Damn the Rejections, Full Speed Ahead***

Writing Alchemy

How to Write Fast and Deep

Memoir Edition

Matilda Butler and Kendra Bonnett

**Knowledge
Access
Publishing**

Writing Alchemy: How to Write Fast and Deep
Memoir Edition

Video content is available via QR codes or at the links specified. If you access video content through a mobile device, message and data rates may apply. Video content may not be available indefinitely.

To receive a free weekly digest of the memoir writing blog with tips, prompts, and book marketing ideas, sign up at: http://WomensMemoirs.com

Readers should be aware that Internet websites listed in this work may have changed or disappeared between when this work was written and when it is read.

Publisher's Cataloging-in-Publication Data

Butler, Matilda. / Bonnett, Kendra.
Writing alchemy: how to write fast and deep / Matilda Butler and Kendra Bonnett.
p. cm.
Includes bibliographical references.

ISBN: 978-0-9841278-4-9

1. Authorship. 2. English language--rhetoric. 3. Exposition (Rhetoric). 4. Narration (Rhetoric). 5. Autobiography. I. Title.

Printed in the United States of America

15 14 13 12   1 2 3 4 5 6 7 8 9 10

BOOK AND COVER DESIGNS BY REES MAXWELL

Table of Contents

Introducing *Writing Alchemy*— Far from Writing as Usual

Welcome to *Writing Alchemy: How to Write Fast and Deep*. You are about to embark on a writing adventure unlike anything you've ever experienced. But please, don't take our word for it.

When we sent Advanced Review Copies of our book to some authors we know, we were blown away with their responses. Not only were they supportive, they saw in *Writing Alchemy* exactly what we had hoped. Here are some of the words they used in their testimonials: Evolutionary...Essential...Invaluable...Engaging...Innovative...Indispensable...Magical...Productive...Enjoyable...Grand.

Writing Alchemy Delivers on the Promise

We wrote *Writing Alchemy* for everyone serious about their writing... from the writers just starting out and looking to learn their craft to aspiring memoirists working on their first manuscripts to established authors with several books already published. But how do we know that Writing Alchemy works, that it delivers on the promise? We asked our students.

Here are a few of their comments that will give you an idea of what you can expect to achieve as well:

Writing Alchemy is helping me make my writing more interesting.

We all want the people who read our stories to find them engaging. You'll find that your interest-factor goes way up when you show with detail. It doesn't take flowery descriptive words or metaphors steeped in literary reference; just good detail clearly written.

I discovered a system I could work my way through with every turn of the page.

We call Writing Alchemy a system because it helps you work your way through a story or scene. It shows you how to dig into your thoughts and memory for the details that make characters, their actions and their surroundings come alive. Writing Alchemy is not formulaic writing; rather it stimulates you to tell your story and develop your own style.

With the help of Writing Alchemy, I've given up stream of consciousness for Deconstruction.

Deconstruction is the heart of the Writing Alchemy system. It helps you think through the five essential elements of writing--character development, emotions, dialogue, sensory description and time and place--and use them in your writing. Deconstruction moves you away from writing off the top of your head to becoming more deliberate and in control.

I now have the tools to dig deeper into my characters and bring out both the good and the bad. Writing Alchemy has given me the means to deliver real characters to the page.

While you need to start with a good story, it's the strong, multi-dimensional characters you develop that are going to carry the action. And it's not enough to develop them in your head; you need to share their personalities, their behaviors and the motivations that make them believable to your readers.

The stories that seem so clear in my memory have been hard to put on paper. With Writing Alchemy, I've found the healing strength that comes from writing the truth.

One of our students wrote us to say that she had been "telling all my memoirist friends that I've just been through another $50,000 worth of therapy with your lessons!" As many of you well know, memoir writing can be a way to work through some of the toughest experiences life can throw in your direction. Writing Alchemy will help you work through your thoughts and emotions and get them down on paper once and for all.

While our students enjoy telling us that this is a powerful approach to writing, like all good writers they also show us...every time they write and share a story.

Finally, Writing Alchemy is Ready for You.

And now it's your turn. As you are about to discover, Writing Alchemy delivers on so many levels. In the pages that follow, you will find the tools, exercises and processes that together form a system that will have you:

- Showing, not telling your story.
- Taking control of your writing process--what we call purposeful writing.

- Building rich, multi-dimensional characters.
- Digging into and working through emotions.
- Writing powerful dialogue.
- Taking your readers from casual bystanders and bringing them into your scenes.
- And finding greater satisfaction with your writing than ever before.

We can tell you that this is an exciting, revolutionary system. But that's just telling. Dig into "Getting a Head Start on Writing Alchemy" right now and share the enthusiasm that our students feel. Do all the exercises, and by the end of Chapter 1 you'll be applying Writing Alchemy to your own stories. But don't stop there. Keep going as each successive chapter takes you deeper and deeper into the power of detail. The more you use Writing Alchemy the more it will transform your writing, connecting you with your story and your readers with your prose.

It's time now for you to move far from writing as usual.

-Matilda and Kendra

Register Your Copy of *Writing Alchemy* Today

Register Now To:

- Be among the first to know when we open up new Writing Alchemy events
- Get the inside scoop on techniques and writing tips
- Receive discounts on Writing Alchemy classes, workshops, workbooks and other tools that will help you get the most from this revolutionary system for writing
- Participate in free webinars
- Watch interviews with memoir authors

You will only have access to these benefits if you register your copy of Writing Alchemy.

Register using a QR code reader, or by visiting the following link:
http://WomensMemoirs.com/register-writing-alchemy

Here are several more ways to connect with Matilda, Kendra and other memoir writers:

http://WomensMemoirs.com: Here you can read our blog, sign up for the Blogcast (latest posts are delivered to your email). Be sure to click on "Free for You" where you'll find several free ebooks and videos.

http://LinkedIn.com: We have a Women's Memoirs group on LinkedIn where you can share ideas, experiences and writing success with other writers.

http://Twitter.com/writingalchemy: Get instant updates and links for writing ideas and inspiration.

Examine Separately—My Fast-Talking Sister Martha; Anger and Regret Toward Aunt Elizabeth; Uncle George's Reply "It's Past Time to Go;" Acrid Scent of Singed Hair Clinging to My Mind; The Log Cabin with Cracked Window From that January Afternoon in 1968—Then Write the Best Memoir Possible.
                                    —Matilda Butler and Kendra Bonnett

Getting a Head Start on Writing Alchemy

So you have a story to tell. Congratulations. Few things are more satisfying or more basic to our human condition than the desire to share our stories with family, friends, members of our writing groups, even complete strangers whom we hope to entertain, inform, inspire and even instruct through our books. Early cave dwellers carved their stories on rocks. Native people painted their stories on animal skins, wove them into rugs and passed them along in the oral tradition. In that tradition, we continue to share our inner-most thoughts—some born of imagination, other out of experience. Even as modern writers, our goal remains to tell the best, most engaging story possible.

Think for a minute of yourself in the role of reader. What do you like? A story that captures your interest from the first page? Better still, the first sentence? You want characters that come alive—practically leap off the page and speak to you directly. Think of the best books you've read. They're the ones that linger. The characters and events stay with you for days after you finish reading. Have you ever found yourself daydreaming and wondering what the people in a story are doing now? We have, and that's when we say, "Wow that was a great book!"

A Great Book is the Gold Standard

A book that takes up residence in our thoughts for awhile might be called the gold standard of writing. And while we all aspire to achieve it, most of us worry that we'll never get there. Okay, we may not all be destined to be the next Ernest Hemingway or an up-and-coming Elizabeth Gilbert (author of *Eat, Pray, Love*). Our books may not become optioned for movies. But that doesn't prevent us from writing with style, clarity and vividness. We have it within us to engage our readers. It takes practice. Lots of practice. English novelist Joan Aiken, author of more than 100 books, including *Mansfield Revisited* and *The Wolves of Willoughby Chase* series, perhaps said it best, "As cows need milking and sweet peas need picking, so writers must continually exercise their mental muscles by a daily stint." The ancient Greek philosopher Epictetus was more succinct: "If you wish to be a writer, write."

Perfect Practice

These are words for writers to live by...and practice by. But it takes more; it takes knowing *how* to write. Vince Lombardi—legendary coach of the Green Bay Packers—put his finger on our challenge when he said, "Practice does not make perfect. Only perfect practice makes perfect." Reading helps us recognize perfection (or near perfection). It's an essential component of our training and an exercise we must perform throughout our writing lives. We also read books about writing, take writing courses, attend workshops, join writing groups and, if we're lucky, go off to a writers' retreat for some intensive focus on our craft. This is how we acquire the tools and learn the techniques of our passion.

The Problem: Opportunistic Writer

There's just one problem. Maybe you've noticed it in yourself. Whatever we studied most recently becomes the focus of our writing. If you take a class in dialogue, you probably tend to concentrate on writing dialogue. If you attend a workshop on character development, then characters become your main concern. Sound familiar?

The problem is that good writing is a beautiful blending of ALL the essentials—character development, deep emotional exploration, powerful dialogue, vivid sensory detail and a well-developed sense of time and place.

Knowing that you need all these elements can turn you into their slave. Imagine yourself writing along. You have a wonderful story with a strong theme and message. So far, so good. As you're writing in narrative form, suddenly you think, "Oh my, I've just finished four pages and I haven't written a single line of dialogue." So you dash out a few lines of dialogue, breathe a sigh of relief, congratulate yourself for remembering and go back to writing more narrative. Next you remember that you need to keep developing your characters. Again you shift gears and dig a little deeper into your characters. Then it's back to the story, when you suddenly think to include a couple breathtaking descriptions and maybe throw in a metaphor for good measure.

The Solution: Writing Alchemy

If this sounds even slightly like your writing process, then you're not in control. The techniques and the elements of your writing are calling the shots. You're along for the ride. You're an opportunistic writer. This is where Writing Alchemy, our revolutionary writing system, puts you in charge. Writing Alchemy will turn you into a purposeful writer. For the purposeful writer, every subtle detail about a character, emotional element, bit of dialogue, sensory description and connection with time and place becomes deliberate. You include each of these when and where it belongs because you know it will enhance your story and connect you to your readers. This is a point we will return to throughout this book.

What Is Writing Alchemy?

So what exactly *is* Writing Alchemy? It's more than another tip or technique. It's a totally new system for taking much of what you already know about good writing and giving you a way to use it effectively. It's more than a system to use what you already know. We cover new ground and give you scientific concepts for taking your characters and emotional development, dialogue, sensory detail and time and place in new and fresh directions. Much of our material is built on research found in the social sciences and only now applied to writing. But the key to Writing Alchemy is how it enables you to dig into the five essential elements of writing by showing you how to pre-write, if you will; what we call DECONSTRUCTION.* And then write with intense purpose—CONSTRUCTION. By now you have the first hint of what we mean by our subtitle, *How to Write Fast and Deep*. Fast? As you learn the Writing Alchemy system, you may wonder at our use of the word *fast*. We use the word in two ways, but for now we'll just focus on the first of these. When you *pre*-write, you are saving yourself the need to do as many *re*-writes. This means you can complete you memoir in a considerably shorter time and with less frustration. As you near the finish line, you'll see that Writing Alchemy is indeed a way to write fast.

And deep? By the end of the chapter, you will understand not only that you're digging into your subject in a deeper way than ever before but also that the depth adds a richness and clarity to your writing. Then as you work through Chapters 3-7, you'll be energized by the even greater depth you can achieve with your writing.

*Because Deconstruction and Construction are key components of our Writing Alchemy system, we have capitalized the terms in their noun and verb forms throughout this book.

Jumping Right In

We call this first chapter "Getting a Head Start" because we want to get you started using Writing Alchemy's Deconstruction/Construction process immediately. We want Writing Alchemy to excite you as much as it does us. We want you to discover right off just how easy and transformative the process is. You don't need to go through the entire book before you start using Writing Alchemy. This simplified version will get you started right now. By the end of this chapter, you will have successfully applied this new writing system to a scene or vignette.

In subsequent chapters we'll dive deeper into the process and give you suggestions and examples for applying Deconstruction and Construction. We'll also delve into each of the five essential elements of writing and present new techniques and ideas for bringing greater depth and detail to your writing. This is where we'll introduce concepts we've adapted from the social sciences. You can think of Chapters 3 through 7 as *power tools* for your writing that will open your mind to new possibilities and fresh ways to connect with your readers and draw them into your story...and it's fun.

Writing Alchemy in Use

Our students blow us away with their writing once they start Deconstructing their stories. For one thing, their characters come alive. Student memoir writers often fall short when it comes to describing themselves and others in vivid word pictures. With Writing Alchemy, that changes. As instructors, nothing is more rewarding than watching a memoir student bring her characters—and particularly herself—to life with imagery, emotion, motivation and language. Students who struggled with dialogue suddenly find themselves using this essential element of writing to move events forward and turn narrative into action that engages the reader. And so it goes for changes in each of the five elements.

While this edition of *Writing Alchemy* is specifically for memoir writers and many of our examples are taken from memoirs, the information is appropriate for writers of all genres. You can apply it to every scene, vignette or chapter you write. It works with short stories, essay writing, screenwriting, fiction and creative nonfiction writing.

When we first developed our Writing Alchemy system, we thought we were on to something special. We were sure once our students began to Deconstruct. And now we get to share it all with you. You'll see Writing Alchemy transform your words into rich, engaging and readable stories. That's the alchemy at work.

Have Fun While You Write

One more thing before we get started. In her book *Writing Past Dark: Envy, Fear, Distraction, and Other Dilemmas in the Writer's Life*, Bonnie Friedman wrote, "Successful writers are not the ones who write the best sentences. They are the ones who keep writing. They are the ones who discover what is most important and strangest and most pleasurable in themselves, and keep believing in the value of their work, despite the difficulties." In other words, practice and believe in the power of that practice. And the best way to keep practicing is to find the pleasure, the fun, in writing...even when it's difficult.

We believe that making writing as much fun as possible will encourage you to practice and that through practice your desire to write will blossom into a passion. At that point, drive and the determination to hone your skills will transcend even the need for fun. And you will truly be a writer. In the meantime, writing tools like our StoryMap: The Neverending Writing Prompt™ (http:// womensmemoirs.com/the-writers-store/books/) can help. This is the fictive town of Five Points, Oklahoma, replete with a town square, streets, and an array of somewhat fanciful shops and business owners (characters) that we've laid out on a colorful 11" x 17" map. StoryMap will help jumpstart your imagination and get your creative juices flowing. We've included people and places, bits of dialogue, sensory and emotional references to remind you to weave all five into your writing. The fanciful names and business ventures you'll find lining the streets of Five Points should have you laughing as you push through barriers—be they lethargy, time or writer's block—and just write.

You can use StoryMap to dash off a quick scene told entirely through dialogue, describe one of the local businesses using the five senses, develop a colorful character study, and even practice writing about yourself (sometimes hard for writers new to memoir) by placing yourself in the middle of the action in Five Points. Our students are using StoryMap, and believe us, when they get to writing about the events, characters and activities they envision going on in our little town, they have eclipsed anything even we imagined.

8 Head-Start Steps to Your First Scene

Whether you're writing a scene, a vignette or a chapter, Writing Alchemy uses the same simple steps:

Step 1: Write a Synopsis

Step 2: Understand the Deconstruction Process

Step 3: Create Characters (Deconstruct)

Step 4: Uncover and Track Emotions (Deconstruct)

Step 5: Tell It in Dialogue (Deconstruct)

Step 6: Evoke the Five Senses (Deconstruct)

Step 7: Specify Time and Place (Deconstruct)

Step 8: Understand the Construction Process and Write Your Story

Obviously, Step 2: Understand the Deconstruction Process isn't repeated each time you sit to write your next scene. However, we want to give you the "lite" version of this step now so that you'll begin to understand how Deconstruction works. We go into more depth with the Deconstruction process in the following chapter.

Let's get started.

Step 1: Write a Synopsis

What happens in the scene or vignette or chapter you are going to write? We've chosen to standardize on the word *scene*. If you are not used to thinking of scenes, which are most often thought of in the context of scriptwriting, and prefer vignette or a chapter having multiple scenes, then use the word with which you are more familiar. However, you should not be working with a section larger than a chapter. A synopsis can be of varying lengths. For our purposes here, think of this as a paragraph. If you show the paragraph to someone, they should be able to read it and know what you're writing about. Consider the story essentials—who, what, where, when, why and how—and use as many of these as are appropriate. Be clear on what your scene is about.

We want you to start with the synopsis so you always remember that the essential element of writing is the story itself. It's why you're writing. And bringing this up at the beginning of the process gives us the opportunity to acknowledge what is included and what is excluded from this book. We have chosen to focus on the five essential elements of writing—character, emotion, dialogue, sensory description and time and place. But what about story structure and plot? They are equally important and are the focus of the next two books in our Book Alchemy series. Writing a synopsis will keep you focused on your story. For without a story, why write?

A further point of this first step is to put you on firm footing. Only by knowing where you're going will you ever get there. It all begins with a statement about your content, about your focus. If you have ever worked with clay, think of this as pulling a chunk from a larger block. You immediately know that the piece in your hand, the piece that you're already starting to roll in the palm of your hand, is the totality of your future cup or vase. You don't have to worry about the rest of the block. You don't have to have the details: You don't need to know the final design or the color you'll paint this work of art. You only need to feel the size of the piece with which you'll be working.

Example: Camilla Thomas-Pinfield attends the funeral in Brookwood Cemetery, Surrey, England, of her great aunt Sophia Longworth Brimble and runs into her cousin Prentis Brimble. Memories flood her brain and overtake any sense of propriety.

Now Get to Writing!

1. In five sentences or fewer, write a synopsis of your scene so that it is firmly in your mind.

2. Try writing a logline, a one sentence description that includes the protagonist (who), action (what/how), to whom, location/time (where/when) with what result (why). Again, remember, don't get caught up in details at this point. That comes later. This is just the synopsis, the storyline of a scene you will write as you work through the steps in this book.

Step 2: Understand the Deconstruction Process

We are surrounded by constructs. "For example," says Matilda, "from the vantage of my desk, I gaze at a favorite chair. In reality it's a combination of bamboo frame with a coffee-tinted stain, cane back, gray linen cushions trimmed in a pink Fortuny fabric, metal hardware and plastic foot under each leg. The chair sits next to my beautiful yet simple desk. It's such a functional piece of furniture. In truth, it's a piece of etched glass, rescued from a hotel demolition, supported by two old metal file cabinets that I spruced up with black Hammerite spray paint." Both the chair and desk are constructs—wholes composed of parts. The parts are so seamlessly integrated that the viewer only sees a chair and desk.

Similarly, story is a construct. It's made of many parts. The story as conceived by the writer is quite different from the final product enjoyed by the reader. If you are going to build a story instead of a chair, you need to focus separately on each essential element of writing before bringing them together to create a final product—a story—that others will perceive as a whole.

Dictionary.com defines a construct as an "image, idea, or theory, especially a complex one formed from a number of simpler elements." This definition matches well with our concept for

Deconstruction—that before writing a complex, full narrative, we must first fully develop each of the simpler elements separately.

You might think of Writing Alchemy as part science and part art. The science is the process for Deconstructing your story into each of the five elements of writing:

- Character
- Emotion
- Dialogue
- Five Senses
- Time and Place

The art of Writing Alchemy is the depth, detail and freshness you bring to the process.

Step 2 is one of understanding rather than writing. An easy way to think of Deconstruction is to imagine you're going to bake a loaf of bread rather than write a scene. You need to assemble the ingredients first: flour, water, yeast, salt. These are the Deconstructed elements of a simple loaf of French bread. The qualities of each ingredient—whether organic, fresh, filtered (as in the case of the water), locally produced or handcrafted—are the variables (the details) that determine the final product. For example, flour isn't just flour. It could be whole wheat or bleached white. It could be a mixture of gluten-free flours such as almond, coconut, brown rice and tapioca flours. Those are the kinds of details that you provide when you Deconstruct.

In Steps 3-7, we'll give you a head-start method for Deconstructing each of the five elements of writing, one per step. Deconstruction is the heart of Writing Alchemy; it's the key to transmutation—to borrow a word from the ancient alchemist's lexicon. It's a system for pre-writing your story that results in less time spent later in rewriting. You may lament the time and attention to detail that goes into the pre-writing steps. Our students sometimes do. But you'll find, as they have, that the rewards outweigh the initial consternation. Our students end up writing with a grace, a level of detail and clarity they often didn't know they possessed. And they cut their time rewriting significantly. One of the benefits of Deconstruction is its ability to slow writers down and allow them to focus on their words and thoughts...to become purposeful writers.

Step 3: Create Characters or People

Characters are the first element in your Deconstruction. Your objective is to make the real people in your memoir come to life, to breathe, to move, to interact with others in genuine ways that your readers will believe. Developing the people in your memoir in a step separate from the story's action enables you to achieve this goal. Don't fall into the trap of thinking that just because these people are real, they will seem real to your readers. Making three-dimensional characters is *your* job. The reader only knows as much as you reveal.

Even if you're not planning to publish your memoir and are writing only for your family, you still need to develop rich, well-rounded characters. Your children certainly know a lot about you and what you look like, but if you're writing about your childhood or young adult years, remember that your children didn't know you then. And there are your grandchildren and great grandchildren who may someday read your story; your character needs to jump off the page so these future generations will see you as your children do now. And if you are writing for publication, the need for strong character development is even greater for no one in your audience of readers will know you.

For the head-start method, we want you to begin simply. In Chapter 3, we'll go into techniques that will enable you to develop much richer characters. But even the simple approach will transform your writing. As with a play script, list the people or characters in your scene. Then identify each person with the following information:

- Full name and short or nickname used in scene
- Relationship to others in scene and to the author who, in memoir, is the primary character
- Age in the scene
- Physical description (be descriptive with enough detail to trigger your memory when it's time to Construct/write)
- Other characteristics—especially distinctive ones such as tics, traits or habits

Above all, remember that it is detail that brings people to life for the reader. In this case, the devil is not in the details, but the very soul of your character most certainly is.

Example:

NAME: Camilla Thomas-Pinfield

NICKNAME: Milly

RELATIONSHIP(S): Great niece of Sophia Longworth Brimble (deceased), cousin of Prentis Brimble, wife of Reggie Thomas-Pinfield and mother of Alice and William.

AGE: 47

VISUAL
DESCRIPTION: Milly is 4'9" with thick red hair cut short and stylish; typically dresses in Liberty of London cotton print dresses and, in colder weather, colorful Harris Tweed skirts and jackets. For the funeral she wears an uncharacteristically somber charcoal-gray silk dress suit under a classic Burberry trench coat belted tightly at the waist. Like most Brits, she likes hats and tops her funeral ensemble with a dark gray, wool cloche with a wide, gray, grosgrain ribbon band and bow.

Her blue eyes shine through the thick lenses of her wire-frame glasses.

Although she is slender and strong, with the physique of a horsewoman, she has a slight limp in her left leg. Fox hunting, she explains, and assumes you'll understand the meaning of that. Still she moves with grace and style.

Her only jewelry is an antique diamond and gold wedding ring set, said to have once belonged to the Duchess of Grafton.

OTHER DETAILS: Milly enjoys people and loves to talk. People gravitate to her so easily she seems to travel with her own pack. She draws great energy from this entourage of friends, family and hangers-on. Her parties are the social events of the season around the Surrey countryside.

Milly is slow to anger, quick to praise and always happy to share a kind word. But still waters run deep. When old wounds rise up or new hurts (other than her husband's affairs) finally bring her to anger, her response is lightning fast. Her tongue rapier sharp.

Not one for tea and cakes, Milly prefers a strong, peaty single malt (Talisker or Lagavulin)...on the rocks. One cube, please.

Milly's son and daughter are her greatest source of pride and her favorite topic of conversation. At the same time, much of the warmth has gone out of her marriage. She tolerates (actually pretends to not notice) Reggie's incessant flirtations, dalliances and extra-martial escapades. As long as he's by her side at parties and social outings, she doesn't much care what he does. As she likes to say, "The money's mine."

Now Get to Writing!

1. Make a list of the people in the scene using your Step 1 synopsis.

2. Then using the points above, describe each person. Begin with yourself. If someone reads your physical description can she close her eyes and see you? Be sure to think about the essence of each person. Imagine the person before writing your list of characteristics. What is unique? What makes that person distinctive from everyone else in the scene?

3. While a story, scene or vignette might have one person, it's more common to have two to four people. At the other extreme, you might choose to describe a large party. But even in a crowd scene, only a few people will have the spotlight shine on them. Not everyone is important to the develop-

ment of the story. Not only do people have different degrees of importance, but a reader can only keep track of a few people. By the time you can write enough about every person to make them memorable to the reader, you may have delayed the development of your story unnecessarily and probably destroyed your connection to the reader.

Step 4: Uncover and Track Emotions

Emotions are our second element in story Deconstruction, and every story and scene has some. Even the apparent lack of emotion is a significant aspect of emotion. While it is possible to tell a story and ignore emotions, the result is a flat tale that rarely resonates with the reader. Throughout each day, we experience a legion of emotions from joy upon waking and seeing a sunny day out the window to anger when the car won't start and we realize we'll be late for work to sadness when a phone call tells us of a best friend's diagnosis of terminal cancer. This range of emotions could be likened to a musical score. The same note does not repeat over and over again. There are high notes, mid-range notes and low notes that create their own compelling music. Even the length of the note varies from the longest whole note to the very brief 64th note.

So it is with our emotions. Our subjective reactions to events, situations, even thoughts and memories result in psychological and physical changes that in turn direct our behaviors. Some emotions stay with us all day while others are fleeting.

When Deconstructing the element of emotions, tell your story from the emotional point of view of each main character. Imagine a play in which you must portray each character. When you are, let's say, John (Person 1), you may be happy, then worried, shocked and finally angry as you go through the scene. When you are Madison (Person 2), you may enter the scene embarrassed, then become surprised, irritated and jealous as you play out the scene and interact with the other character(s), events and actions. One person may go through 10 emotions in a scene while another may only have two. While there are no rules, it is reasonable to say that a person rarely stays in the same mood all the time. If you have not been considering the emotions of your characters, then you are ignoring one of the elements that lets readers understand, empathize with, even dislike the people in your story.

To help you consider the huge range of emotions, here are some of the words we use to describe emotional states of mind:

Vocabulary of Emotions Adoration...Affection...Alarm... Alienation...Ambivalence...Anger...Annoyance...Anticipation... Anxiety...Apathy...Appreciation...Attraction...Awe...Bliss...Boldness...Boredom...Calmness...Caring...Caution...Cheerfulness... Closeness...Compassion...Confusion...Contempt...Contentment... Courage...Cruelty...Curiosity...Delight...Depression...Desire... Despair...Disappointment...Discovery...Dislike...Disgust...Doubt... Dread...Ecstasy...Elation...Embarrassment...Empathy...Emptiness...Enjoyment...Enthusiasm...Envy...Epiphany...Euphoria... Exasperation...Excitement...Familiarity...Fanaticism...Fear... Friendliness...Frustration...Generosity...Gladness...Gratification...Gratitude...Greed...Grief...Guilt...Happiness...Hatred... Homesickness...Hope...Hostility...Humiliation...Hurt...Hysteria...Inspiration...Interest...Irritation...Isolation...Jealousy...Joy... Kindness...Longing...Loneliness...Love...Lust...Melancholia... Modesty...Nostalgia...Obligation...Optimism...Panic...Patience... Pessimism...Pity...Pleasure...Pride...Rage...Regret...Rejection...Relief...Remorse...Repentance...Repulsion...Resentment...Righteous Indignation...Sadness...Satisfaction...Scorn...Self-pity...Serene... Shame...Shyness...Submission...Suffering...Surprise...Suspicion... Sympathy...Tension...Trust...Understand...Vengefulness...Wonder... Worry...Zest

This list of emotions is just the beginning. In Chapter 4, we'll introduce you to information on the science of emotions that will help you dig deep. For now, you'll find that even at this introductory level you'll be adding an element that will transform your writing.

Now Get to Writing!

1. Go back to the synopsis of the scene you are writing. With that firmly in mind, consider the first character—*you*. Think through each emotion that you had in the scene. List them in order as you mentally work through events in the scene. You don't have to make this up. This is, after all, memoir. Try to visualize events as clearly and authentically as possible.

2. Now go to the second person in the scene and try to imagine what her or his emotions were. Sometimes these emotions will be in response to your own. If you're thinking, but

I can't possibly know the emotions going on inside others, try to recall body language, behaviors, bits of conversation. These are visual and aural manifestations of emotion that will help you get inside the emotional state of others.

3. Go through the emotions of each remaining person in the scene, writing them down in the order in which they occurred.

Remember just create a list of emotions for each person in the scene. Don't write paragraphs. That will come later. Devote your time to seeing the emotions of the scene play out in your mind and recording them.

Step 5: Tell It in Dialogue

The third essential element for you to Deconstruct is dialogue. Now that you have the people in your scene clearly in your mind (and captured on paper) and have told their story and documented their emotions, you've begun to define the multiple layers of your scene. The story is starting to get interesting. In Step 5, it's time to tell that story again, but this time solely through conversation. Think dialogue.

Believable dialogue is hard to create.

Believable dialogue is hard to create because it's always a balance between the way people actually speak and what we think we hear. In your quest for accuracy, for example, you may be tempted to write a long paragraph just as you think you first said it and then follow that with a second, equally long, logical paragraph of response by another person in your scene. In truth, conversations among two or more people are rarely long, orderly or even polite. We interrupt each other; we go off on tangents; we speak in *non sequiturs*. Don't believe us? Try setting up a recorder in a room and let the conversation begin. When you play it back, you may be shocked by the rapid pace of give and take and even the sentence structure that if written word for word might make you sound less than literate.

On the page, we want dialogue that sounds real without being so real that the reader loses the point or becomes bored to the point of tears. It'll take some practice, but here's a fun exercise that can help: Imagine your scene or vignette has just been optioned for a movie. You are barely over your excitement and celebration when you're invited to write the screenplay version. Panic. Do you feel your stomach doing somersaults yet? Swallow hard, and start the first scene, the one in your synopsis, writing it entirely in dialogue. For now, don't worry about the formalities of how a script needs to look. Just let your characters talk you through the story. Think about what you need to include in order to convey information about the people and the plot. Think about unique speech patterns. Think about moving the story forward through dialogue. Don't waste words on "Hi. How are you?" "Fine. How are you?" Make the dialogue do real work. Dialogue is the power tool among our elements of writing, but all too often we forget to plug it in.

Writing powerful dialogue takes practice. Kendra recalls a time when her plane out of San Francisco was delayed. With time to kill, she stopped at the airport lounge for a single malt. "I met a woman sitting in the bar," she explains, "who was waiting for her fiancee's plane to land. We talked for at least 30 minutes, and in that time I got her life story. The woman had incurable cancer, and even though she probably had only a year to live (two at the most) she was getting married." Kendra was so taken with the emotional story that she wanted to get it on paper. The moment she was settled in her plane seat, she started to write. "I wanted to capture the emotion and decided the best way would be to tell the entire story in dialogue. It was a fabulous exercise for writing dialogue and one of the best short pieces I've ever written." Dialogue can convey so much more than just conversation.

Think about other more recent conversations you've had with your characters. This will help you capture a character's natural style, language and phrasing. If this doesn't work, try recording your conversations with the characters in your memoir. You won't always be able to do this, of course, but when you can it's an invaluable resource. And it will get you started.

"But I don't remember the exact words." This worries our memoir students a lot. They often object to using dialogue because they want to be truthful and, as they say, "But how can I be true to a scene when I can't remember the exact words?" We hear this question a lot. Students who are writing memoirs want to be truth and worry that inexact dialogue compromises that truth. We'll say more about

"But I don't remember the exact words."

this later. For now, just know that your job is to capture the best and truest essence of a scene or event. If you do your job well, are fair and honest in your recollection, no one—not even the original speakers—will question or find fault with the words you have emanating from their lips.

In Chapter 5, we'll share information about types of dialogue and what the science of conversation tells us that we can use as writers. For now, just follow the *Now Get to Writing!* instructions and you will have your third head-start Deconstruction.

Now Get to Writing!

1. Once again, go back to your synopsis. Think about the people in the scene and their emotional states. Now write the scene using only dialogue. Remember, in this movie version of your scene, the reader will only know what the characters say.

2. If backstory needs to come out, then one character can convey it through conversation to another character or can use internal dialogue to reveal it. Do not include descriptive paragraphs in this exercise; only dialogue.

Step 6: Evoke the Five Senses

We live in a sensory rich world. Our very existence is dependent on our use of the five senses so why would we leave them out of our memoir? Answer: We shouldn't. Better answer: We must never, ever omit sensory detail. Now that that is settled, can you list the five senses? You probably said sight, sound, smell, taste and touch. But as if it weren't as plain as the noses on our faces, we sometimes forget to include scents and odors when describing a scene. And sometimes a character will be lacking one or more senses—most often vision and/or hearing. Don't forget that people learn to compensate by developing new ways to accomplish everyday tasks and that the remaining senses often become stronger and more sensitive.

Just for fun, here's a quick exercise to get you focusing on your senses: Describe your appearance to a person who has been blind since birth. We're emphasizing the "blind since birth" aspect because she'll have no reference for the many natural shades of skin color. Red lips? What's red? If you've ever seen the movie *Mask* (with Cher and Eric Stoltz), perhaps you can recall how Eric's character, Rocky, conveyed clouds to the blind Diana. He let her squeeze a big wad of cotton. He used the sense of touch to describe the soft, billowy fluffy image of clouds. Brilliant. Now back to you. In describing yourself, what would you say?

Let's put all the senses in the context of a simple scene. Consider a typical morning in Matilda's home: The sound of the alarm jars her awake (*sound*), her fingers blindly reach for, find, and push down the knurled button (*touch*) that brings respite from the buzzer. Her eyes open and search for her mother's hand-me down, spring-wound clock to confirm that the dreaded hour of arising is at hand (*sight*). She thinks, how could it have come so quickly? Just then a smile crosses her lips as the aroma of Peet's dark, rich, decaf French Roast coffee reaches the bedroom (*smell*), telling her that the automatic coffee maker is performing its daily duty without complaint. Getting up isn't that bad, she thinks. Soon she can breakfast on Trader Joe's gluten-free toaster waffles with crunchy pecan pieces and warm, fragrant maple syrup that Kendra sends from Maine (*taste with a little bit of smell thrown in for good measure*). She can practically taste the concoction even before she throws off the dark blue comforter, swings her legs to the edge of the bed, pulls herself upright and anticipates the feel of the cold wooden floor beneath her feet (*touch...again*).

If we've done our job right, in this brief paragraph you not only heard, touched, saw, smelled and tasted along with Matilda but the description of sensory details has awakened your own memories as well. That's the power of the five senses. Our memories and those of our readers are triggered by the activation of specific areas in the cerebral cortex where each sense registers information. Use your storytelling ability to evoke memories and perceptions by engaging with your readers through sensory perception.

In Chapter 6, we'll give you the tools to understand how the five senses operate in the body and how you can use them more powerfully in your writing. For now, here are a few points to get you started:

- **Sight:** Did you know that 80 percent of all information processed through the brain is visual? As a writer that means that creating pictures through words is crucial. When thinking of sight you might consider the big picture, or a specific focus, or even a color.

- **Sound:** What kinds of noises are part of the scene? Is the noise comforting or alarming? Loud or soft? Near or far? Moving? Even silence is worthy of note to help the reader share the moment with you or your characters.
- **Smell:** The language of smell can be elusive. How do you write about what you smell in the room or on another person? Places are rarely devoid of scents; these might range from the stench of stale cigarette smoke to the brisk aroma of a cup of freshly brewed mint tea. Does the smell of eggs and bacon fried hours ago for breakfast still linger in the room? One useful categorization of smells includes: fruit, floral, vegetal, animal and grilled aromas. A familiar smell can often be recalled by simply naming it, such as the smell of fresh cinnamon rolls or the mouth-watering, room-filling aroma of turkey roasting in the oven on Thanksgiving. In memoir, creating a list of smells helps to bring back memories and aid recall.
- **Taste:** As with smell, you don't always have to craft an adjective-rich sentence. Sometimes just mentioning the dark chocolate truffle or the sauerkraut will be enough. It all depends on the context, of course. You may be tempted to skip consideration of taste because your story doesn't have anything to do with food. But remember that taste is often used metaphorically: Her tennis racket has a sweet spot that she knows how to use effectively against her opponent. When his boss fired him, Joe felt bile rise in his throat. Jennifer experienced a bitter-sweet moment when she opened her email from Allison.
- **Touch:** If scent is overlooked, touch is often just plain ignored. Yet skin is the largest of our sensory organs. Did someone hug you when you were worried? And in doing so, did he pat you on the back or gently caress your arm? Did you scrape your knee when you fell? How did that feel? Was that green wool dress your mother loved to see you in as a child scratchy against your skin? Try to remember the variety of ways that touch—from the welcoming to the warning—interacts with your story.

Now Get to Writing!

1. In your fourth pre-write of the scene, consider the five senses and write about each. This is like a mini-deconstruction within a Deconstruction because you should write the scene using sight, then go back and write the sounds of the scene,

and continue repeating the scene until you have examined it through the lens of each of the five senses.

2. You don't need to write well-structured paragraphs. Just write sentences or jot down phrases that capture the sensory detail of your scene—from opening to its conclusion.

Step 7: Specify Time and Place

Our lives, our actions, our thoughts, our experiences are all shaped by and in time and place. This pair of elements nourish each other... like fraternal twins.

The places we write about were only like that at a certain point in time. And the time we write about influenced our feelings about place. In some memoirs, time and/or place may be central to the theme. It would be impossible, for example, to write about your experiences at Woodstock from August 15 through August 18, 1969, without an almost equal focus on time and place. Hey, it was the `60s! The history of that event has become almost larger than the event itself or any one person's experience in attending Woodstock. In this case, your story must be woven into that time and place in history.

Similarly, Matilda might write about a trip she took to visit her mother in Oklahoma City. She could describe the time they had together and what they did. She could even mention that her visit was unexpectedly extended by five days. But the significance of the extension is lost until Matilda mentions that her flight back to California was cancelled along with all other commercial flights in the hours immediately following the crash of American Airlines Flight 11 and United Airlines Flight 175 into the World Trade Center, American Airlines Flight 77 into the Pentagon, and United Airlines Flight 93 into a patch of farmland in Shanksville, Pennsylvania.

As this real story unfolded, Matilda was already packed and driving her 92-year-old mother to the upholsterer who was redoing a pillow for her favorite wrought iron kitchen chair. As she stood in the craftsman's workroom, she watched his small television set show the planes crash into the World Trade Center over and over. Matilda: "I remember my sense of panic and the urgent need to call my partner, aware that in California he might not yet know the news. Unable to imagine that flights would be cancelled for many days, I worried that he and our son would board their plane to New York City on the following day to carry through on a long-planned, father-son trip. The time and place influenced my reaction to the 9-11 tragedy in several ways, and to this day they shape my memories of Oklahoma City and my multi-day return to California on Greyhound buses."

In some stories, time and place are not particularly important. In others, they are the background, the setting...the context. Time and/or place are responsible for shaping a person's behavior. And, occasionally, time and place become characters in the story revealing their own personalities. You never really know how important or unimportant this element pair is until you De-construct for them. Often we simply do not know how much our stories have been influenced by either of these elements until we focus on them. At a minimum, writing the time and place and mentally transporting yourself there will help you remember more details, anchor your narrative, and ensure that your reader shares the experience with you because she understands your specific where and when.

...occasionally, time and place become characters in the story revealing their own personalities.

In Chapter 7, you'll learn about subjective and objective time and place as well as the science behind how they influence or determine our behaviors. For now, do your final Deconstruction in the ***Now Get to Writing!*** exercises.

Now Get to Writing!

1. Think about your story synopsis. Ignore people, emotions, dialogue and the senses for the moment and focus exclusively on time. Pinpoint the time at the beginning of the scene and the time at the end. What else was going on at that time? Did any major events influence your memory of the story? Is the story being told within the context of the times or independent of external events?

2. Write down the details of where your scene takes place. You might need to do some research to learn more about what the place was like--especially if you're writing about your childhood and you were too young to know much about it.

Step 8: Construct Your Story

Congratulations. You have successfully Deconstructed your scene. In later chapters, we'll delve into the social sciences behind each of these elements so that you can Deconstruct in deeper, more sophisticated and powerful ways. But for now, you have five separate perspectives on your scene.

With the hard work behind you, you're ready to begin the Construction step—the writing. Spread out your five written Deconstructions on the desk in front of you. In artist's parlance, these are your paints. But instead of a colorful array of hues and tones squeezed out on your palette you have words, details thoughts and memories. You're about to paint a word picture that is richer, more descriptive, more compelling and engaging than anything you have ever written. You didn't rely on just any old colors: these are the precise shades and tints (details and insights) that you've mixed yourself.

As you prepare to write, don't forget to refer back to your synopsis. You're in writing mode now. And even as you rely on your Deconstructions to help you decide how and when to introduce the various elements and what details to include, keep your focus on the story.

Example: To get you started, let's walk through your first Construction together.

- **Start by reviewing your Deconstructions.** Did any of the five elements seem especially strong? For example, did the story reveal itself through your focus on characters? Perhaps in Deconstructing the dialogue you discovered an intensity or poignancy you hadn't expected. Or maybe you've seen that yours is a story that has to be seen to be appreciated, and the five senses will dominate your descriptive writing. Circle the thoughts, ideas and phrases that you want to include in your writing. Make a list of these creative bits. What do you see? A fresh way to tell your story? Maybe you'll have an epiphany and someone's behavior that you haven't understood all these years will suddenly become clear or a character's motivation for action can now be expressed in dialogue or through character analysis.

- **Craft your opening lines.** Can you find your strongest element among your Deconstructions? Is it a bit of dialogue? A thoughtful insight to a character? Do you have a description of time and place that will make the reader forget everything in the present in order to accompany you on your story's journey?

- **Read and re-read your Deconstructions.** By now you know the story of your scene quite well. One or more of the elements has probably triggered additional memories and specific details. When this happens, write them down in your notes for the appropriate element. Don't worry about where you will use them during the creative process. We recommend that you sleep on your Deconstructions. Not literally, of course. Let your creative subconscious help you.

- **As you work, apply your writer's eye.** Blend the elements of your Deconstructions to shape your construct. Remember Matilda's desk and favorite chair? That's the seamless result you're striving to create. Remember the ingredients for bread— the flour, water, yeast and salt? When you combine them into a dough, they form something new, something that is more than the sum of its parts. By taking all the time you need at this stage, you allow the ingredients of your story to mingle and meld. You allow your best ideas to take hold.

- **Carefully consider your closing lines or paragraph.** A story must never simply run out of steam...or words. You need a strong conclusion. If you're writing a chapter in a longer piece, you need to conclude the section but leave open the possibilities for the next story, the next chapter. Keep your readers engaged to the last sentence.

- **Only use your best material.** Your Deconstructions are your worksheets. They help keep you from accidentally leaving something out of your story. At the same time, just because you included a thought or detail in your Deconstructions doesn't mean you need to use it in your story. You're a purposeful writer now. Fully in control of the writing process.

Now Get to Writing!

1. Read through your Deconstructions.
2. As you Construct, give yourself time to truly create. Your Deconstructions are not exercises to be stored and forgotten. Use them as if you are ordering from a Chinese menu... a little something from column A, a whole lot of column B, with a touch of column C on the side. Use whatever works for this particular scene. An artist uses his paints creatively. He adds more paint if needed and doesn't declare his work

complete simply because he has used up all his paint. Take only the best and consider expanding when more detail is needed.

Congratulations. You have completed the first stage in your journey to becoming a purposeful writer. Before you move on, we want to be perfectly clear: We're not suggesting that you be formulaic in your use of Writing Alchemy. The outcome is completely subjective, based entirely on revelations and decisions you'll make once you take the time to Deconstruct your story elements. Writing Alchemy simply gives you a way to slow down, look at your story from five different perspectives, and find the detail as well as the heart of your memoir.

Congratulations

Are you beginning to see why we call this way of writing fast and deep? At the beginning of the chapter, we mentioned one meaning of fast—not needing to do as many revisions and rewrites when you use Deconstruction. That saves you time in the long run. We also hinted at a second meaning of fast, and here it is: Deconstruction makes getting started less intimidating. It's easy because you won't struggle with your narrative style or word choice. You won't stare at a blank piece of paper or computer screen and wonder what to write first. When you start a new story or scene, you have a starting point: Your synopsis. And from there you begin Deconstructing your characters. Then you'll move on to emotions. And so on. The Writing Alchemy system gets you started quickly and keeps you moving forward.

What's Next?

By now you may be wondering about the origin of the concept for Writing Alchemy. Where did it come from? What does it mean to me as a writer? Is this just one more tool to learn and then forget about? We'll answer your questions in Chapter 2 as we delve into Deconstruction and show that it is not just a post-modern term but a process that every writer needs to understand and use.

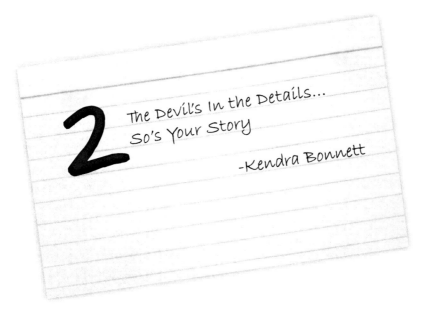

2

The Devil's In the Details...
So's Your Story

−Kendra Bonnett

Deconstructing the Five Essential Elements of Writing

Ask an author about writing, and you'll hear enough carping and complaining to make you want to toss away your Thesaurus and apply for a job cleaning sewers. I'm exaggerating, of course. Well, at least a little bit. After all, as the great sportswriter Walter Wellesley "Red" Smith was often credited with saying, "There is nothing to writing. All you do is sit down at a typewriter and open a vein." Admit it, sometimes writing seems just that hard.

"There is nothing to writing. All you do is sit down at a typewriter and open a vein."

Red Smith isn't the only one to decry the gut-wrenching horrors of writing. Novelist Jessamyn West wrote, "Writing is so difficult that I feel that writers, having had their hell on earth, will escape all punishment hereafter." Author and social critic Dorothy Parker wrote, "If you have any young friends who aspire to become writers, the second greatest favor you can do them is to present them with copies of *The Elements of Style*. The first greatest, of course, is to shoot them now, while they're happy."

Do a Google search on famous quotes about writing, and you may even begin to wonder why anyone chooses to write. Maybe we should all just sing a few bars of "Mamas, Don't Let Your Babies Grow Up to Be Writers" and move on to other professions and avocations.

But here's the rest of the story. Red Smith, for all the buckets of blood he claimed to have expended, wrote for the *Milwaukee Sentinel, St. Louis Journal, Philadelphia Record, New York Herald Tribune* and *The New York Times*. In time, he became a syndicated daily columnist and a freelance writer, wrote five books, and was the first sportswriter to win a Pulitzer Prize.

Jessamyn West was no slouch herself. She was a scriptwriter in Hollywood and wrote more than 20 books, including the autobiographical *To See the Dream* (1974). And Dorothy Parker—the literary luminary with the razor-sharp wit—was a founding member of the Algonquin Round Table and a popular and frequent contributor to *The New Yorker*. During a stint in Hollywood, she received two Academy Award nominations for screenwriting.

So maybe the truth is that the writing life chooses us. We're destined to write and have no way to escape. It's possible that all great novelists are born storytellers. Some memoir writers are seeking the restorative healing that can come from putting their pain into words and literally and figuratively closing the book on that chapter of their life. Others are consumed by their desire to share their experiences with others in the hope of helping, inspiring, teaching or encouraging their readers. So for all of us driven by some inner need to write, we can only accept our fate and spend the rest of our lives trying to connect with our readers and write the best prose possible.

...the writing life chooses us.

Matilda and I wrote this book because we believe our Writing Alchemy system offers techniques that will let you get much closer to your goals. Let me explain by way of sharing some of our backstory. I'll start with my own:

From the time I was little, I loved telling stories and making up word games for my own amusement. In fact, one of my early games is the basis for our writing tool, StoryMap: The Neverending Story Prompt (http://womensmemoirs.com/the-writers-store/books/). But I wasn't what you might call a motivated writer. Dutiful was more my style. I was about four when I learned the alphabet and six, and in first grade, when I wrote my first sentence. It was a paltry little thing, something on the order of Jane watched Spot run. But I had the basics of subject, verb and object, and I was off and writing...although not by choice.

By third grade I was writing the ubiquitous "What I Did On My Summer Vacation" stories and the equally bromidic weekly "What I Did Over the Weekend" themes. I was the grade-school equivalent of Sergeant Joe Friday. "Just the facts, Ma'am." First this happened and this happened and then that happened. No dialogue. No color. No character development. The writing was pure torture for me because 1) I was frustrated that nothing in my writing instruction had equipped me to capture all my many colorful summer adventures in any meaningful form and 2) even I found my prose boring.

But I did what I had to do. With tense fingers cramping as I clenched my yellow Dixon Ticonderoga pencil, I scratched out whatever words came to mind. My only objective was to complete the assignment. Done. End of story.

Only it wasn't. Because from my first stories of summer exploits and weekend activities, I was expected to graduate to creative writing. My sentences grew longer, my vocabulary larger, but my writing remained pedestrian. By seventh grade, we had learned to diagram sentences; I still can't tell you why. And by high school we were reading great literature from around the world with the expectation being that something good might rub off. I can still recite the first 15 lines of Chaucer's *Canterbury Tales* in their original Middle English, but that talent has never helped my writing.

The change began for me in graduate school. As a history major, I had a lot of papers to write, and because I enjoyed the material, I naturally became more thoughtful, more attentive to the writing. In turn, I began to receive compliments (and high grades), which encouraged me to work even harder. And with more effort on my part, the writing continued to improve. A most satisfying cycle was developing.

Jump forward a few more years and, history degrees in hand, I went looking for a job. I ended up working as an editor/writer for an educational non-profit in San Francisco, and Matilda was my boss. She was program director for the Women's Educational Equity Communications Network, and she had a problem. Her contract with the Office of Education included an aggressive schedule of print deliverables, but my predecessor had not kept up. Matilda, her staff and I worked hard to catch up, and by the time my job ended, I felt I had found my calling. I also could see how much I didn't know. If only I'd put more of myself into those themes back in third grade.

I felt I had found my calling.

I thought what I needed was more education so I made an appointment with the head of the Berkeley School of Journalism. He and I talked for almost an hour, and during that time he convinced me I had all the formal education I needed. "Clearly," he said, as he spoke through hands steepled in front of his nose, "you know how to write. There's really nothing we can teach you." He shook my hand and sent me back out into the world with one word of advice... practice.

And that's what I did. I read about writing and took any and all freelance editing or writing jobs, no matter how little they paid. I wrote newsletters, instruction manuals, promotional copy for software packages, press releases and marketing materials; I rewrote other people's writing; and I continued to edit. By the time I was 32, I was editor of *Digit*, a children's computer magazine, and Simon & Schuster was about to publish my first two books. But writing is a journey, and I was still very near the beginning of my trip. I was, however, improving. I was also getting better-paying jobs, and throughout this time I continued to read about my craft and take writing workshops. And everything I wrote was a form of practice for the next piece I'd write.

From San Francisco, I eventually headed back home to the east coast and writing jobs in Manhattan. Now, here I am today with almost 30 years of practice behind me—and that's not counting grade school, high school and college. And I'm going to admit something to you. I'm still learning and still practicing, and I doubt that will ever change.

Matilda and I reconnected professionally around 2005 to collaborate on Matilda's project to write the collective memoir of the generation of women born during World War II. By the time our award-winning book, *Rosie's Daughters: The "First Woman To" Generation Tells Its Story*, came out, we were also teaching and coaching writers who were trying to finish their memoirs. And a funny thing happened. We began to see an interesting pattern in the kinds of writing problems that plagued students. Furthermore, upon close examination, we saw them to be the symptoms of an almost universal problem: the tendency to "tell" rather than "show."

You'll may even recognize some of the symptoms in your own writing:

- Eschewing simple, straightforward, descriptive writing for elaborate metaphors that *seem* more sophisticated and literary.
- Relying on lazy adverbs to give your story emotion rather than using the kind of detail that lets readers reach their own conclusions. (e.g., Angrily Jane said, "Get out of my room!") Readers would prefer to know what Jane's anger looked like.
- Avoiding detailed character descriptions for the people in your memoir and thinking that's okay because you're writing about real people.
- Forgetting to include the most basic information about yourself—the main character.
- Omitting any details about the setting for your story.
- Focusing on the action of your story—the sequence of events—and ignoring the sensory details. In other words, by not stopping to smell the roses, you make it impossible for your readers to smell them as well.

http://womensmemoirs.com/deconstruction-1

Now here is the really amazing thing we discovered. Our students—all adults, most of whom have been writing for years—actually know a lot about writing. They've taken other writing classes. They read books about writing. Many belong to writing groups. And practically all knew that they suffered from show-don't-tell-itis. What they hadn't been able to figure out was how to solve the problem. That was when Matilda and I made it our mission to find a solution. We'd talk for hours: about students' frustrations with their writing and the fact that *knowing* what to do wasn't really the issue. It was the writing itself—the execution—that wasn't working. We'd critique their

...here is the really amazing thing...

work, point out places where they had told and not shown. We even rewrote sentences and paragraphs to illustrate what we meant. Our challenge, however, always remained the same. How to give our students something that could guide them when we weren't around to help.

The Origin and Development of Writing Alchemy

And so things continued for months. We talked about developing a new approach to writing that would address show-don't-tell-itis. But what? And how? We didn't want to rehash the same ideas we could find in a couple dozen other books. If their approach was so effective, we reasoned, then why did we see the same problem crop up over and over in our students' writing? No, we needed something new. Something different. And until we could find it, we left our idea for a book simmering on the back burners of our minds.

On one of my visits to Matilda's home—she was still in California at the time—her husband treated us to an evening concert in San Jose's Le Petit Trianon, the performing art center housed in what may be the best example of classical architecture in that city. The Ives Quartet was debuting a new piece they had commissioned, and the composer, Dan Becker, was present to talk about his work. He explained how he deconstructed the elements of his composition into their most basic forms—rhythm, harmony, melody. He wrote the piece once just using rhythm. He had the quartet play the piece for us just as they played it for him after he first wrote it. Then he took the element of harmony and wrote the music just using harmonies. Again, he had the quartet play the piece, originally for him and now for us. And finally, he took the element of melody and wrote the piece using just it. The quartet again played the piece for him and for the final time for us. Then fully understanding each of the deconstructed elements he went away for the fourth time and composed the piece that we would hear played in its world premier that evening.

Originally, Becker called the three pieces "Flour," "Water" and "Yeast," believing that when he combined them in the final and official composition that he intended to call "Time Rising" he would see the elements come together—rising just as bread does. And, just as bread is more than its ingredients of flour, water and yeast, so would his piece be more than his deconstruction of rhythm, harmony and melody. Matilda and I looked at each other when he finished speaking and mouthed in unison, "That's it."

If you've ever been to a casino when a gambler hit a super jackpot and the alarm bells assaulted every ear drum in the place—well that's what it sounded like inside our heads. We knew in that instant we'd found our solution, or at least the beginning of our solution. It took some time before we had Writing Alchemy fully developed. But the idea was conceived that evening.

> "That's it."

Becker told us that he later changed the name of the three pre-pieces (the equivalent of what we call pre-writing) to "Sky," "Wind" and "Wing." He thought those more appropriate for a music metaphor, just as he called the final composition (the Construction in our terminology) "Fly" rather than "Time Rising." Becker was the springboard that moved us away from a book that might have been just one more collection of writing tools and suggestions and toward a revolutionary new writing system that puts the writer in complete control.

Not long after, I left for Maine and home, and Matilda and Bill drove to Ashland, Oregon, home of the famous Oregon Shakespeare Festival. The ideas that we had been discussing took their next leap forward during that time. Although it is now obvious that the five elements of writing are character, emotion, dialogue, senses, time and place, it wasn't all that clear in the beginning. We had a couple of these elements in place by the time I left. However, it was after watching *King Henry IV, Part I* in the outdoor Elizabethan Theatre followed by a backstage tour where all the magic and business of the theatre were discussed that Matilda fleshed out the five elements. She called me immediately afterward, excited that we'd cleared another hurdle.

Once back in California, Matilda put together a brief overview of our concept in a few PowerPoint slides and introduced Writing Alchemy to her local students. She asked them to try Deconstructing their next assignment before writing. It worked. Every student saw dramatic improvement in her writing. Our mission had now been defined. We expanded the depth of the material, drawing on my background in both history and writing and Matilda's background in the social sciences and writing. We refined our approach and continued to teach. And so the cycle has continued. Even now, with the book finished, we still rely on our teaching to help us further refine the Writing Alchemy system.

Benefits of the Writing Alchemy System

After creating Writing Alchemy, Matilda and I next struggled to find the right word to describe it. Is it a technique? A formula? A method? A program? Not exactly. We felt a bit like Goldilocks and her twin sister as we worked our way through the options. One word was too specific...another too confining...or too rigid. We finally settled on the word "system" because while Writing Alchemy is a simple, organized set of steps, it will never lead to formulaic writing. As the gag line goes in the Johnny Depp *Pirates of the Caribbean* movies, so too with Writing Alchemy: it's not a code...more like a set of guidelines. You will not come away writing the way we do or any of our other students. Rather, you will have a system that brings out your own creative inspiration, your own colorful details, your own style. Writing Alchemy stimulates you to use your inner writer to find your own unique style and voice.

The fact is, good writers all have a system. It may be intuitive. It may even come naturally although probably most have worked hard to develop their craft, their style, their voice. Rather than a fill-in-the-details tool or rigid method that dictates a typical set of results, Writing Alchemy reflects the

...good writers all have a system.

organic, non-linear nature of writing. It adapts to the many ways individual writers choose to work. Most of all, it's a reminder to slow down and collect your thoughts before starting to write. That is, after all, the secret to learning to show and not tell.

Essential Elements of Writing

So what does it take to write like a pro? Here are a few of the components of writing: Theme. Message. Voice. Plotting. Narrative. Style. Story Structure. Grammar. Point of View. Motivation. Alignment. Explicit v. Implicit Characterization. Topic Sentence. Opening Paragraph. Transitions. Metaphors. Similes. Research. Organization. Spelling. First Draft. Revision. Proofing. Critique. Closing.

You're probably looking at this list and saying to yourself, "No wonder my writing is falling flat...I'm not doing half this stuff."

All of these are important. Theme, message, forms and devices as well as temporal span are some of the elements in story structure and will be the focus on our next book Structural Alchemy. Sensemaking, openings and closings, as well as narrative arc are key to your story's plot and will be included in our third book Plot Alchemy. In *Writing Alchemy*, we have chosen to focus on the five essential elements of writing. Do these well—integrate them into your writing with all the detail you can muster—and you will engage readers. Whether you are writing a memoir, a company biography, a keepsake for your children and grandchildren or the Great American Novel, you need these five essential elements of powerful prose to breathe life into your writing:

- **Characters** developed with a precision of detail that gives birth to a complete, three-dimensional person.
- **Emotions** identified and so vividly expressed that readers empathize, understand, even believe they *know* the characters.
- Strong **Dialogue** that communicates while moving the story forward and captures the tension, emotion and pacing in a scene.
- Sensory detail that draws on all **Five Senses** to paint a scene so vibrant and alive that readers don't simply picture it in their mind—they see, hear, smell, taste and touch the author's world.
- A **Time and Place** described in detail to give a story context and verity and to show how the characters and story were shaped by them.

Applying these five elements is the science of making the essential connection with readers. Weaving them into your writing with attention to detail so as to make readers care, that is the art. Writing Alchemy is the easy and natural system for bringing the art and science together.

Deconstruction Learned at My Mother's Knee

Until I was five, we lived in a large garden apartment in the heart of town. I had the opportunity to watch both my parents at work because our home doubled as my doctor father's office. By day, our

TV room was his patients' waiting room. Each night, my bed was rolled in and unfolded in his examining room.

Did I say bed? It was more like a cage with a lock on it to protect me from getting curious and playing with Daddy's medical instruments. What my parents didn't learn until I was about three and a half was that I was a baby Houdini, Willie Sutton and Doctor Dolittle rolled into one little package. Each night, I'd pick the lock, escape from my confinement and spend time doctoring my toy stuffed animals.

But what I remember most was watching my mother paint. She was a commercial artist, and her art table was set up in their bedroom. I loved watching her preparation. In those days, she worked in casein, which is a water-based, rather chalky precursor to acrylics. She'd take out a fresh paper palette, then start selecting her colors—red, blue, green, yellow. Only she didn't have just one red or a single blue. Her paint drawer was filled with a rainbow of options—Naples Yellow, Cadmium Yellow Medium, Cadmium Yellow Light, Yellow Ochre...Cerulean Blue Hue, Cobalt Blue, Permasol Blue...even black came in shades. She would take her time, think about her picture, hold different tubes up to the light and finally pick just the right shade to suit her need.

Once she'd made her selections and squeezed a small amount of each onto the palette, the magic began. I watched her mix a dab of blue with yellow to create a beautiful shade of green that reminded me of the grass in the park. She added Cadmium Red Extra Scarlet to Titanium White to make pink. With a fine, badger-hair brush, she'd swirl the paint, sometimes add a touch of Rose Red, other times create a wash by thinning the paint with more water. It was like watching an alchemist at work.

Deconstruction is your path to finding your inner writer...

All these years later, I think of my mother's paint palette and I see how Deconstruction can give you a palette of word pictures to blend into your story. Deconstruction is your path to finding your inner writer and becoming an artist of words.

Deconstruction Defined

You might think we chose to describe our system as "alchemy" because it has the power of transmutation. That is, to change your writing and turn your words into gold. Well, yes, in part this is true. Our students all see significant change in their writing from the first time they use Writing Alchemy. The real transformation with Writing Alchemy, however, is the change that occurs when you metamorphose from being an opportunistic writer and grow into a confident, deliberate, purposeful writer.

But lest you fear that alchemy is too mystical, too shrouded in miracles and unattainable results, let me reassure you. Writing Alchemy is all about the change in the writer; the system itself is simple. Alchemy is defined as the "spagyric art" whose process requires both disintegration AND union (in Latin, *Solve et Coagula*). Separate and then join together, and that's exactly what you do when you apply Writing Alchemy. It's a two-part system of Deconstruction and Construction: First you break down (Deconstruct) your story into its five essential elements of writing. Then with your palette of word pictures, descriptions and detail spread out in front of you, you're ready to write (Construct). We'll cover Construction in Chapter 8, and in the intervening chapters, we'll share tools, techniques and fresh ideas for getting more out of the five essential elements of writing. We'll show you how research from the social sciences can provide you with new insights that will improve your writing.

Deconstruction's Pre-writes Mean Fewer Rewrites

Yes, you read that right. Deconstruction will save you time. To Deconstruct your story, you'll need to take five, separate passes at writing your story. But before you go throwing that Thesaurus out the window again (trust me, you don't want to do that because you're only going to have to retrieve it) and go running off to that job in the sewer, consider this: Five passes that result in detailed notes that make it easier to write a solid first draft may reduce the number of rewrites and subsequent drafts. That's significant and the reason we think of Deconstruction as a form of pre-writing and Writing Alchemy as your path to writing faster.

For many authors, rewriting is a big part of their writing. Don't take my word for it. I'll let them tell you in their own words what they go through for their art:

I have to start with Ernest Hemingway. Ever spare and succinct, he summed up the mess that could be your first draft without

Writing Alchemy: "The first draft of anything is shit." He certainly doesn't mince words.

The popular author of books for children and young adults, Judy Blume, seems to relish the rewrite: "I'm a rewriter. That's the part I like best...once I have a pile of paper to work with, it's like having the pieces of a puzzle. I just have to put the pieces together to make a picture."

You want to talk about hell on earth. Poet John Ciardi used to endure many passes before he found his rhythm: "Spontaneous is what you get after the seventeenth draft." Next.

"Writing is rewriting," says former Assistant Attorney General for Ohio Richard North Patterson. "A writer must learn to deepen characters, trim writing, intensify scenes. To fall in love with the 1st draft to the point where one cannot change it is to greatly enhance the prospects of never publishing." Good advice, and I can only believe that with 19 books to his name he keeps his rewrites to a minimum.

The late Michael Crichton had a similar take: "Books aren't written—they're rewritten. Including your own. It is one of the hardest things to accept, especially after the seventh rewrite hasn't quite done it."

Dean Koontz has a different process: "I don't write a quick draft and then revise; instead, I work slowly page by page, revising and polishing." Nora Roberts, on the other hand, says, "I generally write a first draft that's pretty lean. Just get the story down."

Now, Jacqueline Susann had a methodical approach that seems a bit like Deconstruction in reverse: "The second draft is on yellow paper, that's when I work on characterizations. The third is pink, I work on story motivations. Then blue, that's where I cut, cut, cut."

Australian novelist Colleen McCullough has a slightly different approach: "Once I've got the first draft down on paper then I do five or six more drafts, the last two of which will be polishing drafts. The ones in between will flesh out the characters and maybe I'll check my research."

If you're not totally put off by the thought of seemingly endless rounds of rewrites, then maybe you can handle the words of Irish-born novelist Pete Murphy: "Rewriting is like scrubbing the basement floor with a toothbrush."

About now, I suspect pre-writing through Deconstruction—even with five passes—is looking pretty reasonable. I'm having fun with some of these quotes, but the fact is rewriting is a necessary, often laborious, part of writing. With Deconstruction you may not feel quite as much like Sherman marching through Georgia, burning and, in your case, revising everything in your path.

Deconstruction's Deceptive Simplicity

You're about to become hooked on the sheer simplicity of Deconstruction. If you've completed Chapter 1 Head-Start, then you already know how easy it is to get started with the system. You've seen, too, its flexibility. Deconstruction conforms to however you choose to work. If you're about to start your first Deconstruction, you'll find that you probably need no more than 30 minutes to grasp the concept and start making substantive progress pre-writing your story.

But be prepared to change how you work forever. You'll spend days, weeks and months discovering and going ever deeper into each of the five elements. Whenever you think of new categories of information that you want to include in your Deconstructions, just add them to your outline. Every writing course you take or book you read is compatible with Writing Alchemy. When you learn about a new technique, add it too to your Deconstruction steps.

Don't be surprised if you spend the rest of your writing life using Deconstruction and adapting it to your needs. That's what makes this so deceptively simply.

Begin Deconstructing Your Story

As you begin the Deconstruction process, commit to spending as much time as you need to dig deep into the recesses of your mind. This is not a race. Describe details out loud, if it helps. Talk with friends and family members who were there. If you include their memories and images, make a note of the source, especially if their recollection is at odds with your own. This may be important to the story.

Focus on one element, one scene, one character at a time. Don't blend. But if something important to your description of a different element happens to pop into your head, make a note so you don't forget, then come back to it at the right time. Above all, remember that this is a hands-on process. You have to write things down if you're going to have the necessary reference material in front of you when it's time to Construct (write). How you choose to capture the information is very individualistic. The format for your Deconstructions must work for you.

http://womensmemoirs.com/deconstruction-2

Step 1: Write a Synopsis. There are two kinds of synopses. The first is the one you wrote in Chapter 1 Getting a Head Start on Writing Alchemy where we had you create a brief synopsis of a scene in your story. We wanted you to spend enough time thinking about what you were going to write so that you could boil it down to the basics. The objective of the chapter/scene synopsis is to:

1. **Identify** the main character(s), put them in time/place and define the main event (action). More specifically, provide the who, what, where, when and how.

2. **Articulate** the point of the story—why you want to write it and why anyone would want to read it. When you think about it, that's pretty important because if you can't sum up the point of the story, you're going to have a hard time writing a strong conclusion, and your story is going to end by:
   • Slamming into a brick wall at 75 miles an hour (abrupt)
   • Sailing off a cliff a la Thelma and Louise (vague, although in their case it *was* pretty cool) or
   • Collapsing like a tire with a slow leak (weak).

3. **Insure** that the size of the story matches the size of the project. This is harder than you might think. The problem is when you write with the depth required to bring your story to life and engage readers, you're going to use a lot of detail. So if you want a scene to come in around 2,000 words, say, then the scene needs to be very focused.

Whenever Matilda and I teach Writing Alchemy: Head Start, we have our students submit their synopses before they start writing, and we send back 90 percent of them with the caution to think smaller, focus more and narrow the scope. For example, if a 62-year-old, black man decides to write a story about his experience being the first student of color at a small Midwestern college, that's a book-length memoir. It's not possible to write anything meaningful or compelling in 2,000 words, or even 5,000.

But, if this same person decides to write about the day he arrived on campus, checked into his dorm and met his white roommate from Macon, Georgia, for the first time, that could be well handled in 2,000 to 5,000 words.

The second type of synopsis is the one you write when preparing to write your book-length memoir. As you might expect, this one will be longer. You'll want to define the theme and message of your book, and if you don't understand the difference, take a look at Chapter 8. I've briefly explained both. You'll also need to mention the main characters and time and place (the years you'll be covering and the primary locations). And don't forget to include your objective. Just as you need to think about the point of each chapter and scene, you'll want to determine up front the point of the whole book. In fact, if you know how you want to break the book into chapters, include a chapter list and the point of each one. If you don't yet know this, you can always add this information later.

When you are ready to start Deconstructing your first chapter, you'll want both your book synopsis and chapter or scene synopsis on the desk in front of you.

Step 2: Create Characters. For readers to connect with your story, the people you're writing about need to come alive and be believable. Readers need enough physical detail to pick them out in a crowd. In Chapter 3, Matilda will take you through character development in depth. You want to spend a lot of time thinking about your characters. What do they look like? Do they have unusual habits or quirks? What makes them tick? What are their personalities?

Tips: Some writers Deconstruct characters by making a table with boxes for Name/Nickname, Relationship, Physical Description, Personality and Behavior/Motivation. Others write a detailed character sketch for each of the main characters. Most make bulleted lists with words and phrases that will help them recall the important details when it's time to write.

Step 3: Uncover and Track Emotions. When thinking through a scene, you need to capture the mood. Is there anger in the air? Is everyone happy and having a good time...except Uncle John who is off sulking in the corner? If the mood is mixed, what is each character feeling? The interesting thing about emotions is that they can change in a flash. It's not unusual for the mood and tension and emotions of the people to change several times in one chapter or scene. This is what you're looking to capture in your Deconstruction. In Chapter 4, Matilda shows you both the science and the art of emotions.

Tips: When listing your emotions, if you think of a good example (something said, a look or action) that will illustrate a particular emotion, write it down because good writing is about showing, not telling. Readers don't want you to tell them that Mary was euphorically happy; they need to know that she did cartwheels down the length of the bowling alley. (I actually know someone who did that.) You show the emotion; let the reader say, "Wow, she was really happy." List the emotions in the order they occur. This will make it easier for you to track them when you're writing. You could even create a timeline that ties events to changes in emotion.

Step 4: Tell It In Dialogue. Most writing students have trouble with dialogue. Either they try to avoid it as much as possible or they include every inconsequential exchange between characters—stuff that in writing dialogue is a throwaway. In Deconstructing dialogue you're looking for three things:

1. **Powerful examples** of conversation or exchanges among your characters. "Bye, Dad, see you tonight" doesn't make the cut. But when Anne's mother was dying and said, "Anne, for the past 45 years, we've argued about everything from the proper temperature for tea to the color of the walls in your bedroom, but through all through it all, every night just before I closed my eyes to go to sleep I thanked God you are my daughter. I love you," that's dialogue.

2. **Scenes** that are better told through dialogue than narrative. Unless everyone in the room is asleep or reading, there's bound to be some conversation. Sometimes the exchange is so dramatic that it should be written entirely as dialogue. By making

yourself work through a scene using only dialogue, you'll be able to identify those scenes that benefit from a lot of dialogue and write them into your story.

3. **Conflict** and **tension** that you can best express through conversation. There's a lot more to dialogue than, "Hello, how are you," and in Chapter 5 I have many more tips and techniques for Deconstructing dialogue. You're going to be able to use dialogue to bring scenes to life, move the action forward and provide great insight into people.

Tips: When you write a scene only in dialogue, experiment with the attributions (the he said/she saids). See if you can capture the exchange with as few attributions, also called dialogue tags, as possible.

Step 5: Evoke the Five Senses. We see, hear, smell, touch and taste 100s, maybe 1000s, of times each day, and yet the experiences are often so subtle or ordinary that we ignore them in our writing. But these are the very things that put readers into your scene. If you do this Deconstruction with a careful "eye" for detail, you'll have many sensory experiences on which to draw when writing. You won't use them all, but you'll be able to identify the best, the most iconic. Matilda helps you go into depth with the Five Senses in Chapter 6.

Tips: Close your eyes when Deconstructing the senses, you'll "see" the scene better in your mind. Focus on one sensory experience at a time. Smell everything...the cigarette smoldering in the ashtray, the candle burning on the mantle, the odor of dog food on Rover's breath when he jumps up to greet you and tries to lick your face. Touch is one we often overlook, and yet our hands are almost always engaged and touching something. Feel the ribs of your corduroy slacks, the deep etching in the cut glass goblet you hold to toast the birth of your nephew, Ethan's whiskers when he kisses you.

Step 6: Specify Time and Place. This element pair is critical to your stories. If Sunshine shows up in a miniskirt in a scene, readers are going to have different opinions about her if she's wearing it to church, wearing it in the dead of winter while walking down Fifth Avenue without a coat or wearing it to an LA disco party. And speaking of Fifth Avenue, New York City's Fifth Avenue is nothing like Fifth Avenue in Seattle. For one thing, Seattle's Fifth Avenue doesn't have an Apple Store.

As for time, if a mother named her daughter Sunshine in 1933, that would be unusual and probably tell readers that Sunshine's mother listened to quite a different drummer than her peers. If Sunshine's mother was a flower child who used to live in a commune in Ohio, we might be surprised if she didn't name her daughter Sunshine or Moonbeam. In Chapter 7 Matilda will give you more insight into time and place and help you see that they work together to shape behavior.

Tips: When Deconstructing for time and place, write down all the facts then spend some time thinking about time and place in the context of each of the other elements. For example, if you're writing about San Francisco in the 1960s and looking for sensory details, try to recall the scent of marijuana in the air at the corner of Haight and Ashbury Streets. Don't forget about the conversations you heard, especially the Hippie slang that was slipping into everyday language—phrases like "Right on man." "You dig?" "I'm bummed out." Emotions, too, were part of the times—mellow, stoned and freaked-out come to mind (no, I wasn't there).

Step 7: Analyze Your Deconstructions and Construct Your Story. If you put enough time and energy into your Deconstructions, you're going to have a lot of material for your story. Oh the word pictures you're going to paint using the colorful, vivid details spread out on your paper palettes. But just as the artist doesn't keep painting until the last bit of paint is used up, you're going to be selective in what you choose to incorporate into your writing. Only use the best, most evocative dialogue, the most interesting and pertinent sensory detail and the emotions that capture the mood. Study your character Deconstructions and begin thinking about how you're going to reveal a person's physical aspects and personality through the course of the story.

It's time to get started. Use Chapters 3 through 7 as you Deconstruct each element of your story. Then move on to Chapter 8 where I'll help you understand the Construction process.

What's Next?

By now you understand the need to describe the way each character looks. But when is that not enough? How much more do you have to put into a Deconstruction of each person in your memoir? What tools and techniques can help you describe your characters in full? Do you really have to fill out one of those character interviews that are so popular on the Internet? Chapter 3 will answer these questions and give you the best that the social sciences have to offer to writers in the development of character descriptions. We think you'll be surprised and pleased with what you find. And you just may learn something about yourself and others in your memoir.

References and Resources

Dillard, Annie. *The Writing Life*. New York: Harper & Row, Publishers, Inc., 1989.

Goldberg, Natalie. *Writing Down the Bones: Freeing the Writer Within*. Second Edition. Boston: Shambhala Publications, Inc., 2005.

Gornick, Vivian. *The Situation and the Story: The Art of Personal Narrative*. New York: Farrar, Straus and Giroux, 2001.

King, Stephen. *On Writing: A Memoir of the Craft*. New York: Pocket Books, 2000.

Tiberghien, Susan M. *One Year to a Writing Life: Twelve Lessons to Deepen Every Writer's Art and Craft*. Cambridge, MA: Da Capo Press, 2007.

Traig, Jennifer (ed.) *The Autobiographer's Handbook: The 826 National Guide to Writing Your Memoir*. New York: Henry Holt and Company, 2008.

Ueland, Brenda. *If You Want to Write: A Book About Art, Independence and Spirit*. Second Edition. St. Paul, MN: Graywolf Press, 1987.

3 Wise Grandmother, Brutally Cruel Mother with Dyed, Flaming-Red Hair, Silly Sister, Compassionate Husband, Dysfunctional Relationships
—Matilda Butler

The Element of People and Characters

Long Island Sound beckoned. The kayaker scanned the sky. She followed the bright rays of sunlight down to the horizon, watched as they dissolved what just an hour before had been a heavy blanket of fog covering the water. Wisps of wind skittered over the water leaving patterns of ripples and swirls on the glassy surface. Where wind, sun and water met, icy hot diamonds flared, forcing her to all but close her right eye against the glaring reflection. She didn't narrow her eye on purpose; it was her natural reflex whenever the sun was too bright...painfully bright. She wouldn't have thought about it today as she readied her turquoise Cobra Navigator-XF for a morning paddle. But as she pushed off from the shore of Hawthorne Beach, she recalled the words. "You squint just like your father," her mother used to say. Grateful for the memory, her face beamed with joy. Yes, her father had had the same habit...same eye even. She missed Moo and Daddy with all her heart. Now only the stories remained.

As we prepare to dive into character development, let's take a moment to consider the paragraph above. In just a few lines, we know:

- This is a woman who likes to kayak.
- She lives near or has access to Long Island Sound, which

probably means she lives in New York, Connecticut or Rhode Island.

- She has a characteristic facial quirk, passed down through her father's DNA, that makes her right eye squint in bright sunlight.
- Both of her parents have died.
- She was very close to them.

Characters Matter...

The above details are interesting. But do they provide enough detail to satisfy readers like us? Can we really "see" the kayaker...enough to pick her out on a crowded beach? Do we identify with her situation...her emotions? Most important, do we care?

The answer, quite clearly, is no. While we know some interesting details, there's so much more that we don't know. Other than her gender, we have no clue what our kayaker looks like: Is she young, old, in between? What color is her hair? Her eyes? Even though we may sympathize with her feelings of loss—especially those of us who have lost parents—we don't have enough of a connection to get emotionally invested in our kayaker. We don't *feel* her pain. This is a half-baked character...and all too typical of the shallow character development we see among memoir writers.

As Mark Twain wrote, "The test of any good fiction is that you should care something for the characters: the good to succeed, the bad to fail. The trouble with most fiction is that you want them all to land in hell, together, as quickly as possible." Our takeaway is this: Even clear, well-written prose won't make up for a lack of detailed description.

So let's go deep and mine our characters for all they have to offer...

So let's go deep and mine our characters for all they have to offer...and keep our characters out of Twain's purgatory. We'll start by Deconstructing our characters with an eye for defining their physical attributes. Then we'll turn to the social sciences for help in delving into our characters' behavior and the psychology and motivation behind their actions. We'll come out of this as more knowledgeable writers who can better fulfill the promise of our craft.

...Because It All Begins With Characters

Kendra and I take our lead from the great Russian novelist Ivan S. Turgenev who wrote, "I never started from ideas but always from character." For this reason, we start all our story Deconstructions with the characters because people are central to our stories. Yes, every story needs a plot and action, conflict and resolution, but stories happen *to* characters and are driven *by* characters. While characters in memoir are real people that the author knows, when we cut across genres, characters can be almost anything. In Rita Mae Brown's Mrs. Murphy mystery series, Mary Minor "Harry" Haristeen shares top billing with two talking cats and a Welsh Corgi. Readers of these stories know as much about her animal friends— physically and behaviorally—as they do about Harry herself. They come to respect the intelligent Mrs. Murphy (tiger cat); laugh at the pudgy, self-absorbed Pewter (gray cat); and love the loyal and brave little Corgi, Tee Tucker.

Even an inanimate object can become a character in the hands of a skilled writer. For proof, you don't have to look further than Stephen King's Christine—a red-and-white Plymouth Fury with a "drive" for vengeance...and murder.

But for our purposes here, we're going to focus on human characters—both real and fictional. I emphasize "real and fictional" because memoir writers often are hesitant to apply the techniques of character development to real people—living or dead—including themselves. But when writing for readers, even for family members, it's critical to create a picture of a character that has depth and detail.

...memoir writers often are hesitant to apply the techniques of character development to real people...

Readers need to picture the person in their mind's eye. Even when they can refer to photos, children like to "see" and understand personality of parents, especially the descriptions of when their parents were young. And subsequent generations definitely need the visual reference. Characters must come alive. They need to rise up off the page and stand on their own as fully formed people we want to know more about, as people about whom we have an emotional response—love, hate or something in between. Let's consider this description from Thomas Hardy's book, *Tess of the D'Urbervilles*:

... middle-aged man was walking homeward from Shaston to the village of Marlott, in the adjoining Vale of Blakemore, or Blackmoor. The pair of legs that carried him were rickety, and there was a bias in his gait which inclined him somewhat to the left of a straight line. He occasionally gave a smart nod, as if in confirmation of some opinion, though he was not thinking of anything in particular. An empty egg-basket was slung upon his arm, the nap of his hat was ruffled, a patch being quite worn away at its brim where his thumb came in taking it off.

Memoir writers are even more hesitant to get into the psychology and motivation of their characters, but these are exactly what readers need if they are going to understand, empathize and connect with the people in a memoir. It's this reluctance that leads me to draw on examples from fiction, rather than memoir. Fiction writers have a better understanding of the need to get inside their characters' heads and so provide us with the best examples of in-depth character development. They know how to create characters with whom readers connect. As memoir writers, we should learn from the best. Let's get started.

When Kendra and I were discussing the many facets of character, she mentioned that her mother used to tell her, "I know I've read a good book when the characters keep coming to mind weeks after I've finished the novel." Now that's impact. And in response to this conversation, we began looking into some of the great characters in literature and how the authors created such dynamic, memorable figures. Here are two examples:

Let's turn first to Margaret Mitchell's *Gone With The Wind*:

Scarlett O'Hara was not beautiful, but men seldom realized it when caught by her charm....it was an arresting face, pointed of chin, square of jaw. Her eyes were pale green without a touch of hazel, starred with bristly black lashes and slightly tilted at the ends. Above them, her thick black brows slanted upward, cutting a startling oblique line in her magnolia-white skin...Her new green flowered-muslin dress spread its twelve yards of billowing material over her hoops and exactly matched the flat-heeled green morocco slippers her father had recently brought her from Atlanta. The dress set off to perfection the seventeen-inch waist, the smallest in three counties, and the tightly fitting basque showed breasts well matured for her sixteen years. But for all the modesty of her spreading skirts, the demureness of hair netted smoothly into a chignon and the quietness of small white hands folded in her lap, her true self was poorly concealed. The green eyes in the carefully sweet face were turbulent, willful, lusty with life, distinctly at variance with her decorous demeanor...."If you say 'war' again, I'll go in the house.

She meant what she said, for she could never long endure any conversation of which she was not the chief subject. But she smiled when she spoke, consciously deepening her dimple and fluttering her bristly black lashes as swiftly as butterflies' wings.

Can you see Scarlett sitting on the front porch of Tara with the Tarleton twins? My ellipses indicate that these descriptive passages were spread out across several pages. This is key to any exposition of character in your story. You don't want to do a core dump of everything you have or know about a character. Spread it out. Let aspects of your characters be revealed throughout the course of the story or scene. Mitchell choose to give readers a very complete visual picture of Scarlett in the first chapter; she spent the rest of the book building on what we are first told. And Scarlett remained true to form to the end.

Now, let's turn to Mark Twain and his description of Tom Sawyer from the pages of *The Adventures of Tom Sawyer*:

There was a slight noise behind her and she [Aunt Polly] turned just in time to seize a small boy by the slack of his roundabout and arrest his flight....

"My! Look behind you, aunt!"

The old lady whirled round, and snatched her skirts out of danger. The lad fled on the instant, scrambled up the high board-fence, and disappeared over it....He's full of the Old Scratch, but laws-a-me! he's my own dead sister's boy, poor thing, and I ain't got the heart to lash him, somehow....

He was not the Model Boy of the village. He knew the model boy very well though--and loathed him.

Within two minutes, or even less, he had forgotten all his troubles. Not because his troubles were one whit less heavy and bitter to him than a man's are to a man, but because a new and powerful interest bore them down and drove them out of his mind for the time...This new interest was a valued novelty in whistling, which he had just acquired...Diligence and attention soon gave him the knack of it, and he strode down the street with his mouth full of harmony and his soul full of gratitude....

The more Tom stared at the splendid marvel [of a new boy in town], the higher he turned up his nose at his finery and the shabbier and shabbier his own outfit seemed to grow....

Again, the bits I've selected are spread out across the book. Each scene, each adventure either gives us (the reader) greater understanding and insight into the indomitable, lovable scamp Tom Sawyer or reinforces our picture of him and ensures his enduring place in literature. Twain was a master at dialogue and dialect, and Kendra will come back to discuss this in greater detail in Chapter 5. He also told his stories less through detailed physical description and more through action. In Twain's case, actions really do speak louder than words. We come to know Tom through his activities, the snippets of personality that Twain reveals, and his conversations.

But enough about the masters for the moment. Let's focus on what you can bring to your character development in order to create people who come alive and establish an emotional bond between character and reader. To that end, we'll explore five dimensions of character for your Deconstruction—identity, visual description, demographic factors, psychographic attributes and personality. But that's not quite all. We'll also get into motivation. By the time you complete the exercises that follow each section, you will have described at least one person in full—probably yourself. We'll urge you to also describe another person. Using a tool more than once will help you become proficient with the bonus that by the time you are through, you will have a significant portion of your Character Deconstructions finished.

First, A Confession

In Chapter 1, "Head Start," we said that you should never Deconstruct a segment larger than a chapter, and preferably a scene. However, now that we're taking you deeper into the art and science of character, I need to confess. We lied. Well, let's just say we gave you the abridged explanation because there are a few circumstances where you need to Deconstruct at the book, story or essay level...in other words, at the highest, most all-encompassing level. Character Deconstruction is one of those cases, and I think this will make sense to you.

Emotions can change dramatically within scenes and from scene to scene, and dialogue is completely unique to each event. Characters, however, don't really change. They may grow up, grow older, get married, become sick. They may go from rags to riches and back again, but the basic nature, the psychological makeup and behavior patterns of characters remain largely the same. Even when they appear to change, there is a logical continuum or evolution that can (and should) be traced. Illness may make a carefree young man become depressed and difficult. I suggest to you that the man's nature didn't change as much as the situation brought out something that was part of his underlying personality all the time. As you can imagine, developing a character over time and circumstances helps you create a rich, realistic and believable portrait. And that captivates readers.

Each character in your memoir needs to be fully developed during an initial story-level Deconstruction. Once you've thoroughly examined and described your primary characters, you can gradually reveal them during the course of your memoir. If you try to Deconstruct characters scene by scene, chapter by chapter, you lose the opportunity to build on revelations and delve into the deeper psychological and motivational aspects of personality. So while you will add specific details when you do the five Deconstructions prior to working on each chapter (or scene), for the most part you'll be deciding which elements of character to reveal and noting any significant changes in health, age, circumstance, as well as describing what the character was wearing at the time. I mean, can you think of any scene in *Gone With The Wind* where we don't know exactly what Scarlett was wearing?

I may seem to be beating a dead horse, but I want to emphasize again the importance of revealing a character's physical description and even quirks initially and the personality and demographics gradually through the course of the story. It's more natural, mirroring the way we get to know people in real life. When you meet someone new, you don't know everything about them in the first five minutes except how they look and if they have any obvious tics or behavioral mannerisms. Author J. K. Rowling, in her first Harry Potter book, mentions Harry's round glasses that are held together with tape because they broke frequently when Dudley punched him. This gives the reader a quick way to identify, to visualize, Harry. It also provides information about the circumstances of his life. And consider the way Nevada Barr handles the main character of her series. In Barr's mysteries about park ranger Anna Pigeon, aspects of Anna's backstory, personality and personal demons unfold across the pages of more than a dozen books.

Three Schools of Character Development

Before looking at the art and science behind character development, let's consider three schools of thought on how to write about people.

School 1—Let the Characters Develop Themselves

Writers who subscribe to this school believe that by starting with a rough story outline (similar to what we're calling the synopsis) and placing a well-developed character in time and place, the character will begin to drive the story, define his/her own behavior and words. Giving characters their head like this, is popular among fiction writers. William Faulkner described his experience: "It begins with a character, usually, and once he stands up on his feet and begins to move, all I can do is trot along behind him with a paper and pencil trying to keep up long enough to put down what he says and does."

Even in nonfiction, one character may seem to take center stage quite to our surprise. A memoirist, for example, might think her story revolves around her mother's influence only to find out as she writes that her father was the dominant force in her life. And then there are always the writers who just start writing with the belief that whatever they need to say will come out. If this works for you, Deconstruction will enhance your results.

School 2—Learn As Much As You Can About Your Characters Up Front

Writers who like this approach go to great lengths to build a complete picture of their characters before they start to write. To collect the necessary background information, they "interview" their characters to learn everything from likes and dislikes to attitudes to favorite color to childhood pets to astrological sign to mother's maiden name. "Before I write down one word," explained Norwegian playwright Henrik Ibsen, "I have to have the character in my mind through and through. I must penetrate into the last wrinkle of his soul."

You might wonder how writers can interview a fictional character. They create detailed lists of questions, which they go through and answer, or they rely on one or more of the character questionnaires available online. Just type "character questionnaire" into your search engine, and you'll find plenty of resources—many of which are free.

Memoirists often think that because they know the people in their story, they don't need to build detailed character studies. We disagree and suggest that if you like the interview approach, then give it a try because it can help you slow down and take the time to recall as much detail as possible about the people in your memoir. Of course, this style may not work for you and definitely isn't needed. You'll find that our exercises will help you fully develop each important person in your memoir.

> *Memoirists often think…they don't need to build detailed character studies. We disagree.*

One small warning: If you decide to download questionnaires from the Internet and use these to stimulate your interviews, don't fall into a trap of always starting with the same set of questions. You run the risk of devolving into a formulaic model for character development. These questionnaires are useful tools, but be sure to always keep your focus fresh and unique. Different hair colors, accents and favorite colors are not enough. You need to look for the truly unique in each person. Making questionnaires just one element of your character Deconstruction can help you avoid formulaic descriptions.

School 3—Start With a Character List

Novelist Carolyn See provides a third approach to character development. In her book, *Making a Literary Life: Advice for Writers and Other Dreamers,* she encourages writers to create a list of the most important people in their lives. See says writers should work quickly, without expending a lot of thought, and suggests that the list include about 10 people. Then each person should be described in a few sentences. Next See urges writers to create a second, even shorter list of people who give them "the willies."

These two lists—about 15 people in total—will provide fiction writers a starting point for all character development. Each person on your list is already a cluster of physical description, personality, behaviors and attitudes. If you are writing fiction, it is easy to morph them into fully developed people for your book because they are already real, already coherent. In other words, you don't have to take one trait from column A, a second from column B, and so on. You don't have to interview your person and perhaps make up some of the responses. See believes that the people on the list will provide a lifetime of material for building characters. You don't need to start from scratch with each new story you write.

As a memoir writer, you can use Carolyn See's exercise as a way to identify the people who will be the most important (primary) characters in your story. The few sentences you write about each person serve as a good initial take on them and will fit into the more extensive profile you will develop during the Deconstruction. It also will help you identify which people belong in your book and keep you focused. This technique described in School 3, combined with the approach in School 2, will help you avoid flat, formulaic characters.

http://womensmemoirs.com/character-1

A Fourth School of Thought for Character Development

All three approaches just mentioned—let the characters develop themselves, learn as much as you can about your characters up front through an interview process, start with a character list—have aspects that commend them; there is no right or wrong about these choices. You might even decide to mix and match techniques. We'd like to add our own school of thought: For each significant person in your memoir, focus on the essence of the person and the turning point or major event that made that person who she or he is.

For example, Kendra says that it was her love of Colonial American History that shaped her college career and ultimately helped to develop her love of writing. She told me that it was a trip to Fort Ticonderoga in Upstate New York when she was six that was the turning point. She says, "I remember walking into a cool, stone-walled room deep within the fort. It was dark but for the glass cases filled with old Revolutionary War uniforms. Soldiers wore those clothes while fighting for our nation's independence, I though. In an instant, history came alive for me; it was a mesmerizing moment."

If you don't know how a particular person in your memoir became who she is, and can't ask, then determine the person's major impact on others as that reflects the person's strengths and weaknesses. The character's development begins with this core, this essence, and other facets grow outward from here. Let me give two more examples. The first tells of a turning point that shaped a fictional character; the second looks at a real person's major impact.

Sue Grafton's Kinsey Millhone (protagonist in Grafton's alphabet mystery series) has her own Wikipedia entry that reads:

> Kinsey Millhone was born on May 5, 1950. Her unusual first name was her mother's surname before her marriage to Kinsey's father. Kinsey lived with her parents until they were killed in a car wreck when she was five and survived in the car for several hours before she was rescued. She then moved in with her aunt (her mother's sister) Gin, who was the only relative still in contact with her mother, the rest of the family having disapproved of the marriage and cut off contact with her. From her Aunt Gin, Kinsey acquired various eccentricities, including a liking for peanut-butter and pickle sandwiches....

The entry goes on from there, and I urge you to look it up. By the time you've finished reading her brief profile, you'll think Kinsey is a real person. You'll know her height, weight, hair color and style, clothes, health fitness routine, food preferences, education, profession, marital status and more. However, it is the death of her parents when she was only five and her upbringing by a reclusive aunt that shaped much of Kinsey's personality and adult behavior. The childhood tragedy is the turning point.

My father, Edward Ainsworth Butler, is the source for my second example, which focuses on the impact of a person rather than a turning point. I've taken this entirely from my own memories and experiences:

- Edward Butler's impact was his capacity for unconditional love. I don't know why he was like that or if there was a turning point that made him that way. Perhaps it was just his personality. Perhaps he had a role model when he was young. All I know is that by the time I was a teenager and old enough to reflect on him as someone who was more than just my father, his love of people and willingness to love them—no matter what—ruled his life. It affected everything from his home life and his relationships with his six brothers (many of whom he helped financially even though he was the next to youngest and not wealthy by any standard) to his business career, which included owning his own company, and even his openness with strangers in the grocery store line. Expressing unconditional love got him in trouble sometimes because others took advantage of him, but that was still the essence of the man.

...he valued honesty in all aspects of his life.

- Of course, there was much more to him than his unconditional love. For example, he valued honesty in all aspects of his life. When a number of people in parallel businesses were caught in a sting operation and sent to jail, my father wasn't even investigated. He had never gotten involved in bribes and payoffs because of his personal moral code.

- But he wasn't all positive traits. He was also an alcoholic, and that created chaotic times when I was young. But somehow you loved him anyway. After all, he was willing to look past your mistakes and problems so you felt you should look past his.

- Physically, he was short by today's standards, about five and a half feet, and bald from a young age. I have a treasured photo of him holding me in his arms when I was six months old, and you can already see the pattern of his future baldness. This physical trait has given my sons much to discuss and tease about as each measures the other's receding hairline.

- His grandchildren remember that he almost always had on a freshly laundered white dress shirt no matter the occasion—baking, gardening or grocery shopping. Even a blue dress shirt seemed too casual to him. When we took clothes to the funeral home for his final dressing, one family member said, "I'll go get his blue shirt with white collar. It looks practically new." That idea was vetoed by the rest of us. It looked the best because he didn't like to wear blue. So why put him in that for eternity? We selected, instead, an older, worn, but freshly laundered and starched white dress shirt. That's what he wore most days. A child of The Depression, he would have been offended had we purchased a new shirt for his funeral.

- For 27 years and 9 months, his regular morning trip to the office included a stop at Shirley's Dry Cleaners where he left the previous day's suit pants to be pressed and picked them up on his way home in the evening. He was careful with money and didn't have them cleaned until absolutely necessary, but the crease was pressed professionally each day. The way he looked mattered to him, in part, because he was not a professional. His company sold Caterpillar, and later Euclid, road construction equipment. He was often in the field but had a professional look in his mind that he created with the clothes he chose.

- For as long as I can remember, he wore Allen Edmonds lace-up shoes. When I commented about this luxury given his carefulness with money, he always said, "If you take care of your feet, your feet will take care of you."

If I were developing my father as a character in my memoir, he would be all of this...and more. But at his core, my father was the embodiment of unconditional love.

As you consider this fourth approach, you may wonder if a person can have more than one essence. Sure, that's possible. But don't allow yourself to be lazy. Try to determine the *core essence* because it will let you explain your character more clearly.

Now Get to Writing!

1. Before we turn to the deeper dimensions of character development, take 10 minutes to write the turning point in your

life. This is your memoir, and it's time to begin the Deconstruction of you as a person. What changed you and put you
on a new life course, or what factors caused you to be the
person you became?

2. Now, consider the second most important person in your
   memoir. If you don't have the information available to
   write about the turning point, describe the impact the
   person has on others and which serves as an expression
   of that person's core life belief. You should be able to write
   this in a short paragraph, even a few sentences. You won't
   have to spend a long time on this as once you focus on the
   person, you should know what to write almost immediately.

The Five Dimensions of Character

You're a memoir writer, but for a moment let's consider the different challenges that fiction writers have when crafting their
characters. We'll then tie this back to memoir in a moment. Fiction writers have to create believable, motivated characters with
whom readers are willing to become emotionally involved. The
operative word for fiction writers is *creating*, then describing, a
strong, coherent character. If truth is stranger than fiction, then
the fiction writer has the bigger challenge to create characters that
readers won't reject.

Memoir writers have a similar responsibility. Technically, this
is easier because they only have to *describe* believable, motivated
characters with whom readers are willing to become emotionally
involved. The danger, however, is that memoirists *know* their characters so well—at least on the surface—that they often forget to
provide enough detail. But they have an obligation to set up characters that readers can get to know, and that's true whether writing for
family or publishing for an audience of strangers.

The fact is, I've rarely read a novel that doesn't describe each
character to some degree when he or she first appears in a scene.
Then, as the story unfolds, I continue to learn more about the character. However, I've read memoirs in which I have no idea what the
individuals even look like, let alone understand their behavior or
motivation. It becomes all about the actions rather than the characters. As readers, we want to care about the people and believe in

them. You have to ask yourself, why should a fictional character be more vivid in our minds than a real person? Obviously, none. To fix this, you need a laser-like focus on your characters. And it starts when you fully Deconstruct each character for the five dimensions: identity, visual description, demographic factors, psychographic attributes and personality.

Let's begin to dig deeper into our characters.

Character Dimension 1—Specifying Identity

Identity is the simplest aspect of character; it's also our starting point. As they say in the Army, just name, rank and serial number. In our case, we'll focus on each person's name and relationship to others in the story. Even minor characters need to be identified for readers. You don't want any vague references floating around. Since this is the Deconstruction stage, write everything down. You're not required to use it all in the final writing, but at least you'll have all the information at your fingertips. In your memoir, for example, you might mention your Uncle John only in passing. But your Deconstruction should include your uncle's full name, any nicknames and his relationship to other family members, such as: "John is my father's eldest brother and is married to my mother's second cousin."

Now Get to Writing!

1. Before continuing your character Deconstruction, take the time to write a brief synopsis of your entire memoir. Unlike the Head Start first chapter, which focused on a scene, this synopsis needs to capture the essence of your entire story or book. Include the time period you are covering, the message you want to convey to readers and a very brief storyline. You should be able to do this in a couple of paragraphs. With synopsis in hand, it's easier to determine which characters need to be included in your book.

2. Once you have your synopsis, write your name and any nicknames. Next to that describe the relationships that exist between you and other people in your memoir. You may find that it helps to go ahead and create a list of all the people you believe will be significant in your memoir (the major characters) and then go back and start filling in the relationships.

Character Dimension 2—Specifying Visual Description

Later, as you begin to dig deeper into the other four elements of writing you'll begin to notice some overlap with character development. Emotion, for example, is certainly an aspect of character; dialogue helps to move the story forward while telling us things about the speaker. And a case can be made that how a person looks is part of the five senses. But we'd all feel cheated if we ended the Deconstruction of our characters and had no idea what the people looked like. So we make physical description part of character development.

While it's important to create a visual portrait of your characters, it's not about throwing in every detail that comes to mind. Be selective and have an objective. There's no right or wrong here. You're looking for an approach that best serves your goals. Here are two approaches that help to explain what I mean:

- **At first glance:** Imagine that a man has just walked into the room. What's the first thing you notice? Maybe he has a limp, and that limp is significant. Or maybe it's the fact that he has gray hair yet appears to be a very young man. What's the second thing you notice? Perhaps it's his icy blue eyes. Third? Well, when another character engages him in conversation you learn he has a French accent.

- Don't worry about Deconstructing a comprehensive checklist of all possible physical characteristics. Just write down those that make an immediate impression; you can always come back and add more. Then give some thought as to why certain physical features stand out. Does the person try to cover them up or try to enhance their impact? If in doubt, write down too much rather than too little. Just don't feel bogged down by the task.

- Let me give you a personal example. I remember attending a library meeting a few years ago. A woman walked up to me and said, "You must be Matilda. I've been wanting to meet you." I didn't have a name tag on and so asked how she knew me. She replied, "Oh, you're wearing black. I heard you always wear black." Without getting into the backstory, it is true that I do wear only black (with a little white thrown in occasionally for variation). In parallel to the movie title *Dances with Wolves*, I've come to think of myself as She Who Wears Black. In describing myself in a memoir, I'd be remiss if I failed to mention my clothing.

- **Enhance the story:** Work the character description into the story in a way that reveals something about the person AND the story. In *The Help* by Kathryn Stockett, the narrator is a maid in Mississippi in the early 1960s. She has been hired to take care of the house and the new baby. The mother, Miss Leefolt, doesn't know how to get the baby to stop crying and quickly hands her to the maid. The following description begins on the first page of the book:

> Here's something about Miss Leefolt: she not just frowning all the time, she skinny. Her legs is so spindly, she look like she done growed em last week. Twenty-three years old and she lanky as a fourteen-year-old boy. Even her hair is thin, brown, see-through. She try to tease it up, but it only make it look thinner. Her face be the same shape as that red devil on the redhot candy box, pointy chin and all. Fact, her whole body be so full a sharp knobs and corners, it's no wonder she can't soothe that baby. Babies like fat.

Notice how the description of Miss Leefolt is integrated into the storyline. The narrator could have talked about her clothes, tone of voice, height and a dozen other things—all valid physical attributes, just not relevant to the story. Instead, she treats the reader to a colorful physical description of Miss Leefolt that is a delight to read, helps explain (at least from the narrator's perspective) the distance between mother and child and tells us something about the story and where it's going.

Details, details, details.

Now think about your memoir. Once you are established as the main character, it will be easy for you to later Deconstruct chapters and scenes and focus on specific characteristics of hairstyle, wardrobe and other small details that change.

Details, details, details. That should be your mantra. It's the little things that often help to bring a character to life for a reader. Do you wear rimless eyeglasses that you frequently adjust? Do you have bangs that are just a little too long, thus reinforcing your habit of pushing them back with your left hand? Did you have a hard time losing that extra 23 pounds after the birth of your first child, which stretched the seams of your favorite azure slacks almost to the bursting point? Did you give up on wearing earrings because your earlobes are attached rather than free hanging? Once you get them written down, some of these details may seem irrelevant to the storyline of your memoir. That's all right. You don't have to use everything. You also may begin to decide the order in which you want to reveal details as the story unfolds. Aim for a strong, vivid physical description because it is much easier for readers to become engaged when they can "see" the person.

For now, create a series of strong physical descriptions of yourself that map to the passage of time in your memoir. Before writing your memoir, you'll need to repeat this process for each primary character. If you need to describe someone, such as your mother, when she was young and you couldn't have actually seen her, photographs can be helpful. And if you can't ask your mother for details, maybe another relative remembers her as a child and can help. Don't have any information about how she looked as a six year old in 1910. You can find photos of little girls that age in that year, and they can help you fill in details that are likely to be quite appropriate (assuming you have the right part of the country, the right income group, etc.).

Now Get to Writing!

1. Deconstruct your own physical appearance by listing details that describe how you look at the beginning of your story and a second set of details that describe how you look at the end of the story. You already have your synopsis so you know the period of time that your story will cover. If you think you may use flashbacks, then describe yourself at earlier periods as well. Provide enough detail so that a reader could pick you out of a group.

2. Repeat the physical description for a second major person in your memoir. If you have a hard time describing yourself in #1 above, consider describing another person first. Perhaps it will give you the distance you need to then write about yourself to thinking about how other people view you.

3. Remember, details, details, details. Don't get bogged down or feel overwhelmed by this writing exercise. At the same

time, don't skimp on the description or rush to finish it. If you think of details later, return to this exercise and add them.

Character Dimension 3—Specifying Demographic Factors

Demography is usually the study of populations. But in this case we are looking at the demographic variables (the vital statistics) of each person in the story you're writing. This includes *ascribed* facts such as race, gender and age as well as *achieved* or *chosen* factors such as marital status, education, occupation and income.

Not all of this may seem relevant, but as researchers and marketers have found since the 1880 census, demographic information suggests clusters of attitudes and behaviors. In other words, knowing a character is 6 years old or 60 years old in a story segment tells the reader about more than just the person's age. For example, if a person has lost all her worldly possessions in a fire, it is much more devastating for the 60 year old than the 6 year old. Similarly, telling the reader you have recently married for the fifth time or have just been divorced by your husband who traded you in for his 20-year-old secretary is a shorthand that hints at much about you and your circumstance. Or, if I tell you that my father never went to college but that he read throughout his adult life and always sought to learn something new each day, then you have an insight into the type of person he was. But I'm getting ahead of myself because while education is a demographic fact about my father, his reading behavior and attitudes toward learning move us into the fourth dimension of psychographics. So hold that thought.

Now Get to Writing!

1. Deconstruct for demographics. Be as specific as you can about your *ascribed* (race, gender, age) factors and the *achieved/chosen* (marital status, education, occupation and income) factors. Since you are first going to Deconstruct your characters for the entire memoir, you will need to consider the timeframe you have outlined in your synopsis. If you are dealing with a two-year period (e.g., onset and diagnosis of an illness through to recovery), there may not be much change in your personal demographic factors. On the

other hand, you may have experienced major changes, such as a divorce or job loss resulting from the stress caused by your illness. The number of points in time you need to include will depend entirely on the number of years covered by your memoir. While you may not have gone to school during the period covered in your memoir, be sure to include both the ascribed and achieved factors.

2. Now Deconstruct for the demographic factors of the second most important person in your memoir. Be specific. For example, instead of just saying four years of education, write which college or colleges, what major was pursued, whether the education was continuous or if employment intervened. Don't worry about whether you will use all the details. For now, you are anchoring the person. Be just as detailed for the second person as you were for yourself. You might need to do some research. That's all right. Now is the time to gather the information.

Character Dimension 4—Specifying Psychographic Attributes

Aside from your description of the essence of one of your characters, so far you have written only the easily determined facts or what we might call the shell of the person. Now, let's begin to get inside our characters by examining their psychographics—clusters of attitudes, values, interests, activities and lifestyle.

Psychographics and writing? In the 1960s, marketers found they could better predict customer behaviors when they looked at attributes that went beyond demographics. They turned to psychographics—a system for understanding different consumer mindsets—to develop targeted communication campaigns that would appeal to specific customer groups. Writers can use these same psychographics to develop complex, authentic characters who behave in believable ways. Psychographics moves a writer away from making all characters seem alike on the one extreme (do the same types of things, have similar beliefs, react in unidimensional ways) and from being artificial composites of values, attitudes, interests and activities and acting in unmotivated ways at the other extreme. With psychographics, writers begin to have the strength of social science research at their disposal.

As a case in point, I remember when historian Fawn Brodie published her psychohistorical biography, *Thomas Jefferson: An Intimate History*. Among scholars, Brodie's research received a mixed and often critical reception. Literary critic Alfred Kazin called it "fascinating." Detractors like *Times* reviewer Christopher Lehmann-Haupt accused Brodie of seeking out "extremely subtle evidence." But the reading public was captivated, and *Thomas Jefferson* spent 13 weeks on *The New York Times* bestseller list. Psychographics proved to be a powerful draw and commercial success.

An Early Explorer into Psychographics. Psychographic research and analytical tools found their way into the mainstream of consumer and market segmentation work in the 1970s. Social scientist Arnold Mitchell, then a researcher at SRI International (I lived in Palo Alto at the time—near Menlo Park and heard Mitchell talk on multiple occasions), developed one of the best known psychographic systems and brought it to the commercial marketplace in 1978 as VALS™ (Values, Attitudes and Lifestyles). Using statistics to analyze consumer demographics and attitudes, Mitchell divided individuals into nine groups according to their social values: Survivors, Sustainers, Belongers, Emulators, Achievers, I-Am-Me, Experientials, Socially Conscious and Integrateds. When SRI spun off VALS to Strategic Business Insights (SBI), VALS became more clearly focused on psychological (internal) variables, which have the advantage of remaining more constant over time than social (external) values. Strategic Business Insights later reworked Mitchell's original nine lifestyle groups into eight: Innovators and Survivors as the two extremes. Innovators can then be classified as Thinkers, Achievers or Experiences and Survivors can be classified as Believers, Strivers, or Makers. As writers, we can use VALS as a way to go a little deeper into our characters and begin to understand what makes them tick.

Try This: You can take the VALS survey for yourself. Go to SBI's website (http://www.strategicbusinessinsights.com/VALS/presurvey.shtml) and click on "Take the Survey." You'll be asked to answer a short, 35-item test; it's free, and SBI promises you won't be put on any mailing lists. You are asked at the end of the 35th item to provide your sex, age, education and income range. You can add your email but you still get the score if you don't. The results are scored immediately, and you are told your primary and secondary type such as Innovator and Thinker or Survivor and Believer. Click through on each of your VALS types for a short definition and a list of four "favorite things" that might appeal to the type.

- The first type defines a person's primary motivation...what drives his or her ideals, achievement and self-expression.
- The second type measures a person's resources...what kind of consumer she or he is likely to be. Age, income and education are part of the equation, but resources also depend on a person's energy, self-confidence, intellectualism, leadership and impulsiveness (to name a few).

You'll get more out of the concept of psychographics if you take the VALS test twice—once as yourself and then as another person in your memoir. This is good practice for putting yourself inside the head of the people in your memoir.

When I took the VALS test, the results showed that I am an Innovator/Thinker. Their description of Innovator states:

> Innovators are successful, sophisticated, take-charge people with high self-esteem. Because they have such abundant resources, they exhibit all three primary motivations in varying degrees. They are ...the most receptive to new ideas and technologies. ...they continue to seek challenges. Their lives are characterized by variety.

This characterization of me isn't far off. Of course, no test will suddenly reveal a person, but it does help us to understand ourselves and others. You could stop at this point. However, you'll also notice that the VALS test lists four likely preferences. The list was only about half right for me but if I were a baseball batter, hitting 500 would be terrific. The list shows a likely consumer preference for BMW (I'm not a car person and just want something reliable; we have a 2003 Honda CRV), *Wired* (I have had a subscription to it in the past and love to read the magazine when I find one in a pubic place, but found the subscription too expensive. Perhaps I should give VALS half credit for this item), sparkling water (this one is right on; I prefer a non-flavored sparkling water and think Trader Joe's has a good price), a rewarding experience (I include visits to museums on a list of favorite activities and so again agree with this preference).

The list of preferences may not offer a memoir writer much insight. However, the revelation of my receptiveness to new ideas, my desire to seek challenges and my love of variety helps to explain many of my behaviors. These are all true and yet I might not have thought to include them in a description if I hadn't taken the VALS test.

Now Get to Writing!

1. With your VALS results in hand, flesh out your character Deconstructions with attitudes, values, interests, activities and lifestyle.

2. Remember, too, that because you are developing a full Deconstruction for each character, you'll need to take into consideration the timeframe of your memoir. You may want to retake the VALS survey several times. Try to put yourself into the mindset you or one of your characters would have had at key times in the course of the story and answer the questions from that perspective. For example, think back to what you were like when you first married and answer the questions as that person, then recall what you were like when you divorced and take the survey again. Or try to remember what you were like when you graduated from college versus how you thought after 15 years into your career; take the survey from these two perspectives. Use the major turning points in your life to help you select the time periods you want to Deconstruct using VALS. You may be surprised at how consistent you have been over time. Or, a major change in your life may have brought you into a different classification.

Psychographics meets time and place. Before moving on to the fifth, and perhaps the most powerful, dimension of character development, I'd like you to think about this: how people fit (or do not fit) into the places where they live. Although this may seem like a point better saved for your time-and-place Deconstruction, I mentioned that there is some overlap among the five essential elements of writing. This is one of those cases. Consider, for example, a sophisticated man raised and educated in the northeast who moves to a rural, southern town. The town has its own profile, its own cluster of people types; let's say for our example that more than half of the residents are hard-working, blue-collar men and women. The differences between the newcomer and the predominately high-school-educated locals might even help us better understand our man's restlessness and reclusiveness. Our behaviors are influenced by how comfortable we feel in the place where we live.

About the same time that Arnold Mitchell was developing VALS, Jonathan Robbin was starting his company, Claritas (now owned by Nielsen), to market his PRIZM (Potential Rating Index for Zip Markets) system. PRIZM, admittedly more geodemographic than psychographic, is based on 66 (the actual number of clusters changes over time based on the information gathered) colorfully named clusters such as Urban Achievers, Young Digerati, Big Fish/Small Pond, and Mayberry-ville. The clusters are developed using census data at the zip code level along with point-of-purchase receipts, car and truck ownership records, radio and television listening/viewing information, market research surveys, public opinion polls and more.

Try This: Look up the cluster types in the town where your memoir takes place. Go to http://www.claritas.com/MyBestSegments/Default.jsp and click on the box in the right-hand column of the page and enter your zip code. You will also need to enter the randomly generated code used so that spammers can't get into their system. You'll see the top five clusters for your area (listed in alphabetical order not by size). When you click on each of the cluster types, you can read brief descriptions and see the demographics associated with each cluster. For fun, I entered my zip code in Corvallis, Oregon, and the results are: Boomtown Singles, City Startups, Middleburg Managers, Mobility Blues and Sunset City Blues. I laid out some of the key demographics in a table so I could compare across the five clusters. I get a snapshot that defines this wonderful town—ethnically diverse, ranging in age from under 35 (it's a college town) to retired, college educated, and when it comes to incomes and homeownership, we are a mixed bag of upper-middle to lower income, owners and renters.

Now Get to Writing!

1. If this information stimulates more details for your character Deconstructions, add them now. One note. If you are writing about your childhood, these profiles won't be of

much help. PRIZM geodemographics are forever changing; there is no historical data. Even so, you might get some useful background material about the people in your community, which may give you insight into the ideas and values that have helped shape the adult you.

2. Remember that we're now looking at the intersection of people and place. If your memoir involves two or more cities, look each up in Claritas. Then write a comparison of the two places.

Character Dimension 5—Specifying Personality, Habits and Quirks

Identity, physical attributes, demographics and psychographics are all necessary, but it's personality that will put your character development over the top and help you develop interesting, three-dimensional people. Of course, people change over time. Maturing is the word we usually apply. Yet, brain injury not withstanding, personality and even many of our habits and quirks develop early and stay with us throughout our lives. Quirks are great devices writers can use to create memorable hooks to describe a character and help readers to recall or evoke that person the next time you mention her in your memoir. *Does your grandmother wring her hands when she's nervous?* Does your grandmother wring her hands when she's nervous? Does your uncle put away the clean mugs so that all the handles are facing the same direction? When your sister dresses, does she always put on her left shoe first and even remove her shoes and start over if she gets out of sync and puts on the right one first? When your father removes his socks, does he tie them together before putting them in the dirty clothes basket...driving your mother crazy? Each morning, for example, my father patted all his pockets. Like clockwork, he stood up from the kitchen breakfast table and began his self pat down. He was looking for his car keys and could never remember where he had put them. Even now, when I see a man patting his pocket, I'm reminded of my father.

In her memoir, *Dancing In My Nightgown*, Betty Auchard describes her husband's habit of criticizing her driving. He had always been the family driver, but as he became weaker from cancer treatments, Betty needed to drive him. He complained frequently until she could barely stand it. In her description, we begin to know more about Denny as well as Betty.

I protested—"Enough already!"—and put him on a ration of five criticisms per round-trip. My darling Denny tried, but it wasn't easy for him to keep his mouth shut. Out of the corner of my eye, I would notice his hand fly up to issue directions, but he'd catch himself and pretend to adjust his cap or scratch his head. He might start to use a cautionary tone, but instead substitute a fake little cough or pretend that he had forgotten whatever he was going to say. And so it went until he eventually returned to full-time monitoring of every mile I drove.

I tried the honest, up-front approach. "Honey, when I drive alone I have a lot of confidence, but when you're in the car I have none at all. My driving is growing worse. I'm anxious when you're my p-p-passenger [I started to cry right about here] and I dread these trips more than I can possible tell you." The tears I shed were really big, and Denny felt terrible.

He felt so bad that he began to compliment my driving. He praised my ability to stay in the middle of my own lane, my parking skills, my confidence as I passed slow cars, and my overall driving improvement. It was like being patted on the head or patronized, so I never quite got out of my angry mode. I prayed a lot: "God help Denny get off my back, or help me ignore him while I'm driving. I don't want to spend our precious time together being mad." We were in the car a lot, so I prayed a lot!

Denny got sicker as his cancer spread, but he still had a mission concerning my driving. He managed to sneak in a comment - or two, or three, or more -- on every trip to the hospital, and I finally grew accustomed to it after almost ten months of treatment. Perhaps God had whispered to me, "Betty, get used to it. He doesn't have much time left."

Indeed, he didn't.

While quirks and traits can be revealing, and in some cases even fun for both the writer and the reader, it is the underlying personality of the people in your stories that provides the important basis for behaviors and the motivations behind them. Personality is like the water in the pool, creating the context within which a character moves and from which he or she draws energy and actions. We have rich resources to mine; let's dig in.

Temperaments, The Start of Personality Type Theory

Temperament, which in ancient times was considered a medical condition, grew into our modern concept of behavior and personality. Social scientists have shown that most behavior is determined by our personality and that these personality traits remain fairly constant throughout our lifetime. The ancient Greek physician Hippocrates described what he called the four humors (black bile, yellow bile, phlegm and blood), which he believed controlled not only a person's health but also his or her behavior and emotions.

In the 2nd century, Claudius Galenus—physician to Roman emperors—popularized Hippocrates' work and created a list of four temperaments, each thought to be caused by an excess of one of what at that time were believed to be the body's four fluids. Galenus, also known as Galen of Pergamon, wrote extensively and his research continued to be studied by medical students well into the 19th century. His four temperament types are:

- **Sanguine**—a person with too much blood thought to come from the liver was courageous and hopeful.
- **Choleric**—a person with too much yellow bile believed to come from the gall bladder was easily angered and had a bad temper.
- **Phlegmatic**—a person with too much phlegm said to come from the brain and lungs was calm and unemotional, even sluggish.
- **Melancholic**—a person with too much black bile assumed to come from the spleen was irritable and despondent.

Now Get to Writing!

1. Today we generally use the four temperaments as adjectives to conjure up mental images of classic behaviors and emotions. While we no longer believe these types are caused

by body fluids, the terms can help us characterize people, even understand how these stereotypes can get in way of understanding people. To start, write the name of one person whom you think might be described as sanguine. Do the same for choleric, phlegmatic and melancholic.

2. Which of these temperaments best describes you? Of course, you're much more complex than a single temperament, and that's where we're headed next. But let's take this one step at a time.

Body Shapes, Another Precursor of Personality Types

For almost 1800 years, the four temperaments dominated the thinking among scientists and philosophers alike as the basis for defining personality. But in the 1940s, American psychologist William H. Sheldon suggested a shift from looking internally for personality traits to studying the exterior—physique—for clues to a person's character. He described three categories:

- **Endomorphs**—large-boned and fat, which results in jolly types. Think Dom DeLuise.
- **Mesomorphs**—medium-boned, muscular with broad shoulders and narrow waists, which defines tough types. Think Arnold Schwarzenegger.
- **Ectomorphs**—slim with long, thin muscles and limbs, which translates as nerdy types. Think Woody Allen.

Now Get to Writing!

1. Although scientists soon discounted Sheldon's classifications, his stereotypes still influence our preconceptions about people. For each of the three body types, write the name of one person in your memoir you know who might be described this way. Which one are you?

2. Next write several sentences about each person's behavior and personality. Does the stereotype hold true? Do their behaviors appear to match their body type? If so, make note of this in your Deconstruction. If not, you have a great opportunity to describe an interesting contradiction. The muscular computer nerd, for example, with the narrow waist of a body builder and swimmer makes for an image your readers won't soon forget...picture Bill Gates in Arnold Schwarzenegger's body.

Personality Types, The Blossoming of Modern Science

While as writers we can use the physical-personality stereotype or its juxtaposition to our advantage in creating memorable characters, this isn't scientific. It's time we delve into the real science of personality, and for that we must again look inward. As Eudora Welty wrote, "Characters take on life sometimes by luck, but I suspect it is when you can write more entirely out of yourself, inside the skin, heart, mind, and soul of a person who is not yourself, that a character becomes in his own right another human being on the page."

Whether or not you have taken a personality test, you've probably heard of the Myers-Briggs Type Indicator (MBTI). Katharine Cook Briggs had long been interested in human development and designing a tool to help people reach their full potential when, in 1923, she read Carl Jung's *Psychological Types*. His concepts of analytical psychology and archetypes resonated and redirected her own efforts. Together, Briggs and her daughter Isabel Briggs Myers dedicated their lives to refining Jungian theory and applying it in a measurable way to the analysis of personality types.

MBTI theory is based on four pairs of inherent elements:
- **(E)xtraversion** *vs.* **(I)ntroversion**—how a person gets energy
- **(S)ensing** *vs.* **I(N)ntuition**—how a person gets information
- **(T)hinking** *vs.* **(F)eeling**—how a person makes decisions
- **(J)udging** *vs.* **(P)erceiving**—how a person manages her/his lifestyle

These natural preferences (or dichotomies) are not meant to be judgmental; there is no right or wrong. They only help to catalog and measure our natural predilections for thinking and acting. By identifying a person's preference between each of the dichotomies, the Myers-Briggs Type Indicator assigns one of 16 personality types (ESTJ, ESTP, ESFJ, ESFP, ISTJ, ISFJ,etc.). While more than 2 million people take the certified MBTI questionnaire annually, there are free versions available online that satisfy our purposes. I've tested many of the free questionnaires based on Myers-Briggs types of questions and selected two that will provide you with insights into your personality and behavior as well as others in your memoir. You'll need to take

More than 2 million people take the certified MBTI questionnaire annually.

the tests *in the persona of* each of your major characters. For our purposes right now, however, take each test twice—once as yourself and once as a major character in your memoir. You might think you can save time by assigning personality types to your characters just by looking at the four dichotomies and selecting the combination that you *believe* is the best match. Don't. The questions are designed to capture nuance; they may also suggest situations that will help you consider how you or another character will behave under particular circumstances. Take the two tests and save your results because we'll end this section with an exercise in character Deconstruction.

Try This—Personality Test 1: Go to: http://www.teamtechnology.co.uk/mmdi/questionnaire/ and take The Mental Muscle Diagram Indicator™ (MMDI) test. You are given 36 items—each is a pair of statements. Using a six-point scale, you indicate which statement you agree with most. I like this test because it allows you to qualify your degree of agreement rather than give a binary yes/no response. After you take the test, you'll be told how strongly you match each of the four preferences and your most likely personality type. While you can buy a full report, the free information will give you enough of what you need to begin developing a more detailed psychological and behavioral analysis of yourself and other characters in your memoir. Save your results for further Deconstruction.

When I took The Mental Muscle Diagram Indicator, the report showed that I'm an ESFJ. In other words, I'm an E(xtravert), someone who gets energy from being with other people and who directs energy toward the outer rather than the inner world. Obviously, as a writer, I do spend a certain amount of my time in the inner world and I thrive during those hours. But anyone who has ever met me would immediately agree that I'm an extravert. The designation as an S(ensing) person also maps well with my personality. I prefer facts and tangible outcomes any day. As a F(eeling) person, I tend to make decisions based on subjective values versus relying on an entirely logical or fact-drive process. And finally, I am a J(udging) person. This one fits me perfectly. If I need to make a decision, I gather some facts, weigh them, and make a decision. End of story.

My partner, on the other hand, took the test with a resulting type of INTP. Polar opposites. As an I(introvert), he comes home from a party exhausted while I'm wired and full of enthusiasm. As an i(N)tuition personality, he makes decisions after carefully weighing alternatives (this overlaps with his characterization as a P, and in the process considers many possibilities. Recently a table server asked, "Do you want sweet potato hash or a kale salad as your side dish?" I could see him thinking through how each one might taste with his pan seared sea bass. Then the server added, "Or, you can have half and half." This was the kind of decision that was easy and put a smile on his face. His T(hinking) personality trait means that he uses objective logic when making decisions. And finally, as a P(erceiving) person, he doesn't need a fully organized world.

Let me give a quick example of how his composite personality type influences his behaviors. He takes on the responsibility for all our trip planning. His choices of hotels and experiences (music, theater, museums) are superb. No one could do better. But this comes at a high cost. He spends days researching each decision. A few months ago, we decided to go on a month-long trip (the longest we had ever taken) that was part writing retreat and part sunshine seeking, an escape from Oregon's rainy winters. Because I knew how long he would spend on the plans, I decided to take it on. I went to a website that listed privately owned condos available for vacation rental. We had already decided that we wanted to be in the San Diego area and chose Dana Point. A couple of years earlier he had researched Dana Point as an ideal spot for a trip that didn't work out. I felt safe with the choice. I looked through the rentals after ranking them by price since that would be a determining factor. I found one that seemed perfect -- walking distance to the beach and near the bus line. I showed him what I had found and said, "Let's take it." Not surprisingly, he said, "What other rentals are in Dana Point?" That was a fair question since I was the one who had done all the research. I showed him the others that had made it to my short list. He agreed with my choice and I contacted the owner and started negotiating price. Boy, I thought. That was simple. I should do this more often.

The next day, he said, "Here are street maps of the area around the condo. Come look at my computer. I'll show you the condo with the satellite view so you can see what the neighborhood looks like." He even showed me what the walk to the beach would be like, the location of nearby grocery stores and actual bus routes we could take to the San Capistrano Mission and other sightseeing places. By then he had probably spent about three hours and the clock was still ticking. He went on to say, "I'm starting to look at other condos to see if there is a different area where we'd like to be." I reminded him of why we had chosen the condo and that the advantage of a multi-day search didn't seem to outweigh the cost of time invested in a different decision. He finally agreed.

Has he always been like this? Yes. But I could never understand him until I had him take the MMDI personality test. Actually, just before he took the test I had asked him if he thought we should use our vacation money on a special trip or to visit our sons in Arizona and Texas. He replied, "Yes." Let me assure you, I didn't really think that was an appropriate answer to my question. Yet on reflection, I realized it was typical. Once he took the personality test, I began to understand the what and the why of his actions. His behaviors were a reflection of how he viewed the world as influenced by his personality.

Try This—Personality Test 2: Go to: http://www.humanmetrics.com/cgi-win/JType2.asp. The Jung Typology Test™ is a 72-item, yes/no test that will take you about 15 minutes to complete. As with the previous test, the results will identify your personality type and how strongly you scored for each preference. You'll see a brief qualitative analysis of your personality type, which will provide some context. In addition, you can click through to see a list of famous personalities who share your personality type and read more about your type. As with MMDI, Human Metrics offers several fee-based reports, but you should find enough information in the free reports. Save your results.

Once again, my scores showed I am an ESFJ. One of the things I like about The Jung Typology Test is that each element receives a score. Obviously, no one is ever 100% an Extravert or an Intravert. We are simply more one than the other. Here are my scores: 78% Extravert, 12% Sensing, 62% Feeling and 67% Judging.

All of these tests tell you that you may not feel the scores reflect your personality and that they are not guaranteed to be completely accurate. They often urge you to talk with friends after you get your results and determine if they see you in the same way. For me, the scores seem just about right. For example, I am a strong Extravert and indeed that is my single highest score. Previously I said I was an S(ensing) person and felt it right because I prefer facts and tangible outcomes to potential or unknown outcomes. And I do. However, as you can see from this test, I am only 12%

over on the S(ensing) versus (i)N(tuition) side of the dimension. So while I may prefer factual situations, I actually spend quite a bit of my time dealing in realms where simple facts are not known, where theories are relevant and where one has to experiment and see what works.

When writing a memoir, it is tempting to believe that good friends, possibly even relatives (although we tend to know them better) are like us. If we like being with a large group, we believe they feel the same way, etc. This is a natural tendency. Everyone does it. And because of this tendency to see others as having similar personalities, people in memoirs tend to come out as flat. It's why behaviors often seem unmotivated. Yet, when we take the time to understand the different personality types, we can connect better with our readers.

Case in point. My partner and I have been married more than four decades. After he took these personality tests, he said, "I'm sure our results are the same. I bet you are an INTP—well maybe an ENTP."

Dig deeply into character and the memoir you write will be significantly better.

Example: To help you apply Myers-Briggs personality types to your character development Deconstructions, Kendra thought it would be fun to put these two tests through their paces using one of the more interesting characters in modern literature—Oscar Wilde's Dorian Gray. Here's her report. "Admittedly, Dorian had more going on than just personality. The MBTI isn't designed to determine psychoses, psychiatric disorders or psychopathic/sociopathic behavior. That said, I gathered some interesting insights.

"When I answered both questionnaires as I believed Dorian Gray would respond, the MMDI test (Team Technology) defined Dorian Gray as an INFP (Introverted iNtuitive Feeling Perceiving):

- **Introverted** (moderate): concentrates on a few deep issues
- **iNtuitive** (strong): interested in what's not yet known
- **Feeling** (slight): takes personal, subjective view as participant (But because preference is slight, I am including its opposite
- **Perceiving** (strong): flexible, inquiring, spontaneous, keeps options open

"Answering the items of The HumanMetrics' Jung Typology Test as I thought Dorian Gray would resulted a somewhat different personality type: ENTP (Extraverted iNtuitive Thinking Perceiving):

- **Extraverted** (slight 1%)
- **iNtuitive** (moderate 50%)
- **Thinking** (moderate 50%)
- **Perceiving** (moderate 56%)

"Of course, the differences could be that I was dealing with a fictional character that I didn't know in person. However, it turns out that the differences can be explained in other ways. First, consider that Dorian Gray is a classic dual personality—a regular Dr. Jekyll/Mr. Hyde. Second, these two personality types are not all that different. The Jung Typology Test registers only 1 percent Extraverted; iNtuitive and Perceiving are consistent with the MMDI results; and the MMDI indicated only a slight preference for Feeling, so a Thinking preference is not an unreasonable result. The Jung Typology Test doesn't provide simple phrases to define the ENTP, but I did click on the provided link to read a description of this personality type. I found several useful descriptors: "clever," "perverse sense of humor," "quick to spot a kindred spirit, and good at acquiring friends of similar temperament." But one paragraph in particular caught my attention:

> ENTPs are basically optimists, but in spite of this (perhaps because of it?), they can become petulant about small setbacks and inconveniences. (Major setbacks they regard as challenges, and tackle with determination.) ENTPs have little patience with those they consider wrongheaded or unintelligent, and show little restraint in demonstrating this. In general, however, they are genial, even charming, when not being harassed by life.

"Now," Kendra continued, "let's try to validate these test results against Wilde's description of Dorian Gray in his own words. We know Dorian, of course, as the narcissistic hedonist obsessed with preserving his youth and beauty who, once he realizes his sins are relegated to the portrait, abandons any attempt at self control. When not locked in the room upstairs pondering the painting (the mirror of his soul), he is the clever, witty dinner guest or host, full of imagination and ready for anything...for he sees only possibilities. His personality is a pathological mix of introspective idealism, unpredictability, extreme emotionalism and moodiness. Wilde wrote:

> He grew more and more enamoured of his own beauty, more and more interested in the corruption of his own soul....he would think of the ruin he had brought upon his soul with a pity that was all the more poignant because it was purely selfish....He had mad hungers that grew more ravenous as he fed them....He sought to elaborate some new scheme of life that would have its reasoned philosophy and its ordered principles, and find in the spiritualizing of the senses its highest realization.

"The ellipses," Kendra notes, "indicate where I've strung together sentences and phrases from throughout the book. Continuing on, Wilde says:

> ...in his search for sensations that would be at once new and delightful, and possess that element of strangeness that is so essential to romance, he would often adopt certain modes of thought that he knew to be really alien to his nature, abandon himself to their subtle influences, and then, having, as it were, caught their colour and satisfied his intellectual curiosity, leave them with that curious indifference that is not incompatible with a real ardour of temperament, and that, indeed, according to certain modern psychologists, is often a condition of it.

> Yet, as has been said of him before, no theory of life seemed to him to be of any importance compared with life itself. He felt keenly conscious of how barren all intellectual speculation is when separated from action and experiment.

"Finally, here's portrait artist Basil Hallward on the young Dorian:

> As a rule, he is charming to me, and we sit in the studio and talk of a thousand things. Now and then, however, he is horribly thoughtless, and seems to take a real delight in giving me pain.

"All in all, the personality types seem to hold up pretty well."

Thanks Kendra. That was a real challenge to take the personality test not for yourself or someone you know well but for a fictional character. Your findings are quite striking. I think even Oscar Wilde would accept the results.

Now Get to Writing!

It's time for you to add your personality type (and that of one of your characters) to your character Deconstruction and validate your personality type(s) with examples from your life.

1. Write down your results from both tests. If you didn't take them earlier, now is the time.
2. List some of the behaviors that illustrate your personality type. By the way, if you want more background on your personality type, you can try: http://www.mypersonality.info/personality-types.
3. Validate your personality type with examples in your life.
4. Now, repeat steps 1, 2 and 3 for another major person you are developing.

Note: Don't be concerned if your personality type on one test does not match perfectly with results on the other. These free tests are based on MBTI-type questions and are not certified by The Myers & Briggs Foundation. However, even the official MBTI results may vary. First, you need to focus on the preference similarities you do have. Second, you must take into consideration the strength/weakness of each preference. And third, remember that results are age dependent, and preferences become stronger and more consistent as we age.

By the way, if you're wondering just how much MBTI can help with character development, consider this: In 1929 Isabel Briggs Myers wrote a mystery called *Murder Yet to Come*, drawing heavily on her knowledge of personality types and behavior. She won the national Detective Murder Mystery Contest, beating out an early Ellery Queen story.

Try This—Personality Test 3: When you looked at the results from your Human Metrics Jung Typology Test (Test 2) you may have noticed a link to D. Keirsey's type description. If you clicked the link, you'd have been treated to a one-page explanation of your personality type. D. Keirsey is clinical psychologist David Keirsey.

As with any rich research topic, multiple scientists investigate the same general field but from different perspectives. Often, these perspectives come from their own life narratives. In the 1950s, for example, Keirsey started his career as a youth counselor working with delinquent boys, which led him to focus his practice on strategies for cooperation and conflict management. Once he learned about the Myers-Briggs methodology, he saw that its 16 personality types not only were accurate but complemented his own research. He modified Myers and Briggs' four categories of natural preferences, and their focus on how people think and feel, to reflect his own analysis of observable behaviors, which he defined as the four temperaments—Artisan, Guardian, Idealist and Rational—and 16 character or role variants he calls the Keirsey Temperament Sorter:

- **Artisan**—Composer, Crafter, Performer and Promoter
- **Guardian**—Inspector, Protector, Provider and Supervisor
- **Idealist**—Champion, Counselor, Healer and Teacher
- **Rational**—Architect, Fieldmarshal, Inventor and Mastermind

Keirsey correlates his 16 role variants to the MBTI personality types, which makes it easy for you to add another layer of rich character insight. When Kendra tested Dorian Gray, he scored as a Rational Inventor (ENTP). She felt the write up mapped well to the portrait Wilde creates of the infamous Dorian. "I particularly liked this from Keirsey's write-up on the Rational: 'Rationals don't care about being politically correct. They are interested in the most efficient solutions possible, and will listen to anyone who has something useful to teach them, while disregarding any authority or customary procedure that wastes time and resources.'"

You can take a free version of the Keirsey Temperament Sorter II—a 70-item questionnaire—by following this link: http://www. keirsey.com/sorter/instruments2.aspx?partid=0. You are asked one personal item (gender) and then asked to put in your email address. I took this test for the first time more than a year ago and have never received emails. Keirsey operates a legitimate business so if you should receive any follow-up emails, I am sure they will provide an easy way to get off their list. More than the previous websites, this one makes it somewhat difficult to see your free results. However, just read the material carefully and you'll see that you don't need to purchase any reports.

Now Get to Writing!

You'll find rich material on the Keirsey website about personality and character. Here's a link to tables that explain the correlation between Keirsey's temperaments and the Myers-Briggs personality types: http://www.keirsey.com/aboutkts2.aspx. Now it's time for you to enrich your character Deconstructions with this material.

1. Take the test as yourself and add the results to your Deconstruction.

2. Take the test a second time as the second major person in your memoir whom you've been Deconstructing for these exercises. Include the results in your character Deconstruction.

One More Look at Personality Types: Personality Characteristics

In one more interesting twist, we have Travis Bradberry's book *The Personality Code.* His work is based on the research of psychologist William Marston, inventor of the polygraph who created DISC, a personality test [Dominance, Interpersonal (sometimes called Influence), Steadiness, Conscientiousness (sometimes called Compliance)]. Incidentally, you may know Marston by his pen name Charles Moulton, the creator of Wonder Woman.

World War II brought about the sudden need to put large numbers of people into military assignments, both at home and overseas. Just as Myers-Briggs Type Indicator proved its worth during the war, so too did Marston's DISC types, which looked at the interaction between people and their environment and helped the military predict which types of people would work best in certain situations. Fast forward to the present. Travis Bradberry adapted the Marston DISC system to identify 14 personality types and developed the popular IDISC online personality profiler. IDISC—already taken by more than half a million people—works on Bradberry's premise that self knowledge of our personality and the personality of others enables us to make the most of our strengths and compensate for our weaknesses.

Try This: In looking for free DISC tests, I found one that I like at PersonalityStyle.com, and the 24 items will take you only about 10 minutes to complete. Go to: http://www.personalitystyle.com/personality-test-register.php. You will need to register, but as with the

Keirsey people, I have never received any followup emails, but after registration you can easily return and retake the test for all the major characters in your book. Once you complete the questions, you'll be rewarded with your personality type and a one-page write up.

My result said:

<u>Fire of Inspiration</u>

Matilda, as the "Fire of Inspiration," people are often impressed by your charisma, empathetic nature, and determination. ... You're a natural born communicator and an adept social navigator. Where often others will sit by, you will engage new people or invite others in to make them feel at home, and in turn you are seen as bold, confident, and courageous.

You are neighborly, open-minded and able to see the 'best' in others. Once you form a bond with another person, you have no problem talking about personal subjects and extending trust...You genuinely care for others and will go out of your way for them, especially friends.

In general, I'd agree with the description. The statements about "charisma," "natural born communicator," and "engage new people" are behaviors associated with extraversion. So while the previous tests helped me understand my personality type in an abstract sense, this test points to some behaviors that go with my type.

While I believe in the Buddhism philosophy of Be Here Now, I rarely follow it so you can see why I was surprised by the "live in the moment" reference that was also in the report.

Most likely impulsive, you live in the moment and search out new experiences. Seen as relationship-oriented, people are drawn to your energetic optimism and enthusiasm.

Taking personality tests forces you to think about how you operate in different situations. Personal insights gained from these tests cause you to examine your own life as well as write about it.

Now Get to Writing!

1. Take the DISC test as yourself. Pick key points out of your results—points that give you new insights—and add to your character Deconstructions.

2. Take the test a second time as another major person in your memoir. Read the results. What did you learn about the person that you hadn't noticed before? Add this information to your character Deconstructions for this person. The other person, if taking the test himself or herself, might have somewhat different results. However, you can learn more about another person by trying to think and respond in the way that person would. It is a good exercise that reminds you to let individuals shine through in your memoir as if they were on their own.

Two Theories of Needs (Motivation)

By now, if you've been doing each of the Now Get to Writing! exercises, you may feel that you have quite a rich character Deconstruction. And yes, determining each character's personality type(s) provides you with the basis for creating verisimilitude when you write. But we can go deeper into our characters by understanding specific motivations that drive people in our stories. Why does your friend now behave in ways that make no sense to you while before her behaviors made perfect sense? Perhaps her motivations have stayed the same, but in order to reach her goals the behaviors have changed. You were just looking at the behaviors in the early years and thought you knew her motivations. We're about to determine what drives the people in our stories.

Why does your friend now behave in ways that make no sense to you...

Taxonomy of Needs for Your Characters

Here's another social scientist who is of interest to memoir writers. As a child, Henry Murray didn't get along with his mother and frequently felt depressed. This may have been one of the factors that caused him to be attuned to people's needs and dedicate most of his life to seeking answers. In 1919, Murray graduated from Columbia medical school while simultaneously receiving an MA in biology.

Here's where the thread of Carl Jung is again picked up. In 1923, Murray fell in love with Christiana Morgan. Murray was married at the time and was torn between staying with his wife and leaving her for Morgan. His lover, who was enthusiastic about Jung's work, suggested that he seek the counsel of Jung. So he traveled to Switzerland to spend time in analysis with Jung and to study his writings. As one outcome of this experience, Murray continued his study of biochemistry (Ph.D. in 1927) but decided to make psychology his career although he never earned a degree in the field. The decision certainly didn't hold him back. He became the assistant director of Harvard's Psychological Clinic in 1927 where he developed a theory of latent and manifest needs. Ten years later he became the clinic's director. His *Explorations in Personality* (1938), a classic on the psychology of personality, brought him to the attention of the Office of Strategic Services (OSS), the US intelligence agency formed during World War II. The OSS recruited Murray to help with the selection of secret agents by applying his concept that our needs determine our behaviors.

Murray's needs theory gives us a way to appreciate the basis for motivations and understand how needs are manifested in the behavior of people in our memoirs. His research pointed to a taxonomy of five major types of needs, or primary motivators, each having several related secondary needs:

- **Ambition**: Achievement, Exhibition, Recognition
- **Materialism**: Acquisition, Construction, Order, Retention
- **Power**: Abasement, Autonomy, Aggression, Blame avoidance, Deference, Dominance
- **Affection**: Affiliation, Nurturance, Play, Rejection, Succorance/Social Support
- **Information**: Cognizance, Exposition

Individuals are high or low on each of these needs. The question you must ask is, "To what degree?" When you understand your characters' needs profiles, their behaviors become more explainable and, in turn, more believable for your readers.

For example, of the five major needs, my mother must have been highest on Materialism although Information and Ambition (for her husband) were also motivators for her. But only in recent years have I been able to explain some of her behaviors that seemed unfathomable at the time. Here's a favorite story: My father squeezed fresh orange juice for my mother almost every day of their 66 years together. He used a glass hand juicer, most assuredly inexpensive when first bought. Somewhere across those decades, he bought two of these. A few years after my father died at the age of 90, I was visiting my mother in Oklahoma City. I asked if it would be all right if I took home one of the two juicers, explaining that it reminded me of my father. Mother responded, "Oh, you're going to think I'm selfish, but I can't really let you have either one. I continue to use both of them." Well, she was 93 and had arthritis so badly that she had not been able to use the juicers in years. At that time, I just shrugged it off as "the way she was." Murray's needs theory explains that Materialism includes not only Acquisition but also Retention. And while my story involved an item as insignificant as an ordinary kitchen juicer, you can imagine how tightly she held on to her other possessions. Although I used to laugh that she probably thought she could take them with her, I now understand that was part of what kept her motivated and lively until just past her 95th birthday.

Now Get to Writing!

1. Based on your personality type, develop a likely profile of your needs using Murray's list. Think about what you would do under a specific circumstance (behavior). For example, a picnic with friends has been planned for weeks but you are unexpectedly called in to work on that Saturday. How would you react differently if you were high on the need for Ambition versus the need for Affiliation? What does this tell you about yourself? What would you do in this same situation if you were an Extravert versus an Introvert?

2. Develop a profile of the needs of the second most important person in your memoir. Look for insights that will enable you to develop this person more fully in your book. Remember, in this Deconstruction for character, you are developing material that you will selectively use across the entire memoir. Add as many details as you can including examples of behaviors.

3. Now think of a situation where you and the second person are interacting. If you are writing a scene that involves you two, then use that. Otherwise, use the situation detailed in the first exercise. This means you and the second person are at a picnic when you are called in to work. How do you behave (you've already written this)? How does the second person react based on her or his needs? How does that person's behavior or comments affect you?

Organizing Needs into a Hierarchy

People are complicated, especially when we factor in the element of time. Not only are none of us a pure personality type or motivated by a single need but some aspects of our personality are stronger under specific circumstances or at particular times in our lives. Still, the underlying personality types and needs patterns are there, and as writers this is what we must look for in order to create coherent, believable characters. There's just one thing, all needs are not equal, and for help in establishing priorities of needs, we turn to Abraham Maslow, a name you probably know and associate with self-actualizing.

People are complicated...

But let's back up a bit. Until Maslow's research, most psychologists developed their narratives based on working with people who came to them with their problems—the abnormal and psychologically crippled. Part of Maslow's genius was in seeking to understand healthy, well-adjusted individuals who were succeeding in their daily personal and professional lives. Although most of Maslow's research took place from the 1940s through 1960s, his work continues to be relevant today. Most recently, Daniel Pink's book that was #1 on *The New York Times* bestseller list, *DRIVE: The Surprising Truth About What Motivates Us*, draws on Maslow's pioneering work that resulted in the Hierarchy of Needs. Working from the most necessary upwards, Maslow described:

- **Physiological Needs:** These are the most basic for survival and include the needs for air, water, food and sleep.
- **Security Needs:** Assuming that one has adequate oxygen, water, food and sleep not only today but for the foreseeable future, a person next addresses security needs. These include personal safety as well as security for family, employment, finances and health. To the extent that these security needs are not met, a person spends most of his or her energy focusing on this problem. Imagine, for example, that you lived in a war zone. You would be concerned primarily about your ability to go to the market and return with food for dinner without being killed by a roadside bomb. You'd have little energy left for higher-order needs. Closer to home, what if you unexpectedly found yourself unemployed or losing half of your savings in the stock market at a time when you had little new income. You would devote much

of your energy and effort to your financial state because you no longer had financial security.

- **Social (Belonging) Needs:** People desire love and affection for and from friends and family, even co-workers. But unlike the most basic physiological needs, one can live without meeting the need for social contact or love. We're just unlikely to be very self-actualized when we live without the affection and concern of others.
- **Esteem Needs:** With physiological, security and social needs met, we strive for the acceptance of others (family, friends and co-workers) and especially our own self-respect. Without a personal sense of achievement and the respect of others, we feel weak, helpless and risk an inferiority complex.

These first four levels represent what Maslow called deficiency needs (D-Needs). We continually work to satisfy each to a greater or lesser extent; we can never completely ignore them. However, when they are well met, we have more energy to invest in what Maslow called his being needs (B-Needs):

- **Self-Actualizing Needs:** This, the highest level, identifies the need for creativity, spontaneity, autonomy, even peak experiences. One is never self-actualized, but once other needs are being met on a routine basis, a person can focus on the ongoing process of self-actualizing.

Maslow's Hierarchy of Needs is often shown as a pyramid with the more basic needs at the bottom:

Self-Actualizing Needs: Creativity, spontaneity, autonomy, peak experiences

Esteem Needs: Confidence, achievement, respect of others

Social Needs: Love, affection, connectedness with others

Security Needs: Personal, family, employment, financial and healh safety

Physiological Needs: Water, food, sleep

In practice, however, people's needs don't look like a perfect pyramid, and they're often in flux. Consider the needs hierarchy for Nora Helmer in Ibsen's *A Doll's House*. All of her D-Needs (Physiological, Security, Social, Esteem) are met until she realizes that her husband Torvald's willingness to throw her out to protect his honor shows that he is not the man she thought. You may remember that Nora tells him she will leave that very evening, taking nothing with her, and will not seek any money from him. Although she will spend the night with her friend Christine, she then had to consider the real threat to her most basic needs such as food and clothing as well as her higher needs for love and affection. She might be able to rebuild, to satisfy her D-needs and eventually even her self-actualizing need, but the profile of her hierarchy changes drastically when she walks out of her home—or perhaps I should more accurately say for the times—her husband's home.

Interesting, you may be thinking. But how do I use this in my memoir writing? You can apply Maslow's hierarchy of needs to better understand the motivations and attendant behaviors of the characters in your story. Any number of circumstances determine the shape of the steady-state profile of a person, and many others that could create a hierarchy change. When you think about it, you've seen this in your own life. Once you go beyond the basic physiological needs, personality-type factors (such as introversion and judging) or demographic factors (such as age and education) will influence the shape of your needs hierarchy. Then a change occurs. It might be as minor as getting married and losing the security of your parents paying for everything. Or it could be more drastic: on the negative side, a diagnosis of ovarian cancer when you have no medical insurance, a car wreck that leaves your son a quadriplegic, a spouse who dies at a young age leaving you with infant twins to raise. On the positive side, winning the state lottery, coming into an inheritance, getting a promotion or becoming engaged could also dramatically change the profile of your needs hierarchy.

Example: Let's create two hypothetical profiles of a person to show changes that would highlight motivations for actions in a story. Let's call her Barbara, a woman who enjoys her professional career and has just begun to put aside some money so that she can buy her own home. She has few social contacts, actually only one real friend, and is not close with her co-workers. Her family lives on the other coast and with financial constrains rarely visit. But she is competent at work and has recently earned a promotion and salary increase so her self-esteem is flying high. She is just beginning to become more self-aware and has finally taken her creative interests toward printmaking. The new art hobby pleases her, and she has taken several courses; her teachers have encouraged her to develop her talent. If Barbara was a character in a story, a writer might create her profile as I've shown below. Notice that graphically the box for her social needs is quite narrow. Of course, I have to add that *she* may feel she is meeting her social needs since unlike an extravert, an introvert doesn't need as much external stimulation. Below is her profile as it looks from the perspective of the person viewing her. The white areas show Barbara's profile while the gray areas reflect the ideal profile shown previously.

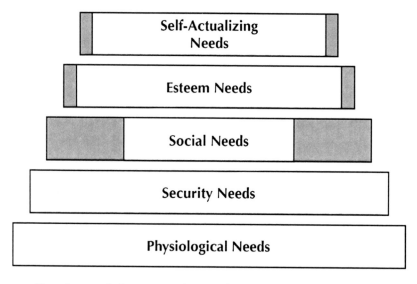

Fast forward three months. Barbara has a new camera and is eager to take photos of snow as a source of inspiration for a print series she wants to undertake. On her way to photograph the newly fallen snow in a nearby mountain range, her car tires spin on a patch of ice and an oncoming car hits her. She survives but is left blind. None of her needs are being met as well as before—from her physiological needs (she continues to have nightmares and her sleep pattern is regularly disrupted) and security needs (she can no longer work, or at least not until she is retrained) to her social needs (she has to rely on others more but has not built the social network that might be able to help her) and esteem needs (her career achievements that meant so much to her are no longer possible). Her self-actualization is all but non-existent (she is no longer able to make prints, her creative outlet).

Barbara must focus on her basic physiological and security needs. Her social needs, while clearly more important to her survival, are unmet and unchanged, and esteem has narrowed dramatically.

Her changed needs hierarchy might look like this:

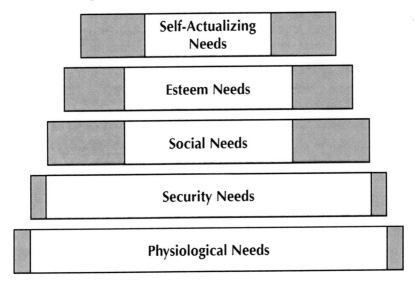

Now Get to Writing!

1. Take two different times in your life and create your own Hierarchy of Needs pyramids. Did the pyramids change over time? How? Why? What events intervened? Add what you have learned about yourself to your Deconstruction.

2. Try doing the same exercise for another major person in your memoir. Look for a critical event or turning point in the person's life. Then draw the Hierarchy of Needs before and after that turning point. How has the person changed? Add your insights about this person to his or her Deconstruction.

And Finally, Adding Enduring Personality Traits

There is one more element of personality that has been widely re-searched by social scientists and may help you as a writer create coherent, motivated characters. This began in a way that as a writer you will appreciate—a study of all the words in the dictionary as-sociated with personality, words that could help distinguish one person from another. Gordon Allport and H. W. Odbert, in 1936, published the result of their personality lexicon that included some 18,000 terms.

Because computers were unavailable to analyze relationships among this large number of words, Allport and Odbert categorized each term in their personality lexicon into one of four groups:

- enduring personality traits,
- temporary states,
- evaluative statements, and
- physical/talent descriptive terms.

Then they selected a subset of terms to represent the range within each of the categories and asked the question, What are the significant personality traits? Research to answer this ques-tion has been ongoing since the 1930s, and today the database stores responses from thousands of people. Although everyone agrees there are many individual personality traits, factor analysis (one statistical way of organizing the data) points to five, higher-order and distinct (little overlap) traits, called simply the Big Five Personality Traits. These traits, for which individuals can score from low to high, are easily remembered by the acronym OCEAN—Openness, Conscientiousness (echo of Marston's DISC), Extraversion (echo of Myers-Briggs), Agreeableness and Neuroticism. Within each is a large number of more specific traits. Here are a few examples:

- **Openness:** People high on this trait may also be imaginative, curious, insightful, adventurous, risk takers.
- **Conscientiousness:** People high on this trait may also be duti-ful, results-oriented, meticulous, disciplined, responsible.
- **Extraversion:** People high on this trait may also be outgoing, energetic, sociable.

- **Agreeableness:** People high on this trait may also be compassionate, trusting, sympathetic, compliant, pragmatic.
- **Neuroticism:** People high on this trait may also be emotionally unstable.

Try This: You can take a 92-item test that will give you feedback on how high or low you score on each of these five personality traits. Just go to: http://www.123test.com/personality-test/

Now Get to Writing!

1. Each of us is a mixture of highs and lows on these traits. Think about these traits and describe yourself in terms of the Big Five based on your scores on the above test. Think through your personality type and see which of these traits provides more specificity so that readers may better understand you. You don't have to write sentences but you might want to sketch out a situation where your trait profile helps you move your story forward.

2. Using the same Big Five traits, describe a second major person in your memoir. The best way to do this is to take the above test imagining that you are the other person. If the other person is agreeable, she or he might be willing to go to the site, take the test, and give you the results.

Now You're Ready to Create Your Main Characters

But wait a minute. Pretend you want to build a frame around your character. Actually a shadowbox would be just about right to hold your character and allow the three-dimensional features. If you are a weekend handy person and work the way I do, you're likely to start the project even before you've designed it adequately. You'll use whatever wood you happen to have left over from a previous craft. You'll get out your wood saw and cut what looks like a 45-degree angle. Oops. Your saw isn't sharp (well, there was that day you couldn't find your hacksaw and cut that metal rod with your wood saw) and now the two 45-degree angles don't really match at the corners of the frame. And so it goes. Nails or screws the wrong size will split the wood, inaccurate measurements will mean the backing won't fit, paint inappropriately applied will run. Around our home we have a saying, "Any project worth doing is worth doing three times." Then we laugh. The first time it doesn't fit. The second time it fits but doesn't look right. The third time it fits and looks great.

Now a master carpenter like Norm Abram of *This Old House* and *The New Yankee Workshop* would only need to make his shadowbox once. He'd begin with a thorough design. Abram said about building a house, "Take the dream as high as you can, then work with the budget realities. Spend a lot of time designing it. Make as many decisions as you can ahead of time so you don't get to the end and find you have no money for carpet. Don't be disappointed when you have to cut back because everyone has to cut back." (Interview with Elizabeth Rhodes, *Seattle Times*, September 10, 1995)

"*Measure twice, cut once.*"

Abram knows the importance of design and making decisions. If you've ever watched him on television, you know that he has more tools than we can imagine and knows how to use each one. They aren't all relevant for any particular project, but they stand by at the ready. He will make a jig specific to the current project, even if that is the only time he uses it. He carefully chooses his wood, measures precisely. "Measure twice, cut once." Then cuts with the appropriate saw, not just the first one his hand touches, then sands and sands and sands. His shadowbox frame could be displayed in the living room with a spotlight on it. Mine, if I manage to get it finished, belongs in the back of a closet.

The difference is planning, attention to detail, having all the right tools available and using them with skill. I might never be a master carpenter but I could improve. Similarly, by showing you a number of tools, teaching you how to use them and providing a process (Deconstruction), we've given you what you need to improve your skills for developing your characters, the people in your memoir. Plus, Deconstruction lets you focus on just one element at a time without worrying about the overarching issues of plot and story structure or the minute details of the actual words, sentences and paragraphs.

You'll find that using concepts and tools in this chapter to Deconstruct all your major characters will let you know them so well that they'll come alive for you and more importantly for your readers. This approach works independent of the school of character development that you favor. If you believe the characters take over and tell you what happens next, Writing Alchemy provides you with a fully developed character who can do precisely that. If you prefer Carolyn See's approach, the tools in this chapter will provide insight into identity, physical description, demographics, psychographics and personality. If you prefer our technique and want to begin with the essence of a person, Writing Alchemy lets you easily add levels to that person's core so that you'll be working with a three-dimensional character. Even if you pursue the interview-the-character school, Writing Alchemy lets you know the character as a whole and then you just add the details that seem important to your storyline.

And live by Norm Abram's words: "Don't be disappointed when you have to cut back because everyone has to cut back." You will have developed characters with such depth that you won't be able to use all the material. Don't worry. This is like creating a real town where the bad guy walks down the street rather than a town with false building fronts propped upright with 2 x 4s. You will know more than the reader will ever be told, but what the reader learns will seem like a bit of time spent with an intriguing person.

Remember that you need to create a complete profile of each of the major people in your book, including yourself. You're Deconstructing at the book level, leaving you only to append details at the chapter/scene level as a character's appearance and behavior changes. At a minimum, you need to create profiles that are true to the people at the beginning of your memoir and at the end. But that really is the minimum. And yes, I know, this may not seem as though you are writing fast. However, this is like Abram's "measure twice." You will save yourself a lot of time, considerable backing up, and months of rewriting if you spend the time now to thoroughly Deconstruct each major person in your memoir.

Once you have the details, you need to think through how to reveal your characters in the course of telling of your story. By the time you begin writing, you should have a timeline or a list of likely chapters, which will help you decide when in the story to show more about each character. The deeper you go into the memoir, the more readers should learn. At first, just a few basics are needed such as identity, relevant demographics and physical description.

The deeper you go into the memoir, the more readers should learn.

Developing the people in your memoir this way is like putting together a jigsaw puzzle until the whole picture is finally revealed. The reward for your efforts is knowing that readers will remain engaged with your story to the end.

A Final Tip. I'll leave you with this: Ask yourself what is known about each character at the beginning of a chapter and what more has been revealed at the end of each chapter. Keep a list as you write. Watch the portrait of each character emerge over the course of your writing.

http://womensmemoirs.com/character-2

What's Next?

Now you can see your characters and have the tools, even online tests, to help you develop and really understand others in your memoir.

So now with good descriptions, with an understanding of how personality factors can drive behaviors, you're wondering what more you need to do?

It's time to move back to the level of a scene or vignette and examine the emotions that you and others experience in the scene you are writing. Just how real are emotions? What do we mean when we talk about emotions? How do we effectively use the element of emotions in writing? How can we incorporate emotions so that our readers are emotionally drawn into our story? We'll share the best of the science of emotions so that you can understand their role in your story.

References and Resources

Auchard, Betty. *Dancing in My Nightgown: The Rhythms of Widowhood.* Las Vegas: Stephens Press, 2010.

Baron, Renee. *What Type Am I? Discover Who You Really Are.* New York: Penguin Books, 1998.

Bradberry, Travis. *The Personality Code*. New York: Putnam, 2007.

Brodie, Fawn. *Thomas Jefferson: An Intimate History*. New York: W. W. Norton & Company, 1974.

Collins, Brandilyn. *Getting into Character: Seven Secrets a Novelist Can Learn from Actors*. New York: John Wiley & Sons, 2002.

Edelstein, Linda N. *The Writer's Guide to Character Traits*. Cincinnati: Writer's Digest Books, 1999.

Engber, Martha. *Growing Great Characters From the Ground Up: A Thorough Primer for Writers of Fiction and Nonfiction*. Albuquerque: Central Avenue Press, 2007.

Lauther, Howard. *Creating Characters: A Writer's Reference to the Personality Traits that Bring Fictional People to Life*. Jefferson, NC: McFarland, 2004.

Pink, Daniel. *DRIVE: The Surprising Truth About What Motivates Us*. New York: Riverhead, 2009.

Roddick, Hawley. *Your Memoirs: Saving the Stories of Your Life and Work*. Lulu Press, 2007. [Note: Roddick discusses both the Myers-Briggs as a tool for writers as well as the Enneagram, a similar tool that we did not cover in this chapter.]

See, Carolyn. *Making a Literary Life: Advice for Writers and Other Dreamers*. New York: Ballantine Books, 2003.

4 Acknowledging Feelings of
Love, Expressing Joy, Dealing
with Anger, Accepting
Sadness, Caving in to Hatred
—Matilda Butler

The Element of Emotion and Affect

Rrrriiinnnggg. Rrrriiinnnggg. I was still dressing for the day, so I picked up the receiver to the phone that sits by the bathtub. It was August 25, 1999, and my sister called to ask if I'd fly to Oklahoma City the next day. She had plans to visit her son in Charleston, but Daddy had just been admitted to Baptist Hospital.

"Daddy's in the hospital?"

"Yes. I'll explain when you get here. I don't think it's too serious but I'd feel better if you were here while I'm gone."

"How long will you be in Charleston?" I saw that my plans for the coming days would have to be changed.

"I'll be there a week. You know, I only get to go once a year."

With that familiar sinking feeling I got whenever Ann reminded me that she spent most of her days making our parents' lives better, I said, "Sure. Let me see what I can do with my schedule and what flight I can get. I'll call you back."

I love my parents and don't like the possible story behind her call. I had flown from San Jose to Oklahoma City in mid-May to celebrate my father's 90th birthday. He was strong and well. Actually, he hadn't seemed to change in a number of years. Denial? Unwillingness to think that my parents might ever die? I don't think so. Even now, a dozen years later, I look at photos of him and see practically no change in his appearance in the last decade of his life. It's true he had finally given up driving—actually my mother took his keys away from him—but due largely to macular degeneration. He remained strong physically and just as strong mentally. He grocery shopped; cooked some—made coffee for my mother each morning so that it was awaiting her when she awoke—visited and kept up with friends; helped maintain the two-plus-acre garden including mulching with the tens of thousands of dried oak leaves that fell each year; and, oh yes, always, always read the newspaper. Even with his eye problems, each morning he read the paper from the first page to the last sitting in his Chinese red chair at the same wrought iron and glass top kitchen table where our family had eaten for decades. A favorite section, if it can be called that, was the obituaries. He combed them each day, and when he saw that a friend had died, he called my sister and asked her to go with him to the funeral.

My father was active and alert in May. We talked frequently on the phone. He was always interested in what I was doing and what was happening on my land. So I wondered that August day how he could possibly be seriously ill. Sure, he'd had prostate cancer but was long past that, and there had been no recurrence. He'd even been in a serious car accident and broken an arm. But nothing much had happened in the past 10 years.

I pushed my fears down, tucking them deep into the recesses of my stomach, and checked online for the best possible airfare. With no advance purchase, the ticket wasn't cheap, but I knew that money shouldn't be an issue at this point. I purchased my ticket and called my sister to let her know I'd show up at the Will Rogers Airport the next day at 4:35 p.m. That would give us time to stop by the hospital, go see Mother and settle in at Ann's house. I'd watch her place while she was out of town.

I pushed my fears down, tucking them deep into the recesses of my stomach...

I have a friend who talks about getting caught in a medical vortex. That's probably as good a way as any to shortcut this description of the days that followed. I'm better at staying up nights than my sister, so I spent every night next to my father. He was always coherent, always thinking about others. I remember him giving me a grocery list of the things that mother liked and suggested that I should pick them up for her. He worried that if anything happened to him, Ann wouldn't have enough money to live on.

This went on several days, and Ann eventually decided to cancel her trip. Fighting the medical establishment takes considerable energy, and two can be better than one. But I figured we were in trouble when my father asked me if I saw the woman driving a Euclid tractor in his hospital room. He had sold large, road-building equipment most of his life but no, I didn't see the woman on the Euclid. Perhaps more bizarre than Daddy's visions was the fact that the doctor didn't want to investigate any of his symptoms. Actually, even now it is too frightening for me to describe all that happened or, perhaps I should say, all that didn't happen medically.

Around 9:30 a.m. on September 1, my sister showed up to relieve me from my night shift. For some reason I stayed. Daddy wasn't seeing anyone that morning although on more than one occasion he had mistaken me for his mother. Later I realized that my hair pulled back from my face along with my rimless glasses did echo the way my grandmother looked. Even now, when I glance up at her picture, I can see the strong resemblance.

I didn't have a cell phone in 1999, but my sister did. When it rang that morning, she said I should answer as she and Daddy were talking. Mother was on the phone asking about Daddy. This was the first time she had called, although she had visited twice. I walked into the hall to talk with her when I heard my sister scream, "Nurse. Nurse."

I knew.

As the nurses came flying down the hall, my heartbeat ratcheted up so high that I could barely hear myself calmly tell Mother that the phone connection wasn't clear and I'd call her back in a little bit. All the remaining activities happened in a haze. The nurses kept saying things like, "Ed, stay with us." I remember thinking it strange to hear them calling him Ed. Somehow it seemed more appropriate that they call him Mr. Butler. My father was in a convalescent home at this point, and someone on the staff called an ambulance to get him to the hospital. I saw Daddy on a gurney as the paramedics rushed him out. My heart raced; my feet did likewise, rushing me to his side. I patted his hand and said I'd see him at the hospital. Then I jumped in the car that Ann already had running. When we arrived at the hospital, we had to check in with the ER administrative staff. It was "wait over here" and "please take a seat" and "someone will be with you soon." A staff person finally informed us that Daddy was dead and that we could go into a room to see him if we wanted.

These memories still hurt. My stomach dropped, opening that deep recess where I had stowed my fear seven days before. It came out and squeezed my heart so tightly that I felt a sharp pain in my chest that stayed with me as we walked into the chilly room where Daddy's body lay. With tears streaming down my cheeks and my nose running, I touched him one last time with my clammy hand. "I love you."

These memories still hurt.

Emotions in Writing

Emotions. Whether associated with traumatic events such as my father's death or ordinary activities such as getting a phone call from a good friend, our bodies are processing emotions all day long. Yet when it comes to writing, many people get so involved in recording the facts and in telling them in an interesting way, that the basic emotional undertone is ignored. But nothing really happens without emotions, which is why working feelings, moods and emotional behavior into our stories is critical. It's hard for readers to become engaged in our stories if we don't expose our emotions and touch their emotions.

That's why Deconstructing for your emotions is so valuable. It allows you to put aside other writing concerns and focus 100 percent of your energy on capturing your emotional states. In this chapter, I'll share information about both the art and the science of emotions so that you'll be better equipped to uncover your emotions and incorporate them into your writing. As we go forward, we'll strive to answer three questions: 1) What do we mean when we talk about emotions? 2) How do we effectively use the element of emotions in writing? 3) How can we incorporate emotions so that our readers are emotionally drawn into our story?

http://womensmemoirs.com/emotions-1

What Do We Mean When We Talk about Emotions?

In the memoir, *Bending Toward the Sun*, written by Leslie Gilbert-Lurie and her mother Rita Lurie, we experience the impact of emotions and their suppression on the lives of three generations. Rita lived through the Holocaust, hidden in a barn attic in Poland with 13 other family members for more than 18 months. Near the end of the time, her younger brother died and soon after her mother died. As they buried her mother, Rita began to cry:

> "Shh! There will be a time to cry. This isn't it," Uncle Max said.
>
> I just watched and listened, in terrible distress, knowing that I was not allowed to say anything. The only way that I could cope at all was to detach myself. That's how I would live a lot of my life afterward--as an observer, plagued with an inability to be fully involved in the present. Suddenly, my mother was gone. In the days that followed, we didn't talk about her death, or the death of my brother. We were all imprisoned in our own private grief, probably feeling that there, but for the grace of God, we went. I was six and a half years old, and felt utterly insignificant. I also felt enormous loss, grief, and emptiness, and clung to that sorrow as a symbol of my mother, because it was better than feeling nothing.

As you can see from this passage, Rita suppressed her emotions, in general, and only "clung to that sorrow." The fears she carried with her to adulthood are passed on to her daughter Leslie, who finally realizes she has passed them on to her daughter. The memoir, an emotional and yet uplifting story, is a lesson in healing. As you read their memoir, you will find emotions buried just below the surface.

As we investigate emotions for your writing, you can quickly identify several states—perhaps anger, love, happiness. And still at the most basic level, we know that emotions:

- Are the expression of our internal feelings;
- Affect our social interactions;
- Manifest themselves in our external behaviors; and
- Change our internal body states, such as blood pressure.

To understand what I mean by each of these statements, think about moments when you have been happy or sad, when you have accepted a situation or were disgusted by it, or when you have been surprised by or anticipated an event. Can you identify your internal feelings? How did your interactions with others change? How did you act? Did you hide your true feelings or let everyone see how you felt? And what kinds of physiological responses did you experience? A change in your breathing, perhaps? Or heartbeat? Maybe your palms were sweaty? Did tears spill down your cheeks?

Author Karen Spears Zacharias, in her memoir *After the Flag Has Been Folded: A Daughter Remembers the Father She Lost to War and the Mother Who Held Her Family Together* eloquently shows us her emotions when her father calls her into the living room to tell her and her 11-year old brother that he is going to Vietnam. Her little sister Linda is just six and is already asleep. Karen, at the age of nine, has no idea where Vietnam was or what fighting communism meant. Still she sensed the danger. She didn't know she would never see him again. This is how she describes the scene:

Did you hide your true feelings?

> "Karen," Daddy said, looking directly at me, "you need to help Mama take care of Linda. Okay?"
>
> I nodded.
>
> I held my tears until after I hugged Mama and Daddy and climbed into my bed. Scrunching myself between the cold wall and the edge of my mattress, I began to cry.
>
> A few minutes later Daddy flipped on the light. On the bed next to mine, curled into a ball like a kitten, sleeping Linda didn't even twitch. "Karen?"
>
> "Yes, sir?" I said as I wiped my nose on the back of my forearm.
>
> "Are you crying?"
>
> "Yes, sir," I replied. I tried to shake the shivers from my neck.
>
> "Why are you crying, honey?" Daddy asked.
>
> "I'm scared," I answered.

"Scared of what?" Daddy walked over and sat down on the edge of my bed.

"That you won't come home!" I wailed. Like monsoon rains, powerful tears rushed forth.

"Karen," Daddy said, smoothing matted hair back from my wet cheeks. "I'll come back, I promise."

Picking me up, he let me cry into his shoulder. He smelled of Old Spice and sweat. "But I need for you to stop your crying, okay? It upsets Mama."

"Okay," I said, sucking back the last sob. I didn't want to upset anyone.

"G'night, Karen."

"G'night, Daddy. I love you."

"I love you too, honey."

He flipped off the light. Grabbing my pillow, I sought to muffle the crying that grown-ups can control but children never can.

As readers, we experience those emotions right along with Zacharias.

History of Emotions

Emotions are as old as the human race. Older, really, because emotions are not unique to Homo sapiens. Trying to make sense of emotions, however, is within our purview. Aristotle was one of the earliest philosophers to describe emotions. He believed there were seven pairs that defined the range of emotional response:

- Mildness/Anger
- Love/Hatred
- Confidence/Fear
- Shamelessness/Shame
- Benevolence/Pity
- Indignation/Envy
- Emulation/Contempt

Aristotle's work influenced the writers of his day and his influence continued for centuries to come. His work unleashed much discussion and writing about emotions and theories as to the source of our emotions. While interesting, we're looking for understanding that will help us better express emotions in our writing, and toward that end we're going to fast forward more than 2000 years to Charles Darwin. In his book *The Expression of Emotions in Man and Animals*, he identified eight universal emotions that he believed were tied to facial expressions: Anger, Sadness, Fear, Surprise, Disgust, Contempt, Happiness and Caring. He postulated that not only were these expressions of emotion found in young and old alike but that animals used the same facial muscles and, as such, these expressions are tied into our survival.

Facial expression and emotion is probably a good place for us to start...

Facial expression and emotion is probably a good place for us to start because like the physical attributes of a character, facial expression is tangible. This brings us to our modern age, specifically the years between the 1960s and 1990s when Paul Ekman, at the University of California Medical School, San Francisco, and other researchers demonstrated five emotions that are definitely pan-cultural—Anger, Fear, Sadness, Enjoyment and Disgust—meaning they are universal across cultures and therefore biological in origin, and four more that probably are—Surprise, Contempt, Shame and Guilt.

While this may sound like stuffy academic research, it's quite relevant to our writing. Ekman's findings next took him into the study of lying and then on to script development. Lying, it turns out, affects our emotions and is revealed in almost imperceptible micro-facial expressions in ways that we cannot control, just as emotions are revealed in our body postures and expressions. Poker players call these "tells."

Ekman found that individuals can be trained to look for the movements in the face that show when a person is lying. In 2009, Fox Broadcasting created a television show, *Lie to Me*, based on Ekman's research. The show's main character, Dr. Cal Lightman, was modeled on Dr. Paul Ekman who was a writing consultant and science advisor to the show. After each program aired, Ekman wrote a blog called "The Truth Behind Lie to Me" on the show's website to describe the research related to the specific episode and any sacrifices that had to be made in order to have a good plot.

Now Get to Writing!

Try the following exercises once a week for four weeks. You will find you are able to pick up on small details and notice subtle differences.

1. Attention to the world around us enhances our ability to write in believable and moving ways. For this exercise, go to some public place and watch people. Take a seat on a bench in your local shopping mall. Watch people interact. What emotions can you observe from their body language and their facial expressions. Make notes.

2. To keep observing without being too obvious, take your computer to your favorite coffee house. Watch for different interactions and make notes in a computer document. Be as specific as possible. When a person is happy, what happens to the face? Write it down. Find five different ways that people express happiness or joy. Look for expressions of frustration or sadness. What does the body do to express an emotion? What does the face do?

3. Once you become alert to the universal expressions of emotions in strangers, turn your study on your family members. In what ways do they uniquely express emotional states? Write down these descriptions. They will be useful as you deconstruct for emotions.

A Vocabulary of Emotion

If we are going to use emotions in our writing, if we are going to consider our emotions and those of our characters in a scene or chapter, then we need a vocabulary. The list below of 115 words, previously shown in Chapter 1 is much more extensive than the small, overlapping lists that come to us through Aristotle, Darwin and Ekman. The emotions they provide are considered to be primary emotions that can be combined with various secondary emotions in order to create tertiary emotions. A list, such as the one below, provides the nuances in our basic emotional states. Do you feel love, affection, closeness to someone? These are all related emotions that define varying degrees of intensity.

Adoration...Affection...Alarm...Alienation...Ambivalence...
Anger...Annoyance...Anticipation...Anxiety...Apathy...Appreciation...Attraction...Awe...Bliss...Boldness...Boredom...

Calmness...Caring...Caution...Cheerfulness...Closeness...
Compassion...Confusion...Contempt...Contentment...Cour-
age...Cruelty...Curiosity...Delight...Depression...Desire...
Despair...Disappointment...Discovery...Dislike...Disgust...
Doubt...Dread...Ecstasy...Elation...Embarrassment...
Empathy...Emptiness...Enjoyment...Enthusiasm...Envy...
Epiphany...Euphoria...Exasperation...Excitement...Fa-
miliarity...Fanaticism...Fear...Friendliness...Frustration...
Generosity...Gladness...Gratification...Gratitude...Greed...
Grief...Guilt...Happiness...Hatred...Homesickness...Hope...
Hostility...Humiliation...Hurt...Hysteria...Inspiration...Inter-
est...Irritation...Isolation...Jealousy...Joy...Kindness...Longing...
Loneliness...Love...Lust...Melancholia...Modesty...Nostalgia...
Obligation...Optimism...Panic...Patience...Pessimism...Pity...
Pleasure...Pride...Rage...Regret...Rejection...Relief...Remorse...
Repentance...Repulsion...Resentment...Righteous Indignation...
Sadness...Satisfaction...Scorn...Self-pity...Serene...Shame...Shy-
ness...Submission...Suffering...Surprise...Suspicion...Sympathy...
Tension...Trust...Understand...Vengefulness...Wonder...Worry...
Zest

This list may help you identify the words associated with emotions you felt in the scene you are writing.

About now you may be wondering if you need to identify emotions. Does it matter? Let me answer by way of an example. In one of my classes, I had each student Deconstruct the vignette she had brought and make a list emotion by emotion. After 10 minutes of writing, we went around the group as each woman read the list she had developed. One woman, writing about a time when her mother was in the hospital, told me she thought she had been in just one emotional state—content and accepting. But as she went through the scene emotion by emotion, she realized that at first she was worried how her mother would be that day, then happy to see her mother's favorite nurse on duty, then frightened by her mother's symptoms and finally anxious about what the future would hold. The rewrite of her vignette was much more powerful because she was more emotionally attuned to the story. It turns out that by accessing our emotions we have a clearer path into our memories.

And science gives us proof. Dr. Candace Pert was the chief of brain biochemistry at the National Institutes of Health for 13 years. Her research, which was the foundation for the discovery of endorphins, focused on mapping biochemicals that are the correlates of emotion. She published her findings in *Molecules of Emotion: Why You Feel the Way You Feel.* Her work is relevant to us because she has demonstrated that emotions are tangible. Although there are many points of interest to writers in Pert's research, let me highlight three items that we know from her work:

And science gives us proof.

- Strong emotions are the key variables that make us bother to remember things.
- Emotional memory is stored in many places in the body, not just the brain.
- Emotional memories are among our earliest memories.

Pert, to illustrate this last point, wrote that one of her earliest memories went back to when she was quite small. She struck a match when her mother was making dinner and inadvertently started a small fire. She vividly remembers the terror on her mother's face as she raced over to put it out with her dishrag. Emotional memories not only are early memories, they stick with us and become part of our long-term memories.

Pert's research provides us with a bonus tip. She found that when a person is in a positive mood, she/he is more likely to recall positive emotional experiences. And similarly, when a person is in a negative mood, she/he will recall negative emotional experiences. Understanding this may help you to use emotions to create a story with real depth and feeling. It also can give you insight into the interaction in a scene. Have you ever noticed that when a person is in a bad mood, he or she is more likely to mention previous bad incidents?

Now Get to Writing!

1. Think back to some of your early childhood memories. Make a list of five of these. Then try to remember details of each one and see how many have a strong emotional component—negative or positive.
2. Next to each item, write down specific details of the memories. For example, if you remember someone smiling, write "smile" and then "happy." If you remember someone yelling at you, then write "yelling" and "anger."

A Tool from the Social Sciences

The Johari Window is one of the social science frameworks that can provide insights for writers. In the 1950s, scientists at the National Training Laboratory in Group Development devised a series of techniques to be used with groups to help people work together. Their work became known as T-groups with the "T" standing for *training*.

Eventually, some of the scientists split off and moved west to found the Western Training Laboratory in Group Development at the University of California. Not long after, their research began to transition away from a sole emphasis on the group to include a greater focus on the individual. Well it was California after all, and we see their interests mirrored in some of the writers of the era. In 1955, when the country was under the sway of the Silent Generation, when most Americans wanted calmness and even blandness after the tragedies and hardships of World War II, when anonymity was considered desirable, there were pockets of experimentation and change such as we find in the writing of Jack Kerouac, Allen Ginsberg and others of the Beat Generation.

Another pocket of experimentation was going on at the Western Training Laboratory. Joseph Luft and Harrington Ingham developed an exercise to help individuals understand themselves in relation to others. Soon the exercise became known as the Johari Window, a combination of the two men's first names. Here's how it works:

The **Self** in the following table (think of this as you) chooses five or six adjectives from a list of 56 adjectives:

Able...Accepting...Adaptable...Bold...Brave...Calm...Caring... Cheerful...Clever...Complex...Confident...Dependable... Dignified...Energetic...Extroverted...Friendly...Giving...Happy... Helpful...Idealistic...Independent...Ingenious...Intelligent... Introverted...Kind...Knowledgeable...Logical...Loving...Mature... Modest...Nervous...Observant...Organized...Patient...Powerful... Proud...Quiet...Reflective...Relaxed...Religious...Responsive... Searching...Self-assertive...Self-conscious...Sensible... Sentimental...Shy...Silly...Smart...Spontaneous...Sympathetic... Tense...Trustworthy...Warm...Wise...Witty

Next, the **Others**—a small group of peers, a group of your friends or even siblings—choose a similar number of adjectives from the same list to describe the person identified as Self. The results are compiled and displayed in a four-fold table (a table with four cells).

Johari Window	Known to Self	Unknown to Self
Known to Others	**Open** Cheerful	**Blind** Spontaneous
Not Known to Others	**Hidden** Nervous	**Unknown**

Those adjectives or characteristics that *both* Self and Others select go into the first quadrant, or cell, of the table. These are Known to Self *and* Known to Others. Another way of saying this is that these characteristics are OPEN, acknowledged by both you and others who know you. For example, I may think of myself as cheerful, and a close group of friends might also select that adjective to describe me. Therefore, the cheerful descriptor goes into the Open quadrant.

My friends, however, may also describe me as spontaneous. But if I don't think of myself that way, then it's one of my characteristics that I'm BLIND to. Others notice this, but I don't. The spontaneous description, therefore, goes into the Blind quadrant.

Each Self knows things that aren't revealed to others. For example, I might describe myself as nervous because that's how I think of myself, especially in difficult situations. I do a good job of hiding my nervousness, so that characteristic belongs in the HIDDEN quadrant.

Finally, there are always characteristics of Self that we don't fully acknowledge to ourselves *and* don't even inadvertently reveal to others. This quadrant with no words in it is called UNKNOWN.

In the Johari Window I've described above, the four quadrants— Open, Blind, Hidden and Unknown—are the same size. In reality, these will vary considerably. Some people are quite transparent about themselves and have a large Open quadrant. Some people, we might call them clueless, are not introspective and will have a large Blind quadrant. And so on.

As writers we can use the Johari Window to give us insight into emotions and the emotional states of ourselves and others in our memoirs. I suggest we make a small change in the original methodology. Instead of a list of 56 characteristics officially used with the Johari Window, you can work from the alphabetical vocabulary list of emotions shown earlier in this chapter or from the categorized list called Emotion Annotation and Representation Language (EARL) developed by the HUMAINE network and listed below. If you are looking for a specific type of emotion, EARL may be useful. If you are simply wanting to remind yourself of the range of emotions possible, then the alphabetical list may be more helpful. You can also consider modifying either of these lists if that makes them more useful for you.

We can use the Johari Window to give us insight into emotions...

- **Negative & Forceful:** Anger, Annoyance, Contempt, Disgust, Irritation
- **Negative & Not in Control:** Anxiety, Embarrassment, Fear, Helplessness, Powerlessness, Worry
- **Negative Thoughts:** Doubt, Envy, Frustration, Guilt, Shame
- **Negative & Passive:** Boredom, Despair, Disappointment, Hurt, Sadness
- **Agitation:** Shock, Stress, Tension
- **Positive & Lively:** Amusement, Delight, Elation, Excitement, Happiness, Joy, Pleasure
- **Caring:** Affection, Empathy, Friendliness, Love
- **Positive Thoughts:** Courage, Hope, Pride, Satisfaction, Trust
- **Quiet Positive:** Calm, Content, Relaxed, Relieved, Serene
- **Reactive:** Interest, Politeness, Surprise

Let's look at the Johari Window profiles for three people, Jacqueline, Robert and Melissa. I'll fill in the details for Jacqueline then let you do the same for Robert and Melissa.

Jacqueline's *Johari* *Window*	Known to Self	Unknown to Self
Known to Others	**Open** Anxious Worried Powerless	**Blind** Relief Hope Courage
Not Known to Others	**Hidden** Angry Fearful	**Unknown**

Notice in the four-fold table, Jacqueline is OPEN to others both in what she reveals about her emotions and in her receptiveness to what others tell her about herself, and her BLIND quadrant is small. Now let's see how this is expressed in her life and story; for our purposes pretend you are Jacqueline. You have just been told that you have cancer. Previously, you had planned to have lunch with a friend, so you go on to the restaurant even though you feel as though you're navigating in a fog.

When you arrive at Salads R Us, rather than hugging your friend Angie, as you normally would, you slump into the chair opposite her. Angie asks, "What's the matter?" With your voice quivering, you say, "I just came from the doctor's office."

As the conversation unfolds, your facial expressions, body movements and vocal tone reveal many of your emotions. Angie empathizes and urges you to talk. Somehow you manage to order and pick at your food but mainly you just focus on the discussion. If you and Angie were asked to name the emotions, you would agree on *anxious, worried* and *powerless*. These emotions are in Jacqueline's Open quadrant. But Angie has been a friend for a long time and knows you well. The longer you talk, the more Angie sees that "old Jacqueline" beginning to reassert—even though it's only been a few hours since you've spoken with the doctor. Angie sees *relief* (from finally knowing what the symptoms mean), *hope* and even *courage* to do what needs to be done. You might not acknowledge these emotions yet, but your words, body posture and facial expressions convey these additional and changing emotions to Angie. Right now they are in Jacqueline's Blind quadrant as only Angie sees them.

You can go on and consider the Hidden quadrant. Are there some emotions that you/Jacqueline already are aware of but don't want to reveal to Angie? Perhaps you are *angry* that your spouse didn't urge you to go to the doctor when you first had symptoms. Maybe you are *fearful* for what your diagnosis might mean for your daughter's health in the future. You don't want to bring up these additional emotions with Angie, feeling that you are already burdening her with your problems.

A person reading this story would connect with Jacqueline and understand a lot more about her because she reveals her own emotional state rather than just communicating the facts of the diagnosis. Here's a question for you to consider: Do you think this type of person generates more openness in those around her? If you or someone else in your memoir is primarily an Open person, consider how this type of person interacts with others in your life story.

Use the Johari Window to Reveal Emotional Depth and Understanding. Writers can use the Johari Window to delve more deeply into emotional states than a simple recounting of one's own emotions. It helps us consider our emotions, which ones we reveal to others versus keep to ourselves. It is also a tool for examining the emotions of others rather than ourselves. What do they reveal to us? What do we know about them that lets us see emotions that they think they are hiding from us? Consider how each of us reveals our emotional circuitry.

Now Get to Writing!

Just as I built the emotional list for Jacqueline and categorized each in terms of how (and to whom) it is revealed, try doing the same for Robert and Melissa. I'll help you get started:

1. Fill in the Johari Window for Robert. Assume that he has just decided to break up with Bobbie, his girlfriend. They

dated for two years and been living together for one year. He discusses his decision with Jack and Samantha, a couple they frequently go out with. Jack had been Robert's college roommate, so he knows his friend well.

Robert's Johari Window	Known to Self	Unknown to Self
Known to Others	**Open** Relief	**Blind** Disappointment
Not Known to Others	**Hidden** Shame	**Unknown**

- Consider the emotions that Robert describes. How does he do this? What might Jack and Samantha understand about Robert's emotions that he doesn't acknowledge? By looking at Robert's Johari Window, you see that he doesn't engage in self-reflection. What emotions might Robert try to keep from his friends?
- If you know someone like Robert, perhaps a brother or a friend or a co-worker, you can substitute my fictional situation for an actual one. Then analyze it. This will help you be aware of point of view because while you don't know what is in someone's head, there are ways that their emotional states are revealed. Become attuned to this and your writing will improve.

2. Fill in the Johari Window for Melissa. She's going to be a challenge because so many of her emotions are HIDDEN from those who know her. Melissa received an email this afternoon saying that she is to schedule an appointment for a job interview. This is a position that she has coveted

for more than a year. She's *thrilled,* but tells no one. That night at dinner, she doesn't even mention the email to her husband. He senses that something is different but knows better than to pry. She often doesn't communicate well. He notices that she is whistling when she sets the table. This is unusual and one of his clues to what he assumes is a *happy* emotional state. Meanwhile, Melissa has memorized the brief email and repeats its message over and over in her head. She can feel how *excited* and *hopeful* she is. She realizes that she's *relieved* to finally be at this stage in the process since she submitted her resume and letter of interest more than two months ago. As it gets later in the evening, her initial euphoria begins to wear off, and she feels a *tension* headache coming on. Now she needs to prepare for the interview and confront the possibility that she won't get the job. She acknowledges to herself that as long as no one was offered the job, she could still have *hope.*

Melissa's Johari Window	Known to Self	Unknown to Self
Known to Others	**Open** Happy	**Blind** Calm
Not Known to Others	**Hidden** Thrilled	**Unknown**

• Do you know anyone like Melissa? Is there someone like this in your memoir? Do you think the person would consistently keep so many emotions Hidden? Or would this be situational and depend on with whom she's interacting? Maybe she doesn't want her family to see her emotions but perhaps she is willing to divulge them to a close friend. Or perhaps just the opposite.

- Imagine you are her husband; try to fill out the Johari Window with the emotions Melissa reveals and how. Does he see a change in her behavior during the evening?

The Johari Window Times Two. When writing a memoir, we can use the Johari Window in at least two ways:

- To examine our emotions in each of the scenes or chapters and determine how much we want to reveal to the reader.
- To consider what we know about the emotions of other people we are including in the memoir. For example, are we making assumptions about the emotions of others, or have we observed behaviors that clearly point to emotions of others?

Let's Be Intelligent about Our Emotions

Emotional intelligence (EI) is a concept developed by Peter Salovey and John D. Mayer in 1990 and popularized by Daniel Goleman in 1995 in his book *Emotional Intelligence: Why It Can Matter More than IQ*, which stayed on *The New York Times* bestseller list for 18 months. Being intelligent (as measured by standard IQ tests) and working hard were thought to guarantee success for most of your life. That's the way I was brought up. Were you? If you had a high IQ and weren't successful, then the fault was clearly with you—you hadn't applied yourself. Studies now show that intelligence, as typically measured, only accounts for a small portion of success. Researchers have sought to understand this gap and are turning to EI as an important component for success. Many of the studies have focused on the workplace where it seems that emotional intelligence is twice as important as a combined technical and cognitive intelligence, and EI is four times more important among leaders in the organization. Stated simply, emotional intelligence matters.

EI also matters to writers. Emotional intelligence is our ability to understand emotions and use that information to enhance thought and behavior. John D. Mayer, one of the early researchers on this topic, wrote on the *Psychology Today* blog (post entitled "What Is Emotional Intelligence and What Is It Not?"):

> High EI people, for example, can accurately perceive emotions in faces. Such individuals also know how to use

emotional episodes in their lives to promote specific types of thinking. They know,...that sadness promotes analytical thought and so they may prefer to analyze things when they are in a sad mood (given the choice). High EI people also understand the meanings that emotions convey: They know that angry people can be dangerous, that happiness means that someone wants to join with others and that some sad people may prefer to be alone. High EI people also know how to manage their own and others' emotions. They understand that, when happy, a person will be more likely to accept an invitation to a social gathering than when sad or afraid.

...we need a deeper understanding of emotions...

As we quickly see, emotions and emotional intelligence mean more than just our emotional vocabulary listed earlier in this chapter. To use emotions fully in writing we need a deeper understanding of emotions in our own lives and in the lives of others. Knowledge of emotions enables us to *show* rather than *tell* about emotions. Read the two sentences below and decide which is more powerful in sharing an emotion with the reader:

1. When I told her the good news, she looked happy.
2. When I told her the news, her eyes sparkled and she raced across the room to hug me.

Clearly it's the second one. Readers don't want to be told someone is happy; they want to reach their own conclusions. You can connect with readers by empowering them to see a scene and make their own decisions.

Knowing how the body responds to emotional states gives us a rich sense of how we can incorporate emotions into our stories. A little background will help. In the brain, there are two almond-shaped structures called the amygdala, an organ that ensures we have the appropriate reaction to potential dangers. The word *emotion* comes from the Latin *motere* (to move) and *e* (away)—to move away. In other words, situations trigger the amygdala to ensure that the body protects itself and moves away from danger when necessary. Consider these emotions:

1. When a person is **ANGRY**, the heart rate increases, additional blood flows to hands (so that a weapon can help you protect your-

Physical responses attached to emotional states

self), the rate of breathing increases, attention narrows to a laser-sharp focus on the target of anger and the adrenaline systems kicks into overdrive, which sustains the initial physical reaction, thus helping to maintain awareness and action. If you want to show that you are angry, you can describe feeling your heart beating faster, your blood pressure increasing or other physiological changes. This is more powerful than telling readers you are angry.

2. **FEAR** is similar to anger but affects the body in somewhat different ways. With fear, more blood is directed to the legs, specifically the large skeletal muscles so that the body can get ready to flee if necessary. Blood is drained from the face, and the body briefly freezes so that the mind can determine its best course of action—flight, fight or hiding.

3. **SURPRISE** is easy to recognize once you know what to look for. The eyebrows lift to let the eyes take in a larger visual field, and the retina receives more light making it easier to identify what has caused the surprise and then make a decision as to whether it is a fun surprise or a dangerous surprise.

4. **HAPPINESS** does not have a physiological parallel. Instead there is activity in the brain that inhibits negative feelings and results in an increase in energy. In our example above, the person who was happy ran over to hug someone. That shows the burst of energy that happiness brings.

5. **LOVE** is a complex emotion that seems to create a relaxation response, a calmness or contentedness that facilitates cooperation.

6. Studies of facial expressions show that **DISGUST** appears with the upper lip curled to the side and a wrinkled nose. It is postulated that the facial movements could come from a mechanism for the body to protect against poisonous smells or to spit out toxic food.

7. The emotion of **SADNESS** is clearly shown on the face—the eyebrows may wrinkle, the mouth drawn into a frown and eyelids drooping. The visual expression of sadness is thought to have the function of nonverbally requesting help and comfort from others. Sadness is usually accompanied by a loss of energy. During this "down time," those with emotional intelligence reflect on the circumstance that created the sadness, consider its meaning and what lessons they can learn for the future.

Sadness, like other emotions, is stored in the body and can come out at unexpected times. I have a friend whose daughter died unexpectedly at the age of 30. The sadness stored itself in her muscles. Almost a year after the tragic death, I gave my friend a massage as a birthday gift. We went together and after an hour, I was dressed and waiting in the front lobby area. Fifteen minutes later, the person who was working with her came out to ask if there was a hurry. I said, "No. I'm reading a magazine." He told me that as he worked with some of the muscles in her neck and shoulders, my friend had begun to cry. A little of the sadness was being released. I know the story of another person who had been going through a difficult relationship and felt sad. He seemed much better. But at the end of a multi-hour bike ride, his stressed body released some of the stored emotions. He suddenly burst into tears and cried uncontrollably. Emotions will come out one way or another.

Goleman suggests in *Emotional Intelligence* that emotions are able to hijack the mind because the amygdala, the feeling brain, takes precedence over the neocortex, the thinking brain. As a writer, you need to engage your audience so that the reader observes and feels each emotion and is taken along for the amygdala's emotional ride. Let the reader *feel* your sadness. Let her want to walk over and put her arm around your shoulder to comfort you. Let him be surprised along with you, not because you say you were surprised but because you have shown your surprise. Let her feel disgust with how you were treated by your spouse or a teacher. And, of course, share the energy of happiness with the reader so that he wants to skip around the room with a shared joy when you overcome your challenge.

http://womensmemoirs.com/emotions-2

For one final look at emotions, Mark Greenberg and Jennie Snell, in a chapter for *Emotional Development and Emotional Intelligence*, suggest four manifestations of emotions:

- **Expressive or motor behavior**—illustrated above by looking at how anger and fear affect not only the physiology of the body but also facial expressions, body posture and voice;

- **Experiential or conscious recognition**—ability to accurately report feelings, which requires an understanding of our body state;
- **Regulatory control**—management of the way an emotion is expressed; and
- **Recognition/regulatory**—ability to recognize the emotional states of others.

Five Final Factors: A Quick Quiz

Studying emotions provides a path to self-knowledge that enables you to create characters with emotions that link the reader to the person. When you Deconstruct for emotions, there are five factors to consider:

A. Expressed Behaviors

B. Intensity and Duration

C. Internal (physiological) Feelings

D. Rationalized Assessment

E. Transparency

Each of the following five paragraphs provides illustrations of one of these factors. Take our quiz. Match the five factors (A-E) above to the five paragraphs (1-5) below.

1. Remember a child or grandchild running to you, arms outstretched, giving you a spontaneous hug. What was the feeling? Did your heart seem to expand with joy? Remember a pet's closeness when you were sad or hurting. What did you feel? Were you comforted? Remember the phone call when you learned of the death of your mother or father or close friend. How did you feel? Was there a physiological reaction to the sadness that was experienced deep in your gut? Remember when you were called back for a medical test. Were you scared about the outcome? Did your palms sweat?

2. Have you ever lost a job and felt despair growing as the search for work went on for month after month? Has a friend ever told you a great joke that evoked laughter but you couldn't remember it well enough the next day to get the punch line right? Or what about one joke that had you rolling on the floor and another that merely bought about a smile?

3. Have you ever been angry with a person but kept it hidden so well that only you knew? Have you ever liked someone but been hesitant to expose yourself by revealing your feelings?

4. Have you ever screamed as an outlet for your frustration? Ever slammed a door because you were angry? Ever embraced a person after getting good news?

5. Have you ever felt your anger was justified because you were sure the other person cheated you? Did you hurt someone because you believed they deserved it?

The answers to our quiz. How well did you do? If you didn't figure them all out, that's all right. Keep our list of emotional factors close by when you Deconstruct for emotions as well as the emotional vocabulary list. Both will help you reach deeper into this important element of Writing Alchemy.

C & 1. Internal (physiological) feelings. The first paragraph provides examples of the physiological changes that accompany some emotional moments. Something makes our heart beat faster, our hands sweat, our knees collapse, our stomach act as home to butterflies. When writing about internal feelings, you might rely on the physiological changes to represent the emotion.

B & 2. Intensity and duration. The second paragraph provides examples of emotions that varied in both intensity and duration. When a writer simply reports that the main character is angry, he hasn't really told the reader much. Has the person been angry a long time? Is the person angry, but only mildly? Maybe the character's words are angry one minute and even joking the next. There are a variety of ways to let the reader understand the character's emotions without explicitly saying, "She was only mildly angry." Stay away from the lazy adverbs and try to get deeper into the emotion and its manifestation both in intensity and duration.

E & 3. Transparency (opaque to clear). The third paragraph represents the extent to which we express or keep hidden our emotions. This is a special challenge to writers, and the Johari Window is one tool that may help you determine how Open, Blind, Hidden or Unknown a person's emotions are.

A & 4. Expressed behaviors. Not all emotions create physiological (or internal) changes. The fourth paragraph illustrates a few of the overt behaviors that share the character's emotion with the reader.

D & 5. Rationalized assessment. The fifth paragraph is an aspect of emotion that helps us keep our equilibrium. We may be mad/sad/angry/frightened, but we're justified by the circumstances.

When we explain a situation to a friend, a situation fraught with emotion, we almost always justify what we felt and what we did because of those feelings. The thinking brain verbalizes what the emotional brain made us feel and caused us to do. A more positive aspect of assessment can be our taking time to reflect and learn and thereby improve our emotional intelligence.

What is Your Emotional Intelligence?

In the previous chapter on Deconstructing character, I suggested several personality tests you could use to help develop rich characters in your memoir. For this chapter on Deconstructing emotion, I looked for an emotional intelligence test so that you could determine how well attuned you are to emotions as they relate to situations. With tests you might use to provide more depth of understanding for your writing, I look for two benefits: 1) The items in the test should help you think about the subject, and 2) the test results should provide you with some insight. It turns out this was a big order when it comes to Emotional Quotient (EQ) tests. After taking many, I finally narrowed it to one test that comes in two versions. There is a quick version available from PsychTests AIM Inc. that includes 10 questions you answer using a five-point response scale that goes from Completely True to Completely False. You can complete the test in no more than 10 minutes, and then you receive your score. To take this abbreviated version, go to: http://www.ei4change.com/testyourei.htm

The complete test is available free from Queendom.com, a subsidiary of the psychometric company PsychTests. This version (106 questions when I took it) takes between 30 minutes and 60 minutes to complete, depending on how long you spend considering the situations presented. Type in the URL to take the test: http://www. queendom.com/tests/access_page/index.htm?idRegTest=1121. The feedback after you complete the test is fairly limited but may be enough to get you thinking. Certainly taking the test will increase your awareness of emotions, emotional states and emotions in various contexts with other people involved.

Now Get to Writing!

You're beginning to get a sense of how to use emotions and emotional intelligence more effectively in your writing. It's time to Deconstruct a scene for emotions.

1. Take one person, perhaps yourself, at the beginning of your scene—the one in your synopsis. Write one or two short paragraphs that express your emotional state at that time. But do not use the word for any specific emotion(s). Let your facial expression(s), body language and dialogue reveal all.

2. If a second person is part of that scene, write a brief paragraph or two that illustrates her or his emotion at the beginning of the scene. That emotion might be in reaction to you, and your reaction might be in relation to what the other person has done. Make all of that known.

3. Move to the end of the scene. What is your emotional state now? Again, show the reader; don't tell. What about the second person? If he or she is still part of the scene, then write about that person's emotions. Of course, you can never really know what a person is thinking. Sometimes a person is good about hiding emotions. But the expressive behaviors of the person will inform your memory of the emotional state.

4. How have your emotions changed from the beginning of the scene to the end? Have you let the reader see this change? Have you increased the size of your Open quadrant in the Johari Window in relation to other people in your scene? Have you shared what is in your Hidden cell with the reader but kept the emotions Hidden from others in the scene? This kind of reflection on past emotions can bring the reader closer to you.

What Else Might You Find?

This chapter has examined our emotions, how to draw on them, and how to use them in memoir writing. We did all of this without discussing the emotional trauma that you or others in your story may have endured as that is an element of story content rather than an element of writing. Even our exercises are directed more at understanding and finding ways to include emotions in our writing and less at the idea that emotions may be the focus of your memoir. However, before we leave this subject, I want to mention the landmark research conducted by James W. Pennebaker. His research demonstrates that writing is healing. His *Writing to Heal: A Guided*

Journal for Recovering from Trauma and Emotional Upheaval is beyond the scope of this chapter, but is an important resource to understand how writing can be an important therapy for emotional abuse. We have an additional brief discussion of journaling and healing in Chapter 8.

What's Next?

Deconstructing for emotions brought you back to the level of the scene. What's the next way to Deconstruct that scene? Dialogue. Dialogue, you see, has a job to do. It isn't there for variation. It isn't something to stick in every once in a while for a break. It conveys emotional states, creates well-etched characters, moves the storyline forward, creates tension, and that's just for starters. What are these? How do you put it to work? What can the social sciences teach us about the functions of dialogue? Ever been caught in a life script such as the "Yes, but..." game? Want to know how life scripts can help you craft dialogue that reveals characters and relationships? Explore these and more issues in our next chapter on Deconstructing for dialogue.

References and Resources

Eckman, Paul. *Emotions Revealed*. New York: Holt Paperbacks, 2007.

Gilbert-Lurie, Leslie and Lurie, Rita. *Bending Toward the Sun: A Mother-Daughter Memoir*. New York: Harper, 2009.

Goleman, Daniel. *Emotional Intelligence: Why It Can Matter More Than IQ*. New York: Bantam Books, 1995, 2005.

Luft, Joseph. *Of Human Interaction*. Palo Alto, CA: Mayfield Publishing Co, 1969.

Mayer, John D. *What Is Emotional Intelligence and What Is It Not?* September 21, 2009, The Personality Analyst blog on Psychology Today (http://psychologytoday.com).

Pennebaker, James W. *Writing to Heal: A Guided Journal for Recovering from Trauma and Emotional Upheaval*. NY: New Harbinger Publication, Inc., 2004.

Pert, Candace B. *Molecules of Emotion: Why You Feel the Way You Feel*. New York: Scribner, 1997.

Salovey, Peter; Brackett, Marc A.; Mayer, John D. Eds. *Emotional Intelligence: Key Readings on the Mayer and Salovey Model*. Port Chester, NY: Dude Publishing, 2004.

Salovey, Peter and Sluyter, David J. Eds. *Emotional Development and Emotional Intelligence*. New York: Basic Books, 1997.

Zacharias, Karen Spears. *After the Flag Has Been Folded: A Daughter Remembers the Father She Lost to War—And the Mother Who Held Her Family Together*. New York: Harper Paperbacks, 2006. [Note: Original title was Hero Mama: A Daughter Remembers the Father She Lost in Vietnam and the Mother Who Held Her Family Together]

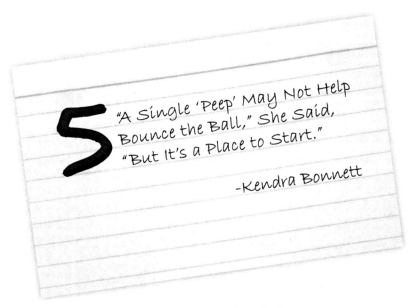

5 "A Single 'Peep' May Not Help Bounce the Ball," She Said, "But It's a Place to Start."

-Kendra Bonnett

The Element of Dialogue

I came out of my room wearing my new blue velvet dress and my first pair of stockings (my mother's, and they had seams). I was going to my first dance.

As I entered the kitchen where my mother was preparing dinner, she surveyed me from head to toe and checked to see that my seams were straight. "You look very nice."

I smiled even though I felt my palms perspiring inside my white cotton gloves.

"Talk to the boys, Kendra. Don't just sit and wait for someone to talk to you."

"Yes, Mommy, but what should I say?"

"Be yourself. You won't have any trouble."

My father walked into the kitchen just then. "Like your mother says, be yourself. You've been chattering since before you knew words. You always have something to say. We can't shut you up around here."

"That's for sure. Just remember that the boys are more nervous than you; they don't have a clue what to say to girls. Start a conversation. Put them at ease. It will all work out."

Even though I knew this was going to be different from talking with family and friends, they were right about one thing. I have been a talker all my life. As I tried to stay calm, I recalled a story my parents had repeated to me dozens of times about how as a baby I entertained myself in the back seat of the car by talking non-stop. Apparently I'd look out the window, point to stars and say, "Staars. Staars. Sharsh [sharp]. Staars. Staars. Sharsh." I'd blabber on like that until I conked out. Hey, I'm a Gemini; I was born to talk.

Hey, I'm a Gemini; I was born to talk.

And I have always had to have the last word. Each Christmas, Daddy would drive us into New York City to look at the holiday decorations in the windows at Macy's, Bloomingdale's and B. Altman. We'd also walk around the giant tree at Rockefeller Center and sometimes have dinner in the city. Mommy and Daddy sat in the front. Niki, Dobie and I piled in the back.

"You stop touching me."

"Keep your foot on your own side of the car."

"Ouch. Mommy, Kendra poked me."

"Shut up."

"Mommy, Kendra said 'shut up.'"

"I did not. I said 'shush up.'"

"Liar."

My mother could tune out our bickering and keep from going insane. Daddy could not. "Not another peep out of anyone," he said on one of our holiday excursions, "or I'll turn this car around and go home."

"Peep."

Daddy did a U-turn on Fifth Avenue, which had two-way traffic in those days, and home we went. I may have gotten in the last word, but three sets of eyes all but seared my skin with the hot looks I got all the way home.

Whether I was testing his authority or just being cute, I can't say. In either case, to my father's credit, I didn't get away with it. And I did what they told me to do that fall evening. I talked to the boys, and they talked back. Being a tomboy, I could talk baseball, sailing, fishing and cars. I started the conversation, and they did the rest. As for those stockings of my mother's, Mary Chapman told me in no uncertain words that no one wore seams any more. That's when I learned about pantyhose.

I remember, too, that from the time we started being around our parents' adult friends my sister, brother and I were taught to speak up when we talked, look the person in the eye and shake hands with a firm grip. We also were expected to hold our own in conversation.

And when we'd have dinner as a family, which with my father's hours at the hospital wasn't often when we were young, should the conversation at the dinner table flag as everyone sat quietly eating, my mother would say, "A-B-C." That was a cue for someone to start up a new conversation.

From a story Matilda tells, her mother was equally determined to have children who knew how to converse: "Ann and I would be in the car with Mother and Daddy, and Mother would engage us in a discussion. She was always trying to civilize our conversational style. Ann and I would tire of her efforts, but she was relentless. The less we would respond, the more she would say, 'Bounce that ball.'   *'Bounce that ball.'* She told us that being a good conversationalist was a lot like being a good tennis player; we needed to send the ball back when it had been served to us. For years, we heard 'bounce that ball' more times than I can count. It certainly lodged in my brain and made me more aware of conversational styles and techniques than any of my friends. It pointed me in the direction of not just talking, but also listening and analyzing conversations."

There's no question our mothers' lessons stuck with us. Even after more than 30 years of friendship, Matilda and I can talk on the phone several times a day and never lack for subject matter. And when we're together in the room, it's difficult for other people to get in a word. We scarcely stop to draw a breath.

Beware. There's Risk in Dialogue

Yes, this is our chapter on dialogue, and I have a lot to say on the subject. On the surface, dialogue is such a simple concept. It's communication, and we've been doing it since we were babies. We use it to converse, warn, yell, insult, joke, encourage, comfort, cheer, greet, gossip, report and so much more. Dialogue has a big job to do...in our lives and in our writing.

Conversation, the antecedent of written dialogue, isn't fluff. It carries risk. As Ronald Wardhaugh explains, in his book *How Conversation Works*, you may get hurt or hurt someone else. Not physically hurt but,

> ...diminished in some way....You may have criticized another or have been criticized yourself; you may have incurred an obligation that you did not seek or made a suggestion that another could not refuse; someone may have complimented you, thereby requiring you not only to acknowledge acceptance of that compliment but to live up to it; you may have skirted a topic which others expected you to confront; you may have offered an excuse or an apology but been left with the feeling that it was not necessarily accepted completely--someone's sincerity may therefore be suspect.

Wardhaugh points out that conversations change the nature of relationships by the feelings they evoke. As such, he cautions us to consider not only the words of our conversations, but "the possible intentions of the speaker, in order to come up with a decision as to what the speaker really means." This last is an important point that I'll return to later in the chapter.

Dialogue, the term we use to describe conversation in writing, performs multiple jobs. It truly is power talk. Never again should you think of dialogue as just a convenient way to break up your narrative. Make it work.

It All Started a Long Time Ago

The use of dialogue in writing goes back at least as far as Plato. He employed Platonic dialogue in nearly all of his writing as a teaching device and means to make the case for his ideas through discussion—almost a controlled argument. He'd start with a character, often Socrates, and have him present an idea and make his case, defending his position against the counterpoint presented by other characters. Plato could have used straight narrative in the form of a treatise, but he found the dialogue to be a more powerful form for engaging readers.

Plato didn't invent the concept of dialogue, which was well known to playwrights, but he was one of the first, if not the first, to use it in narrative writing. Through the centuries, dialogue has evolved into a rich tool for writers. And like Plato, we use it to our advantage. Dialogue:

Plato didn't invent the concept of dialogue...

- Advances the story
- Creates well-etched characters
- Defines relationships between characters
- Conveys emotional states
- Controls a story's pace
- Provides information, background and context to the story, and
- Builds tension

As we start to dissect dialogue and learn to use it as a power tool, I want to begin with how we build tension through dialogue by shaping the voice of each character and controlling how the characters interact (through distance and direction). Tom Chiarella, in his book Writing Dialogue, explains the four basic directions in dialogue.

The Direction of Dialogue

"Some beginning writers confuse tension with conflict," writes Chiarella, "assuming it comes and goes depending on whether characters agree or disagree. Tension is more like the energy between charged particles." Later in this chapter we'll examine the issue of conflict and how you can find and use it; let's turn to the four techniques for building tension into your writing. The four directions are: directed, interpolated, misdirected and modulated dialogue.

Directed Dialogue: This is the simplest, most straight-forward type of dialogue in which the spoken words do all the work. Often used for explanation and exposition, it's a moment in time, and all the action takes place in the present. Although my example shows a basic directed dialogue, it can also have interruptions, changes in pace and tone and more. Let's listen in on a conversation between Ellen and Tom:

"Do you like my new hat?" asked Ellen.

"No," said Tom.

"Well too bad for you because you paid for it," said Ellen.

Interpolated Dialogue: To interpolate, we just have to add a little explanation to our directed dialogue. The spoken words are still there, but we are going to interrupt the simple conversation with narrative used to interpret thoughts and action. You don't want to overuse this dialogue form. Whenever possible, let the power of the words carry the story forward. Here are Ellen and Tom talking again but the dialogue is interpolated:

Pleased after my day of shopping, I couldn't wait to show him what I bought. "Tom, do you like my new hat?"

His reply left me stunned. "Ellen, that's the ugliest thing I've ever seen."

I don't know if I was more angry or hurt; all I wanted to do was lash back. "Well too bad for you, Tom, because you paid for it."

Misdirected Dialogue: I think if you record and listen to many conversations you'll agree that misdirected dialogue is the most like real life. There's back and forth but the progression is not immediately obvious because the speakers are more focused on their own issues and agendas. The speakers are reacting to inner motivation; they often don't answer each other directly. They talk over one another and change subjects without warning. Although the example is our same conversation between Ellen and Tom, misdirected dialogue is often used when there is a three-person conversation as it presents more opportunities for misdirected statements:

"I spent the day shopping for a new hat."

"How will I ever find another job? I'm ruined."

"Isn't this the sweetest little bonnet you ever—"

"I just hope we don't lose the house."

Modulated Dialogue: As memoir writers, modulated dialogue is maybe our most powerful tool because it combines narrative commentary, scenic detail and memories (in the form of thoughts and flashbacks) to interrupt the conversation. Time is actually suspended while the writer reveals memories triggered by an event or comment, explores tensions, advances the plot and/or complicates the present situation.

"Tom, do you like my new hat?"

Looking at her little blue and white hat—more of a cap, really—Tom could think of nothing except that long-ago spring day. What was it now? Twenty years ago? His father had taken him to a ballgame at Yankee Stadium. His father had called it the House that Ruth Built. And he bought him his first Yankee's cap. It was the happiest day of his life. It was time he did the same thing for Little Tom. Then seeing Ellen playing with the angle of her new hat, trying to get it to sit on top of her head just right, he came back to the moment. "You hat is beautiful!" he said.

Now Get to Writing!

As you work your way through the writing exercises in this chapter, you'll probably need to draw on more than one scene from your memoir. You're just not going to find a single one that will work for all the techniques I'll be presenting. Yet at the conclusion of the chapter, I want to make sure that you have fully Deconstructed the scene in your synopsis. So think of these exercises as drawing on your synopsis whenever possible, but using additional scenes when necessary so that you can experiment with the many forms of dialogue. Be sure to choose some scenes or situations that you believe lend themselves to dialogue. Once you have done this exercise several times, you'll find that in future Deconstructions, you will be able to spot whether you could be using directed, interpolated, misdirected or modulated dialogue. Don't assume you know which is right for a while. Make yourself experiment and see what different effects are possible. Meanwhile, you should always be searching for how to make dialogue reveal the people in your memoir.

1. For this first exercise, begin with the scene in your synopsis. Write it entirely as *directed* dialogue. (If you can't make this work, then take another scene that will be in your memoir.)
2. Go back and try the scene as *interpolated* dialogue.
3. You get the idea, now try the scene as *misdirected* dialogue.
4. And, of course, now write the scene as *modulated* dialogue.
5. Which form of dialogue worked best for you? Why?

To Write Dialogue, You Must Understand It

At one point or another, we've probably accused someone we know of speaking just to hear themselves talk. But blathering on isn't the norm. When most people speak, it's because they have something to communicate—a warning, a message, a point of view or an answer in reply to someone asking a question. As writers, we need to learn something of the dynamics of communication to understand what happens in dialogue.

It's time to go deep into dialogue and it shouldn't surprise you that we're going to turn to some of the leading lights in social science research for insight into human interaction, interpersonal communication, transactional analysis and game theory. Their research will give us models and concepts to consider as we Deconstruct for dialogue and determine the best, most effective, way to use dialogue in our memoirs.

Four-Element Model

From three social scientists, we have put together a four-element model of interaction that takes place through dialogue. The process begins with *acquaintance*, moves on to *disclosure* and *co-orientation* and concludes with *exchange*.

Acquaintance: It's simple when it all begins. People need to know each other if they are going to develop any kind of a relationship, even a casual one. In a memoir, we can assume that the characters already know each other, usually quite well, so you might wonder what the acquaintance process gives you that will enhance your ability to write strong dialogue. We start with acquaintance for two reasons: First, a memoir often includes the beginning of a relationship with a friend, a future spouse, even distant relatives who then become part of our story. Second, and the more important reason, acquaintance is the initial building block for relationships and any communication that we'll write as dialogue.

We know how the acquaintance process works from social psychologist Theodore Newcomb's research into communication and its social purpose. The four factors in this process are *proximity* (we tend to know people who are physically near us for educational, vocational, avocational or familial reasons); *reciprocity* (we tend to like people who like us); *similarity* (we tend to know people who share similar values and beliefs); and *complementarity* (the weakest of the four factors but we often become acquainted with people who have skills and abilities that complement our own).

As writers, we need to acknowledge the acquaintance process, even if it's only part of the back story. The fact is, people are unlikely to engage in important conversations with strangers. And when it seems that we do, it is because we have quickly moved through the acquaintance process to disclosure.

Disclosure: "Tell me something about yourself."

"There's nothing to tell."

"Well, what was your childhood like?"

"I don't like to talk about that."

In the previous chapter on emotions, Matilda presented the research of Joseph Luft and Harrington Ingham and their use of the Johari Window, which she used to describe how emotions are shared or kept from others. The Johari Window also serves as a good model for how we disclose ourselves to others. The premise is that there are aspects of ourselves that either are known to self or unknown to self, and these same aspects either are known to others or not known to others. Yes, it's that four-fold table you used in the previous chapter.

Disclosure Johari Window	Known to Self	Unknown to Self
Known to Others	**Open**	**Blind**
Not Known to Others	**Hidden**	**Unknown**

At the beginning of the disclosure process—when you first meet someone—there is little in the Open cell—known to self and known to other(s). Most everything is in our Hidden cell—known to self and not known to other(s). That's what getting to know someone is all about. What we reveal and what we keep back drives our ability to create and understand dialogue. It also drives a story line. Moving forward from a first meeting, we make many disclosures—some deliberate, others not. If we knew everything at the start, we would all make perfect decisions, pick perfect partners and avoid relationship pitfalls. As writers, however, we can apply the pieces of disclosure and show readers through the dialogue how characters learned more in the course of time.

Co-Orientation: To better grasp what is going on in dialogue, we turn back to Theodore Newcomb and his research on co-orientation. Imagine that Jonathan and Marjorie are talking about their daughter's education:

"Elizabeth needs to start thinking about a job after graduation," said Jonathan.

"No, she should go to college."

"But we have to save our money so our boys can go to college. Elizabeth really should go to work."

"Over my dead body."

The process of co-orientation is easily understood if you think of a triangle. In the bottom left and right corners, we have Jonathan and Marjorie. At the top of the triangle, we have the topic of discussion. In this case, it's their daughter's education but the topic might be anything—a person, place or thing. Now draw a line between Jonathan and Marjorie (this is the base of the triangle) and put a plus sign in the middle. They are a loving couple and respect each other in many ways, so it's a positive. However, they disagree on the topic so as you draw a line from Jonathan, on the lower left of the triangle, to the topic at the top, add a minus sign signifying his opposition to Elizabeth going to college. Do the same for Marjorie but use a plus sign because she wants Elizabeth to get a college education.

Had all three signs been the same, plus-plus-plus or minus-minus-minus, then the two people and the topic are balanced. I like you, you like me, and we both like chocolate ice cream. In the Jonathan and Marjorie example, however, and in many life situations, there is no symmetry.

In a different scenario, if we don't like each other but both support the same cause, we would put a minus sign at the bottom and plus signs on both sides of the triangle. Now here's the interesting thing. If the cause is important enough and only the first of many points on which they agree, their personal relationship may change, resulting in symmetry. In the research literature, the co-orientation triangle is often called A-B-X with A and B referring to the people and X the topic.

There are two take away points you can use in writing dialogue:

The topic of a dialogue often represents the source of conflict; resolving the unbalance is what moves a story forward.

As you get deeper into your understanding of the role of co-orientation in dialogue, you'll find that in addition to simple agreement or disagreement, knowledge, attitude and behavior may determine whether you agree (a plus) or disagree (a minus) with another person or persons on a specific topic. This will influence how a disagreement is negotiated in dialogue.

By the way, the story of Jonathan and Marjorie is a piece of real dialogue that marked the turning point in one of our student's lives. When she was a senior in high school, Elizabeth often hid on the steps to listen to her parents talk. One evening, she overheard her parents at the kitchen table discussing her future. Without her mother standing up for her, she never would have gone to college, gotten a Ph.D. or become a college dean. Her brothers, by the way, dropped out of college to pursue business interests. Because of Marjorie's strong stance on the topic and because she and Jonathan had a positive relationship, Jonathan decided to restore balance by agreeing that his daughter should attend college. There is usually some effort to restore balance even if it is an agreement to disagree on a point.

Exchange: The fourth element that drives dialogue comes from the work of sociologists George Homans and Peter Blau. The theory behind exchange is that individuals often engage in and evaluate relationships and decisions based on the personal costs and benefits. For example:

"Hi. I've got to go out of town tomorrow. Will you take care of Leo for me?

"I'd really like to, but I can't."

"I promise I'll pay you back. I'll take care of Alice when you need me to."

"You didn't give me much notice."

"It's just too expensive to use the kennel."

"Oh. All right."

Typically, relationships in their early stages are fairly balanced. We agree to put time into a relationship, and the emotional comforts or benefits seem to equal the cost. We may even feel we get more than we give. That works as long as the other person also perceives that the benefits outweigh the cost in time, money or opportunities lost. When a couple first begins dating and are in the early romantic phase, neither one is thinking much about the ratio of rewards and risks. But once the relationship moves to a long-term relationship, say a marriage, then imbalance can occur. As one woman explained, because she wanted the relationship to work, she kept giving up pieces of herself in order to please her husband. In her words, "Eventually I couldn't find myself." The cost had become too great. She left her husband.

By applying exchange to your Deconstruction of dialogue, you can help readers see the dynamism in relationships and see, perhaps, the hesitancy on the part of people to continue to incur costs when the benefits are minimal. Think about times that have happened in your life. Just remember, there are two sides to most things in life. When you start to apply exchange theory to dialogue in your memoir, try to examine situations from the perspectives of everyone involved.

...help readers see the dynamism in relationships...

Using the Four-Element Model in Memoir Writing

Just as you will be developing an ear for listening to improve the way your dialogue sounds, so too with the social science of conversation. As you better understand the dynamics of conversation, you'll begin to appreciate why you and the other people in your memoir communicate in different ways and how agendas influence what is said. Think back on conversations you have had with parents, children, friends, business colleagues, even strangers. In each case, what was going on? Were you in the process of getting acquainted? Were you or the other person disclosing information that had been hidden until then? Was that disclosure deliberate or accidental? Did you try to reach agreement by changing the other person's opinion? Was your language laced with hidden messages about your perceived cost or benefit of the exchange? Think about these four elements as you listen to conversations, engage in them or write dialogue.

Now Get to Writing!

This exercise may be difficult, but accept the challenge as it will help you build your dialogue muscles. Examine what you learn by doing this:

1. Read through your *directed* dialogue version of the scene in your synopsis. Decide which of the four elements (acquaintance, disclosure, co-orientation or exchange) best defines the dialogue. Write which one is going on and say why you think this is the way you wrote the scene.

2. With your choice in mind, choose one of the other elements (if you wrote the dialogue as disclosure, try it now as co-orientation or exchange as that might allow conflict to come out) and rewrite the dialogue. We tend to think that dialogue is just the way Matilda's mother described it—as a bouncing ball. Therefore, we write it simply and don't use it to reveal what is really going on. This exercise will help you use dialogue in a more powerful and sophisticated manner.

Putting the Games People Play into the Dialogue You Write

Have you ever read dialogue in a book that seemed off? You might not have known why, but you sensed something didn't sound right. Assuming the dialogue is well written, the problem most likely is that we all have a limited number of scripts we use in talking and interacting with people. Quite often we're not even conscious that we're falling into a pattern, but it's there and we are. From our real-world use of scripts, we come to expect a certain flow in the dialogue as characters play out their parts.

Life Scripts

Eric Berne developed the study of life scripts and reported the findings in his book *Games People Play and Beyond Games and Scripts*. Claude Steiner, in his book *Scripts People Live*, and Thomas A. Harris, in his popular *I'm OK, You're OK*, expanded on the original research. These studies come out of transactional analysis. Understanding the scripts that sometimes control our conversations can help you write dialogue better. The dialogue (the actual conversation) is in no way canned; it will be unique to your scene. It's how it plays out that captures the essence of the script. Consider this exchange:

"What shoes do you wear to the gym?" my son asked.

"These flats. The same shoes I wear every day."

"Why don't you get athletic shoes?"

"They aren't comfortable."

"Try one of the good brands."

"That doesn't matter. I have a high arch."

"Shoes have different amounts of support. You should be able to find one that's comfortable."

"The problem is that the top of my foot is so high that the shoes aren't comfortable."

And on and on it goes until someone finally moves the conversation on to another topic. This dialogue comes from the "Yes, but" script, one of the first games that Berne documented. In this life game, the person with the problem will always find a way to reject the advice or suggestion. I'm sure you know people in your life who play this game without realizing it. A few of the other game scripts are "See what you made me do," "Look how hard I've tried," "If it weren't for you" and "I'm only trying to help you." Remember, the people engaged in these dialogues are not deliberately playing a game. These have simply become their life scripts, often learned early in their lives from parents.

Understanding the games/scripts that are part of people's lives takes your writing to a deeper level. This sort of dialogue doesn't seem to advance the story—an important element of dialogue—but it does reveal how people in your memoir interact with others and builds greater dimensionality into your characters. Consider what kind of verbal games are played in your family.

And the above example? It comes from a conversation between Matilda and her son. She doesn't own athletic shoes and wears her flats to the gym. She told me that she wasn't even aware of the script until her partner said, "Well, we get the 'Yes, but' game."

Now Get to Writing!

1. Test the life script concept on someone you know, or even in a group setting. Start a "Yes, but" game but don't tell anyone what you are doing. Start the game with a statement about a problem you have. That usually invites people to start making suggestions to help you solve the situation. Suggestion after suggestion is made, and you continue with your "Yes, but" responses. Note how quickly everyone begins to follow the script of making an additional suggestion or arguing for the previously made suggestion. As soon as you can afterwards, write as much of the conversation as you can remember.

2. Now think about relationships among the people in the scene you are Deconstructing. Can you identify any scripts that might have been used? When you wrote the scene originally as dialogue, you probably used the directed style. Re-imagine the scene in your synopsis while considering such scripts as: "See what you made me do," "Look how hard I've tried," "If it weren't for you," "Yes, but" and "I'm only trying to help you." Even if these scripts don't fit the particular scene you are Deconstructing, rewrite the scene using one of these so that you can become familiar with the way that participants in a conversation begin to talk within the confines of a script. Then, you might want to take a look at one of the books I mentioned above so you can see more of the standard scripts.

P-A-C Ego

In addition to scripts that we have unwittingly absorbed over the years, we learned about roles as we grew up. Berne writes of three ego states or what we might call ego roles—Parent, Adult, Child—that we use in our interactions. When we operate out of our Parent ego, we are relying on behaviors and emotions that we saw our parents use. For example, if we become silent and refuse to talk when we are angry, it is probably a behavior we learned in childhood by observing a parent. On the other hand, when we speak from our Adult ego, we try to look objectively at a situation and react in a rational rather than overly emotional way. The Child ego acts and reacts in ways that are similar to behaviors that worked when she or he was a child.

Adult-to-Adult conversations put aside extraneous emotions that can cloud actions. However, Parent and Child egos often push aside the Adult voice in an effort to get what they want. When writing dialogue, being aware of these egos will bring you closer to what often happens in a conversation.

Thomas Harris explains the P-A-C ego states in his book *I'm OK, You're OK*. He says that the Parent ego relies on *taught* concepts, the Child ego on *felt* concepts and the Adult ego on *thought* concepts. These brief descriptions may help you when you write dialogue to get the distinctive voice of each person.

About now you may be wondering, Which of the three egos should I use in situations? I suggest you start by determining your primary ego state. You can find out by taking the free test at: http://www.transactional-analysis.org. It will take you about 10 minutes to complete the 61 items in this test. On the initial screen, you are asked to choose among taking the test as a Therapist, Teacher or Business. Unfortunately, Writer isn't one of the options, but the questions are the same for all three, so you can choose any to get started.

The difference in the three tests is the follow-up screen that provides a perspective on the test and the way you might use it. Therapist probably provides the most information about the Parent, Adult and Child ego states but you can still read each of them before moving on by clicking on Test Instructions. On the next screen, you are told to indicate your agreement or disagreement with each statement by clicking on the Yes or No response. I found it somewhat hard to take the test in that I couldn't always fully agree or disagree with the statement. My suggestion, since this seems to be the best of the free tests, is that you decide if you are in more agreement or more disagreement with the statement. Then click on the Yes or No.

After you complete the 61 items, your test is scored. You will have three scores, one each for Parent Ego State, Adult Ego State and Child Ego State. You'll probably be surprised that your Adult score isn't higher. I know I was. Transactional analysis helps us see the extent to which our patterns, expressed both in our actions and our conversations, often reflect the Parent or Child ego states. Matilda confessed to me that while she assumed her score would indicate a high Adult Ego State, it actually showed a high Parent Ego State. Once she reflected on it, she realized that was quite accurate, and it helped her to try to tone down the P and emphasize more of the A in her conversations. However, she says that she still reverts to the P state most of the time. I pass this on because it is an indication that when you investigate which of these states dominate the conversational style of each person in your memoir, you will have found a way to more clearly show that person in the dialogue you write.

Now Get to Writing!

1. Does the scene in your synopsis involve you and another family member or close friend? If so, write the scene from the perspective that one or both of you may *not* speak with the Adult ego. Does one of you assume the Parent ego and the other the Child ego? Does the person using the Child ego do this to get her (or his) way? Maybe techniques that were successful as a young child have been translated to be used even now as an adult.

2. If the scene doesn't fit this pattern of individuals, then imagine a scene between you as an adult talking with your mother or father. Do you quickly fall into the Child ego while the other person speaks from the Parent ego? Try to write a brief conversation using the Child and Parent egos. Then rewrite the dialogue where you both use Adult egos. Look at the difference.

What Can You Learn about Dialogue if You Analyze a Conversation?

Deborah Tannen, a linguist specializing in interpersonal communication, has written a number of books for academic and general audiences. Two of her most popular books, *Conversational Style:*

Analyzing Talk Among Friends and *You Just Don't Understand: Women and Men in Conversation,* were on *The New York Times* bestseller list with the second one staying on the list for four years and retaining the #1 spot for eight months.

Tannen has devoted her career to understanding what happens when we talk to/with/at each other. She has examined language between men and women, mothers and daughters, sisters, co-workers and family members (parents, partners, siblings and children as adults). Although she continues to publish new books, I want to take you back to November 23, 1978, when Tannen joined a group of five friends for a Thanksgiving meal in Berkeley, California. With everyone's permission, she put a tape recorder in the middle of the table and later transcribed all the conversations and analyzed them sentence by sentence. She published her findings in *Conversational Style.*

Linguistic Styles

Tannen describes nine linguistic styles used in conversations. I've listed a few that may help as you write dialogue. As you read about the styles below, think about each person involved in the dialogue and how she changes during a conversation depending on the topic and the nature of the relationship to the other person. (I wrote these examples, but have shown them using the same research format Tannen uses in her books.)

Primarily uses personal versus impersonal topics: One person tries to draw another person into the conversation by asking personal questions while the other person gives impersonal responses.

Barbara: What do you do?

Susie: I work downtown.

Shows enthusiasm by frequently interrupting other speaker: The one interrupting (Susie in this example) tries to anticipate the other person's statements and doesn't try to change the topic to redirect or take over the conversation.

Barbara: Didn't I see you last Saturday—

Susie: At the Farmer's Market.

Barbara: Oh you were—

Susie: Absolutely. We always go during the summer, mainly for the blueberries.

Barbara: Well, I just wondered—

Susie: Maybe we can meet there next week.

Asks "machine gun" questions: This style differs from the one above in that one person (Barbara) doesn't try to finish the sentences, she just doesn't wait for answers. She breaks in with a follow-on question while the other speaker is still trying to answer the previous question.

Barbara: Are you going on vacation?

Susie: Sure, we're—

Barbara: When will you leave?

Susie: Well that is going to depend—

Barbara: How do you decide on where you'll go each year?

Susie: This year's choice of Pawleys Island was a matter of finding a place that we can—

Barbara: Have you been there before?

Deepens level of conversation through personal revelations: One person (Barbara in this example) adds personal revelations to help the other person open up and then returns the conversation to the first person (Susie).

Barbara: You look sad.

Susie: I just got off the phone with my daughter. She thinks she's in love, but he's the wrong guy.

Barbara: It's hard to see a child make mistakes—especially when you can't do anything about it. My son is going through a divorce now. His wife is turning the children against him and even against us. Tell me more about your daughter.

Shows persistence: Sometimes one person and sometimes both people in a conversation stay on target and aren't easily budged from what they're trying to say. In this example, Barbara wants to talk about what her daughter is doing and continues to do so even though Susie keeps interrupting. Susie, on the other hand, hasn't seen Barbara in years and doesn't know that she had another child. Neither is dissuaded from the story she is trying to get out.

Barbara: Our youngest daughter—

Susie: Wait!

Barbara: She's just starting—

Susie: I didn't know—

Barbara: ...college this fall.

Susie: Time out. Time out. I didn't know you had another daughter.

The takeaway for us, as writers, is that people have distinctive conversational styles. When writing your memoir, you need to determine the unique ways your characters

...people have distinctive conversational styles...

interact and then let the dialogue unfold within that style. Since you're dealing with actual conversations that may have occurred years before, you'll have to recapture the exchange first, maybe even rough out the dialogue in your Deconstructions then try to dissect the conversation for its linguistic style.

Dialogue and Taking Turns

Then there's the matter of length. Tannen's research shows that a person who wants to keep the attention on herself or himself will speak for a long time without letting another person have a say. A long turn, which is rare, is about 150 words. When writing dialogue, if your character has a long story to tell, you'll want to break it into smaller segments to maintain the feel of a true conversation. A sentence or two—25 to 50 words—is more typical.

Male and Female Dialogue

Before, leaving Tannen's research, let's take a quick look at her findings on differences in male and female dialogue in *You Just Don't Understand: Women and Men in Conversation*. She writes: A man sees himself...

> ...as an individual in a hierarchical social order in which he was either one-up or one-down. In this world, conversations are negotiations in which people try to achieve and maintain the upper hand if they can, and protect themselves from others' attempts to put them down...Life, then, is a contest, a struggle to preserve independence and avoid failure.

On the other hand, a woman, she says, views herself...

> ...as an individual in a network of connections. In this world, conversations are negotiations for closeness in

which people try to seek and give confirmation and support...Life, then, is a community, a struggle to preserve
intimacy and avoid isolation.

While you may be nodding in agreement with this summary of
male and female differences in conversations, you may also wonder
if Tannen is reinforcing stereotypes. She anticipates the question:

Women are also concerned with achieving status and
avoiding failure, but these are not the goals they are focused on all the time, and they tend to pursue them in the
guise of connection. And men are also concerned with
achieving involvement and avoiding isolation, but they
are not focused on these goals, and they tend to pursue
them in the guise of opposition.

The following example from *You Just Don't Understand* illustrates that women and men, operating from their different
assumptions about the purpose and use of conversations, can create conflict even when they don't set out to argue. I'm not implying
that all conversations between the sexes end in disagreements. But
by understanding the gender differences in speech (e.g., men see
talk as part of maintaining their role in a hierarchical society while
women see talk as a way to extend their social connections), we can
write dialogue that better represents the distinctive voices of each
gender. In the following conversation, Maureen and Philip, a married couple, are setting a date for a dinner party:

Maureen: The only weekend we seem to have free is October ninth.

Philip: That's the opening of hunting season.

Maureen: Well, let's do it Saturday or Sunday evening.

Philip: Okay, make it Saturday.

Maureen: Wouldn't you want to be able to hunt later on
the first day of hunting?

Philip: [Annoyed] I said Saturday, so obviously that's the
day I prefer.

Maureen: [Now also annoyed] I was just trying to be con-
siderate of you. You didn't give a reason for choosing Saturday.

Philip: I'm taking off Thursday and Friday to hunt, so I figure I'll have had enough by Saturday night.

Maureen: Well, why didn't you say that?

Philip: I didn't see why I had to. And I found your question very intrusive.

Maureen: I found your response very offensive!

Neither Maureen nor Philip were trying to pick a fight. They had a common objective—choosing a date for a dinner party. But you can see what happened. Each was operating from a gendered approach to conversation.

I'll close the discussion of gendered dialogue with this: The challenge for a woman writing the male side of dialogue (and vice versa when men write dialogue for women) is to overcome the natural inclination to use the same assumptions they make when writing dialogue for their own gender. The more you understand about conversation, the deeper you go in your Deconstruction, the more the people in your memoir will speak in their own distinctive styles. You will have the tools to avoid the common memoir problem of dialogue that sounds all the same, no matter who is speaking.

Now Get to Writing!

Now it's your turn.

1. Do you have a male and a female in the scene in your synopsis? If not, select a scene from your memoir in which a female and male are engaged in dialogue. Because you know yourself so well, it may be tempting to let the second person "sound" like you, just different words. Don't give in to the temptation. Before you begin writing, think about how you use a conversation to accomplish your goal. Do you use the conversation to expand or deepen the relationship? Do you use the conversation to maintain the differences in the relationship? Now ask the same questions of the other person. Having thought through the differences, you'll find it easier to write a page of dialogue with two distinct voices.

2. Deconstruct a conversation to pick up the differences in speaking and communication styles. Identify the common

objective. Then, as you write the dialogue, show how far apart they can get because of their different uses of dialogue.

3. If you can't readily find an appropriate scene in your memoir, practice this technique by making up a dialogue between two people you know. It's helpful to use people you know because you'll have more familiarity with their speaking styles.

The Body Speaks

There is one missing element in our discussion of dialogue—the visual or non-verbal cues. If you sit at a restaurant and look across the room at a table where there are two or more people, you'll see a lot of hand waving, gesturing and, if you're close enough, facial expressions. Owen Hargie, Christine Saunders and David Dickson, in their book *Social Skills in Interpersonal Communication*, describe a number of gestures and movements that people make when talking. An obvious one is head nodding. Let's say that Alan agrees with what you are saying. Rather than making a comment, he is likely to just nod his head up and down. Or, if Elizabeth disagrees with you, she may shake her head sideways. Occasionally, you even may have noticed the odd mixture when a person saying, "Yes, you can do that," will shake her head from left to right. That's probably when the words don't fully agree with what the person is thinking. Using both the verbal and the non-verbal elements is a device you can use in your writing but exercise caution and restraint. You don't want to overdo this. A little goes a long way.

Here are a few of the gestures Hargie lists in his book. No doubt they'll be familiar to you and serve as a good reminder:

Gesture	*Inference*
Hands outstretched	Appealing
Feet-shuffling	Impatience
Shoulder shrugging	I don't know
Drumming table with fingers	Anxious
Shaking clenched fist	Angry
Palms up and facing forward	Stop or wait
Thumbs up	Success
Thumbs down	Loss

Now Get to Writing!

1. As part of your dialogue Deconstruction, create a list of expressive gestures that you make. Engage in some conversations and notice how your body also engages in the dialogue. How do you use your head or your hands? Some people have quiet bodies while others are active with both words and body. Be specific when you write about your body movements.

2. Now take a second person in the scene you are Deconstructing. Does he or she use the body to emphasize words or moods? Close your eyes and see how the person talks.

If you want to explore this topic in more depth, you can pick up a copy of Julius Fast's *Body Language*, the 1970 book that introduced the science of non-verbal communication.

Wrapping Up Dialogue from the Perspective of the Social Sciences

So far, Newcomb, Luft, Homans, Blau, Berne, Steiner, Harris, Tannen and Hargie have given us insights into conversations. They have taken us deeper into what really happens when people talk...beyond the words and all the way to their meaning. Understanding the social science behind speaking and applying it to your writing will elevate your dialogue beyond some lines of he-saids and she-saids. It helps us to know why people speak the way they do, how they negotiate their differences with others, the ways in which relationships and stories unfold or don't, devices often used, how nonverbal clues assist or derail a conversation, what types of games or life scripts are unconsciously played out and how our three ego states (Parent, Adult, Child) can explain why we speak a certain way at one time and differently another time.

You won't be able to apply every aspect of this research to your writing, but it is important to have this in your writing toolkit. Read and learn as much as you can so you can rely on these findings to provide insights for your Deconstruction of the dialogue element. Write real or imagined conversations so that you can see how these different styles can be shown. Anyone can put words on a page; it takes a depth of understanding to fashion dialogue that is true to the people engaged in the conversation. Stephen King reminds us in his book *On Writing*, "It's dialogue that gives your cast their voices, and is crucial in defining their characters—only what people do tells us more about what they're like." Dialogue is one more way we can *show* rather than *tell* and give our readers the information they need to reach their own conclusions, form their own allegiances and create their own emotional bonds with characters.

Dialogue is Not Real...Listen for the Difference

Alfred Hitchcock is reported to have said, "A good story is life with the boring parts taken out." We can rewrite that statement to apply to dialogue: Strong dialogue is conversation with the boring parts taken out. While real dialogue will have lots of "ums" and "I means," you want to select only those elements of dialogue that bring your characters to life. Annie Dillard, in *The Writing Life*, admits, "The written word is weak. Many people prefer life to it. Life gets your blood going and smells good. Writing is mere writing..." Good dialogue is one way we can amp up the written word.

Day-to-day life is where we learn about dialogue. The key to writing dialogue is learning to listen...all over again. This requires you to turn off the filters you've spent a lifetime developing. You know the ones I'm referring to. The filters that eliminate background noises and enable you to concentrate on a conversation you're having, even when you're in a crowded room. The filters that help you ignore accents, speech patterns, dialect and sentence structure and focus on the information. As you develop your ear for conversation, you'll need to tune in to *how* people really speak. You might be shocked by what you hear. Count how often people interrupt one another. How often they speak in unfinished sentences. The frequency with which they repeat themselves. Listen to how many threads can be going on simultaneously in one conversation.

The truth is, real conversation is a mess. It's a testament to our brain that we can cope let alone communicate. And if you don't believe me, get out a recorder and capture a few casual conversations—with everyone's permission, of course. Then transcribe the results. Or, for an easier exercise, turn on your television, put CNN on mute and turn on the closed captioning feature (on some sets this comes on automatically). You'll see the good, the bad, and the ugly of real-time conversations.

The first thing you're going to realize is that you can't possibly write this way and subject your readers to the mayhem. All the rest of your effort is going to go into making dialogue work on paper.

Listen to everything...conversations in a coffee shop or food court. Make notes about gestures, conflict and any apparent efforts to achieve harmony. Listen to radio and television shows because what you're hearing is a hybrid form of conversation. Yes, it's meant to be listened to rather than read so our real-world filters are available to us. But it's still dialogue; it still started out as words in a script. It may sound real, but it's been cleaned up, cleared of verbal debris, sanitized of most of the "ums," "I means" and "you knows" and pruned of the boring parts. Pay particular attention to different styles of speaking in drama, comedy, mystery, news and even talk shows.

Listen to everything...

Set the Stage for the Dialogue and Let Your Character Walk on Prepared

It is tempting to write a piece of dialogue as if two (or more) people have just arrived at this moment in time without a backstory, without preexisting emotions. Yet context often determines how a conversation works out. When you begin to write dialogue, imagine that each person involved is standing backstage. Like a method actor, each is getting into character and mentally preparing to walk on the stage.

Is one person happy? Has she been thinking about how much she loves the other person? Is another angry and argumentative? Maybe he's been worried about financial matters. Did she just return from a fun trip to the beach? Or does she suspect she's pregnant? Is she wondering if her partner is having an affair? Actors bring the emotion with them. It doesn't just happen with the first word. Put yourself in the appropriate mood before you write that first sentence. Even who speaks first will be determined by the context for the dialogue. You might think of the *moment before* as the proximal point in time that drives one person's interaction. Then determine the other person's proximal moment, and you'll have the elements to begin a successful dialogue.

Words to Speak With

He began to think of the fun he had planned for this day, and his sorrows multiplied....He got out his worldly wealth and examined it...enough to buy an exchange of WORK, maybe, but not half enough to buy so much as half an hour of pure freedom....[he] gave up the idea of trying to buy the boys. At this dark and hopeless moment an inspiration burst upon him! Nothing less than a great, magnificent inspiration....

Tom went on whitewashing--paid no attention to the [boy pretending to be a] steamboat. Ben stared a moment and then said: "Hi-YI! YOU'RE up a stump, ain't you!"

No answer. Tom surveyed his last touch with the eye of an artist, then he gave his brush another gentle sweep and surveyed the result...

"Hello, old chap, you got to work, hey?"

Tom wheeled suddenly and said:

"Why, it's you, Ben! I warn't noticing."

"Say--I'm going in a-swimming, I am. Don't you wish you could? But of course you'd druther WORK--wouldn't you? Course you would!"

Tom contemplated the boy a bit, and said:

"What do you call work?"

"Why, ain't THAT work?"...

"No--is that so? Oh' come, now--lemme just try. Only just a little--I'd let YOU, if you was me, Tom."

"Ben, I'd like to, honest injun; but Aunt Polly--well, Jim wanted to do it, but she wouldn't let him; Sid wanted to do it, and she wouldn't let Sid...."

And while the late steamer Big Missouri worked and sweated in the sun, the retired artist sat on a barrel in the shade close by, dangled his legs, munched his apple, and planned the slaughter of more innocents....And when the middle of the afternoon came, from being a poor poverty-stricken boy in the morning, Tom was literally rolling in wealth.

This bit of dialogue is from the popular fence-painting scene in Mark Twain's *The Adventures of Tom Sawyer*. Twain has come down to us as the paragon of dialogue writers, and I have to agree that his crisp exchanges impart a lot of insight into characters while getting the job done and moving the story along. He is also recognized for having one of the best ears for dialect. As you can see from the above piece, his writing is rich in dialect. If you ever wanted to know how folks spoke in southern Missouri back in the 1800s, Twain is your source. He also gives us a bit of good advice. In an 1874 letter to William Dean Howells (known as "The Dean of American Letters"), Twain wrote, "I amend dialect stuff by talking and talking and talking it till it sounds right."

http://womensmemoirs.com/dialogue-1

But for writers in the 21st century, dialect and distinctive speech patterns can be a challenge. For one thing, television and radio have done a lot to even out our diction and accent. Yes, the southern accent is still strong. Yes, in Downeast Maine, where I live, the locals refer to everyone—male and female—as *dear*, and to my ear even pronounce it funny. Yes, people in the Midwest add an "r" to George Washington's name, pronouncing it "Warshington." And yes, as has been true for generations, the kids have their own lingo. But for all that, we in the United States don't have a big issue with the way our fellow countrymen and women speak. So before I launch into some of the vagaries of language, let me give you one rule of thumb: If you can't do dialect, accents or diction effectively, then DON'T. Handling language badly will get you into more trouble than avoiding the issue.

By this point you have a strong sense of conversation and how you can apply it to your dialogue. Just as life scripts, linguistic style, gestures and non-verbal communication help you craft multi-dimensional characters, so too can diction and figures of speech—carefully used—enrich a person's dialogue. Words have three dimensions. As writers, we choose words based on appearance, sound and meaning. This is where the fun begins—when you start listening to your characters' diction. Here are just a few examples:

Mono v. Polysyllabic: Does a person you know use five-cent words with one syllable, such as nope, yup, sure, you bet, or does she go all in for hundred-dollar, multi-syllabic words like supercalifragilisticexpialidocious? Well that may be going to far, but you get my meaning. Using either your memory or by listening to the people in your memoir, see if you notice both types as well as specific words that seem unique to that person.

Pedestrian v. Pedantic: Does one of your characters speak simply or are his sentences and stories always dressed up? Think of this as the difference between saying, "He didn't do it," and announcing, "It is the determination of our august assembled body of jurors that the defendant is not guilty."

Denotative v. Connotative: Choosing the right word can make all the difference in the way your story is understood. And by the right word, I'm talking about knowing both its dictionary (denotative) definition and its emotional or generally used (connotative) meaning. For example, if you write that "they are living together" and mean that in the dictionary sense, your story is likely to be misunderstood because of the connotative meaning of "living together." Similarly, Jimi Hendrix's young audiences understood the connotative meaning of *experience* in his song "Are You Experienced?" just as fans of The Rolling Stones got the meaning of *satisfaction* in "(I Can't Get No) Satisfaction." In all three of these examples, the connotative meanings override the dictionary definition. Be aware of changing meanings of words and phrases or your readers will come away with a different interpretation than you intend.

Slang: Vernacular and slang are often specific to an era, geographic location, industry/field or social class. Here are a few examples: props, ka-ching, 9-11, darn tootin', dork, cool, dope, bummer, weed and outta sight.

General v. Specific: If you want to mention boarding a vessel for transport by water, you will probably say a boat. However, the specific type of boat will significantly alter the meaning of your sentence. For example, saying, "My friend invited me to stay on her yacht" conjures up a very different image than, "My friend invited me to go around the lake in her rowboat." And the sentence, "We decided to take the ferry over to the island" is different still. In almost all cases, the specific word is better than the general.

Wrong Word: While many malaprops are deliberate, a friend of my mother's had a classic case of wrong-word itis. I recall a party at my parents' home one night. The hour was getting late when a couple of neighbors dropped by, and they brought a friend. The friend, a woman, was wearing a particularly startling purple jumpsuit. My mother's friend, who also had a thing for fads in fashion, was quite taken with the outfit and went out of her way to compliment the woman. The problem was her word choice. "Oh how gauche," she said. We were all stunned, but we had to admit, she was right...even though the meaning was not what she'd intended.

Here are a few more malapropisms: "We seem to have *unleased* a hornet's nest." (Valerie Singleton); "He's going up and down like a *metronome*." (Ron Pickering); "Listen to the *blabbing* brook." (Norm Crosby); and my favorite "It is beyond my *apprehension*." (Danny Ozark).

Cliché: Once colorful, figurative language that has lost its freshness becomes trite. It's overuse spoils an otherwise beautifully written memoir. Avoid the cliché and look for fresh, unique ways to express the point you are trying to make, unless, of course, the person speaking is known for throwing around a cliché or two too many. Here are a few common clichés: dead as a door nail, icing on the cake, airing dirty laundry, look before you leap and don't make a Federal case of it. By the way, Warren Buffet likes to play with clichés to give them, if you'll forgive me, a fresh lease on life. Yup, I just indulged in a cliché. Here are three of Buffet's favorites: "I try to buy stock in businesses that are so wonderful that an idiot can run them." "I like to shoot fish in a barrel. But I like to do it after the water has run out." And I particularly like: "Let's not change horses in mid-stream." Reply: "Even if your horse can't swim?"

There are many more examples of diction and figures of speech available. I've only touched the tip of the iceberg. Sorry, I did it again. A simple Google search for "figures of speech" will give you links to several more comprehensive lists.

Two Final Thoughts On Word Choice

I'll leave you with two more points. The first comes from the respected and award-winning memoirist Sue William Silverman, author of *Because I Remember Terror, Father, I Remember You* and *Love Sick: One Woman's Journey through Sexual Addition*, which became a Lifetime Television Original Movie. Silverman has also written a book on the craft of writing memoir, entitled *Fearless Confessions: A Writer's Guide to Memoir*. Given our discussion about dialect, diction and other "broken English," we think her statement is the perfect conclusion: "In all prose, fiction and nonfiction, dialogue works best when it reflects a hint of speech—a suggestion as to how we speak—as opposed to allowing characters (real or fictional) to give speeches."

The second thought comes from me. I love movies both for their entertainment value and what I can learn about storytelling and dialogue. I've noticed in several films where a significant number of the characters are non-English speaking that the writers have used a clever device. When the non-English-speaking characters first begin to talk, they use their native language, and the English is in subtitles. My problem with subtitles is that I'm so busy reading I miss the action on the screen. The filmmakers have solved this for me (and probably you). Rather than use subtitles throughout the film, they ever so gently move into English. The audience gets it that characters are conversing in their own language while they enjoy the convenience of listening to English. You can use a similar technique with your written dialogue. Sprinkle in a few "y'alls," "sight for sore eyes," "scarce as hen's teeth" or other distinctive local idioms or bits of diction--even nonstandard spelling to convey an accent--in the early lines but very quickly start to even out the language so it conforms to a more generic voice. The occasional word or phrase to remind the reader is okay, but not much more than that.

Truth in Dialogue

One of the reasons memoir writers often give for shying away from dialogue is that their stories are true and unless they were standing there with recorder in hand there's no way they can capture the dialogue. They're right, but that doesn't prevent good memoirists from using dialogue. It's too useful a tool to omit on a technicality.

So we do the next best thing. We capture the essence, the intent of the conversation. We include any bits of the exchange that we recall, but we **don't get hung up on every word.** Again quoting from Sue William Silverman's book *Fearless Confessions*, she writes, "I can't even remember the exact words I used ten minutes ago, let alone ten years ago....

We capture the essence...

To write an exact line of dialogue, word for word, isn't the goal of memoir, anyway....Don't you have a sense—if not a factual transcript—as to how various people speak...Don't you have a strong sense of the conversation..." Enough said.

One More Good Excuse to Spend Time Reading

Just as listening is an important technique for learning to use dialogue, so too is reading. For this reason, I'm going to give you permission to read even more. And when your spouse or partner asks, "Shouldn't you be writing instead of sitting around reading?" You can say, "Leave me alone, I'm working." And if you are dissecting the dialogue, you'll be telling the truth.

To get you started, I'm concluding this chapter with some interesting examples of dialogue that I've come across in my reading. Most of these come from memoirs.

Nancy Bachrach's book, *The Center of the Universe: A Memoir*, is the story of her father's death in a fiery explosion, her mother's challenging recovery and the impact of both on the family. Bachrach's perverse sense of humor makes this book come alive...of course, her mother's nature didn't hurt. Here's an exchange that captures the mother-daughter dynamic most effectively. Lola is telling her daughter about an incident on the golf course. Speeding along in her cart as usual, she barely navigates a sharp turn and manages to send her picnic cooler sailing off into the water. As the cooler began to sink, Lola spied the snout of an alligator nearby:

"My cooler! My cooler's sinking! Take this," she said, pushing her ball retriever into his hand. "And hurry!"

"Oh, I don't think this will work, ma'am. The scooper's too small."

"So you'll have to go in, Mario?"

"Oh, I hope not, ma'am. I wouldn't want to do that. I'm scared of alligators."

"I'm sure there aren't any," she told him. "Now hurry!"

"How could you do that, Mom?" I asked her as she proudly recounted the episode. "How could you send that sweet old man into the canal when you'd just seen an alligator?"

"Well, maybe it wasn't an alligator."

"So you were lying to me just now? Or were you lying to Mario at the time?"

"Maybe my eyes were playing tricks on me."

When a liar tells you she might be lying, is she telling the truth? I wasn't sure what to believe.

"You knew you were sending that man into an alligator-infested swamp! You were practically bragging about it a minute ago!"

"Don't exaggerate. It worked out just fine, didn't it? I got my cooler back and I tipped him big. Anyway, alligators never hurt people."

Who's to say why some traits return and others do not, why her instinct to lie is coming back with force but a sense of morality is not? I like to think that the lying part of her brain was so well developed, it was too hard to kill. Maybe that's the essence of character.

In *The Long Hello: The Other Side of Alzheimer's*, Cathie Borrie tells the story of her mother's struggle to communicate and lead a normal life as long as possible. Because communication is such an important component of the disease, she chose to tell as much of the book as possible through their dialogue. As readers, we watch her mother's descent and valiant battle to keep her condition at bay. Because Borrie didn't want to bog readers down with attributions, she used different fonts to indicate the change in speaker. She also only used quotation marks for her lines. The dialogue itself, makes it easy to identify Borrie's Mum:

I call my mother to say goodnight before I leave the dance studio.

"I don't have to be personable all the time, do I?"

Well, on a personal basis...yes, I think you do.

"Oh dear. Well, I'll call you in the morning."

Nighty-night, Hughie Boy. Oh, but aren't you coming over?

"Hughie? Um...I'm at, I just got into bed. Is something wrong?"

I don't know that I want to tell you anything or end up saying anything because as long as I've known when you've asked me anything and I've answered you very nicely, I've got a real boo.

"A real what?"

Boo, boom. I don't think you took it seriously at all. I think it was a big laugh. When you were smallish and growing up and even now I think you would say, 'What do you think of that man, Mum?' and I would say, 'I think he's lovely.' And then you would say, 'Lovely?'

"Oh, I--"

Yeah. No, no, no.

"I'm sorry...I'll try to be more careful."

Well I don't know because I don't know, I don't know you any longer.

This next book is a change of pace. It's one in the series of Lord Peter Wimsey detective novels by Dorothy L. Sayers. The exchange below is from *Clouds of Witness* (1926). Sayers developed a strong character in Wimsey with a distinctive style and voice. As such, she is able to introduce him into a scene without actually mentioning his name. The reader is then treated to a one-sided conversation as Wimsey exchanges pleasantries with everyone assembled; it's rather like listening to one side of a telephone conversation. It's quite different and most effective.

"Who's that, I wonder," said the Duchess.

The door waltzed open.

"Mornin', dear old things," said the newcomer cheerfully. "How are you all? Hullo, Helen! Colonel, you owe me half a crown since last September year. Mornin', Mrs. Marchbanks, Mornin', Mrs. P. Well, Mr. Murbles, how d'you like this bili-beastly weather? Don't trouble to get up, Freddy; I'd simply hate to inconvenience you. Parker, old man, what a damned reliable old bird you are! Always on the spot, like that patent ointment thing. I say, have you all finished? I meant to get up earlier, but I was snorin' so Bunter hadn't the heart to wake me. I nearly blew in last night, only we didn't arrive till 2 A.M. and I thought you wouldn't half bless me if I did. Eh, what, Colonel? Aeroplane. Victoria from Paris to London--North-Eastern to Northallerton--damn bad roads the rest of the way, and a puncture just below Riddlesdale. Damn bad bed at the 'Lord in Glory'; thought I'd blow in for the last sausage here, if I was lucky. What? Sunday morning in an English family and no sausages? God bless my soul, what's the world coming to, eh, Colonel? I say, Helen, old Gerald's been an' gone an' done it this time, what? You've no business to leave him on his own, you know; he always gets into mischief. What's that? Curry? Thanks, old man. Here, I say, you needn't be so stingy about it; I've been travelling for three days on end. Freddy, pass the toast. Beg pardon, Mrs. Marchbanks? Oh, rather, yes; Corsica was perfectly amazin'--all black-eyed fellows with knives in their belts and jolly fine-looking girls. Old Bunter had a regular affair with the inn-keeper's daughter in one place. D'you know, he's an awfully susceptible old beggar. You'd never think it, would you? Jove! I am hungry, I say, Helen, I meant to get you some fetchin' crepe-de-Chine undies from Paris, but I saw that old Parker was gettin' ahead of me over the bloodstains, so we packed up our things and buzzed off."

Mrs. Pettigrew-Robinson rose.

"Theodore," she said, "I think we ought to be getting ready for church."

In her book *Who Do You Think You Are? A Memoir*, Alyse Myers strives to capture the tenor of conversation in her home. The dialogue is straight forward, fairly simple and, I suspect, captures the voices of her mother, father and siblings accurately. Myers includes a lot of brief exchanges that serve to both move the story forward and expand the reader's understanding of the characters. Her mother was the dominant force, but I've selected a brief exchange among Alyse and her sisters after their father died. It's simple, but I think it sounds like children talking, without being over the top:

> "What happened to our daddy?" my youngest sister asked me. "Will he come back soon?"
>
> My middle sister said she didn't think it was fair that I was able to go to the funeral and that she had to stay home.
>
> "Why did you get to go and not me?" she said. "Why do you always get to do things?"
>
> "Why is he dead?" my younger sister asked. "Will Mommy die, too?"
>
> "I don't know," I told them both. "We don't have a father, but we still have our mother."
>
> I didn't have any friends who didn't have a father.

As you become increasingly comfortable with and skilled at dialogue, you may find that it takes center stage in your writing. After Deconstructing their stories for dialogue, we find that many of our students incorporate dialogue as a major element in their storytelling. But don't think you have to use it on every page to be effective. It will all depend on the story and the result of your five Deconstructions.

Jessica Bram, author of *Happily Ever After Divorce: Notes of a Joyful Journey*, uses dialogue quite sparingly. Often she uses one line of dialogue in a paragraph of narrative with no exchange. Other times, if there are only two lines of dialogue, she works these into the narrative paragraph format as well. While this may seem to defy some of the principles of dialogue, she has chosen to describe a conversation and then emphasize a single line or two of the exchange. Here are two examples:

> On one of my teary phone calls to my mother, I lamented the loss of our home and most of all, that dream kitchen.

My mother had an immediate response. "Jessica," she said, "don't you realize? Any kitchen of yours will be wonderful."

• • •

...And of course, he still had that fixation with being on time. "I'll be here to pick them up Friday at five o'clock. Please have them ready so I'm not left waiting in the driveway like last time." Instantly my defenses would spring to attention. "They're not soldiers, they're little boys," I would shoot back. "This isn't the military!" And there we were, sparring again just like in the old days.

Then, just to mix things up, occasionally Bram starts with her embedded dialogue and continues with a standard dialogue format:

One night, several months after Robert's one and only visit to the child psychologist, I stepped into his dark room to put some clean clothes in his drawer. Robert was lying in bed, still awake. On an impulse, I came over and sat down next to him on his bed. "Can I hang out with you here a little while?" I asked. "Sure," he said and moved over to let me lie alongside him.

"Did I ever tell you the story about when my grandmother fell off a sled when she was a little girl in Russia?" I asked.

"Was your grandmother really from Russia?" he asked. "You never told me."

"Siberia. Well, the Ukraine actually. But it must have been a lot like Siberia because it was always snowing." I then proceeded to tell him the story of how after a long trip by horse-drawn sled, her family had to go back to look for my four-year-old grandmother after failing for miles to notice that she was missing. When they retrieved her from the snow and got her back home, they warmed her up by putting her in the oven--or so the story went.

I've taken the following brief exchange from bestselling author Donna VanLiere's *Finding Grace: A Memoir*. Donna is suspicious she's pregnant. She's been nauseous for days, but hadn't yet been to the doctor. Now she must deal with her boss, whom she called The

Skinny Man. He's not happy with her work productivity. Donna is careful not to write The Skinny Man's dialogue to sound feminine; she also allows him to seem more detestable by including both his actions and his proclivity for slang:

> "Is something wrong?" he asked.
>
> "I don't feel well today," I said.
>
> "Well, isn't that a coinkidink because you've been absent from your desk a lot this week." He emphasized week for my sake, just in case I thought it was just today that was the problem.
>
> The Skinny Man was getting under my skin. "I know. I haven't felt well this week."
>
> He leaned in close. "There's a huge *sales frontier* out there that needs discovering." I felt grinding nausea deep in my stomach. Did he just use the term sales frontier? "It could just be me but you don't seem committed to discovering what's out there. Do you need to go talk to the Fat Man [her other boss]?" I shook my head. I think I would have quit that day but if my hunch was right and I was pregnant then I'd need the job till the baby came. "Now" the Skinny Man said, puffing his chest out to the size of a chicken, "are you committed?" I nodded. I loved my clients but calling them ad nauseam had left me dry. "Are we okey-dokey?" I smiled and picked up my phone. He clapped me on the back and squeezed my shoulder. "Later, gator."

For our last dialogue example, I have chosen a passage from Jerramy Fine's *Someday My Prince Will Come: True Adventures of a Wannabe Princess*. Fine uses a lot of dialogue; most of her exchanges are quick. The one I've selected is longer and a very good example of using interpolated dialogue. Notice too that this reads very much like a "Yes, but" life script:

> "I don't think you should go," my mom told me. "I'm really worried you might be caught up in the Y2K."
>
> "What better place to get stuck than in a palace?" I countered.

This conversation was getting ridiculous. It wasn't like I was asking her to fund my plane ticket to Mumbai; I was merely doing the daughterly thing and kindly informing her of my plans. I mean, I was already in London--which was practically *halfway* to India. (And quietly dipping into my new student loan money would easily cover the cost of the flight.)

"I don't think it's safe for you to travel as a woman on your own. You might be forced into a harem or something," she continued.

"I won't be alone! Besides, didn't you try to hitchhike to Woodstock by yourself?" She didn't like being reminded of that one.

"That was different."

"Not really."

"Jerramy, you can't fly around the world on a whim like some spoiled trust-fund kid! You can barely afford to be in London! Every penny you have should be going toward LSE, not wasted on one crazy party after another! You can go to India some other time. It's not like this is a once-in-a-lifetime opportunity."

"Mom! I'm being invited to party with a *royal family* on the eve of *the millennium*. If that's not a once-in-a-lifetime opportunity, what is?!"

"What if you get malaria?"

I was tempted to hang up on her. "I won't get malaria." Seriously, what happened to all the usual do-what-makes-you-happy hippie talk?

"Jerramy, if you go to India, I'll be very disappointed in you." I'm surprised she tried this one. I've never responded to any kind of guilt-related discipline and she knew it.

"Mom, don't worry about me. I'll be perfectly safe. And I'll send you a postcard from the palace." And with that, I said goodbye, called up the London travel agent, and bought my once-in-a-lifetime ticket.

Rules to Make Dialogue Your Power Tool

After that set of exemplars of dialogue, I will leave you to your own reading and discovery. If you've followed the exercises, you now have Deconstructed the scene in your synopsis for dialogue. You've even Deconstructed for dialogue using different techniques. Furthermore, you see how dialogue is such an integral part of our lives.

We start talking in order to communicate what we want. We have a good grasp of conversing, interacting and even conforming to certain life scripts long before we begin to write. It's almost ironic that writing good dialogue can be so challenging. But if you follow a few rules, you can make dialogue a power tool in your writing:

- *First,* become a good listener; pay attention to how people communicate—both with words and non-verbally.
- *Second,* learn to use all four directions for dialogue—directed, interpolated, misdirected and modulated. Not only will they bring variety to your dialogue form but—and this is more important—when matched with the appropriate conversation they can increase tension and help you convey the emotions underlying the words.
- *Third,* before you begin writing, understand what is going on in a scene; apply some of the techniques we've picked up from the social sciences. This will add to your characters' dimensionality and make your dialogue ring true with readers.
- **And *fourth*,** become a student of dialogue; dissect the techniques other writers employ; and determine what works and what doesn't.

As you get deeper into Deconstructing your dialogue, you will need to scrutinize your work. Using dialogue should never be bland, a compromise or something just to break up pages of narrative. Take only the best pieces of your dialogue Deconstruction—primarily that which either adds to the story (e.g., changes the pace, advances the action, increases tension) or enhances the people (e.g., builds multi-dimensional characters, showcases emotions, clarifies relationships).

What's Next?

Up to now, the focus has been on characters, their emotional states and how they communicate through dialogue. Our next element of writing, while it is applicable to people, is more expansive. Look all around you. Take in everything. What does the room look like? Do you smell dinner cooking? Perhaps a pan of kale is starting to burn. Is there a mosquito buzzing nearby or a knock on the front door? How does that apple from your garden taste? Does your hand reach out to touch the soft fur of your British Blue Shorthair cat, Samantha? Join Matilda as she takes you into the rich descriptive world of the five senses. You'll learn how to make your scenes come to life—so much so that readers will feel almost as if they are standing by your side, seeing, smelling, tasting, touching and hearing the same as you.

References and Resources

Barnhart, David K. and Allan A. Metcalf. *America in So Many Words: Words That Have Shaped America*. Boston: Houghton Mifflin, 1997.

Bachrach, Nancy. *The Center of the Universe: A Memoir*. New York: Alfred A. Knopf, 2009.

Berne, Eric. *Beyond Games and Scripts*. New York: Grove Press, Inc. 1976.

Berne, Eric. *Games People Play*. New York: Ballantine Books, 1964.

Blau, Peter. *Exchange and Power in Social Life*. New York: Wiley, 1964.

Borrie, Cathie. *The Long Hello: The Other Side of Alzheimer's*. Nightwing Press, 2010.

Bram, Jessica. *Happily Ever After Divorce: Notes of a Joyful Journey*. Deerfield Beach, FL: Health Communications, Inc., 2009.

Chiarella, Tom. *Writing Dialogue*. Cincinnati: Story Press, 1998.

Chubbuck, Ivana. *The Power of the Actor*. New York: Gotham Books, 2004.

Dawidziak, Mark, ed. *Mark My Words: Mark Twain on Writing*. New York: St. Martin's Press. 1996.

Dillard, Annie. *The Writing Life*. New York: Harper Perennial, 1989.

Fine, Jerramy. *Someday My Prince Will Come: True Adventures of a Wannabe Princess*. New York: Gotham Books, 2008.

Goffman, Erving. *Interaction Ritual: Essays on Face-to-Face Behavior*. Garden City, NY: Doubleday Anchor Books, 1967.

Goffman, Erving. *The Presentation of Self in Everyday Life*. Garden City, NY: Doubleday Anchor Books, 1959.

Hargie, Owen; Saunders, Christine; Dickson, David. *Social Skills in Interpersonal Communication*. Cambridge, MA: The Ware Press, 1981.

Harris, Thomas A. *I'm OK - You're OK*. New York: Galahad Books, 1999.

Homans, George. "Social behavior as exchange." *American Journal of Sociology*, 63 (6) 1958:597-606.

Isaacs, William. *Dialogue: The Art of Thinking Together*. New York: Broadway Business, 1999.

Knowles, Elizabeth, ed. *The Oxford Dictionary of New Words*. Oxford: Oxford University Press, 1998.

Myers, Alyse. *Who Do You Think You Are? A Memoir*. New York. Touchstone, 2008.

Newcomb, Theodore. *The Acquaintance Process*. New York: Holt, Rinehart and Winston, 1961.

Silverman, Sue William. *Fearless Confessions: A Writer's Guide to Memoir*. Athens: The University of Georgia Press, 2009.

Tannen, Deborah. *Conversational Style: Analyzing Talk Among Friends*. Oxford: Oxford University Press, 2005.

Tannen, Deborah. *You Just Don't Understand: Women and Men in Conversation*. New York: Ballantine Press, 1990.

Tannen, Deborah. *Talking from 9 to 5: Women and Men in the Workplace—Language, Sex and Power*. New York: Avon Books, 1994.

VanLiere, Donna. *Finding Grace: A Memoir*. New York: St. Martin's Press, 2009.

Wardhaugh, Ronald. *How Conversation Works*. New York: Basil Blackwell Inc, 1985.

Yankelovich, Daniel. *The Magic of Dialogue: Transforming Conflict into Cooperation*. Austin, TX: Touchstone, 2001.

6

Hot F...
Chil...
Beig...
Rough Nubb...
Ginger

", Soft
...eater, and
...grant

...tilda Butler

Shoreline-Lake Forest Park Senior Center

Date: 4/13 Amt: 20.00 CK# _____

Description: _Writing_

Intl: 7B Rcpt No: 36533 Code: _____

Cash X Name: _Jane Haggard_

The Element of S... ...d Perception

I try to write down al... ...e, smellable facts
as well as what I hear... ...l in front of me, I
have complete access ... ...f how I felt about
a certain incident or ... ...d to have those
thoughts recorded on ... . —*Tracy Kidder*

The warmth of the Californ... ...ernoon sun beckoned
me to open the window. Bu... ...I did, a whiff of acrid
smoke twisted its invisibl... ...e peacefully swaying
birch tree leaves and into ... ...erated days of smoke
residue hanging heavy in ... ...heed fire near Santa
Cruz, although miles away, ...r particles more than
once. One sniff and I quicl... ...ndow sash, slamming
the window closed. "So mu... ...nought.

Curious that winds had ... ...smoke across the val-
ley to us, I grabbed my com... ...o Google, "Lockheed
Fire San—. I never got to fin... ...se nor see the results.
Instead I was interrupted ... ...unding on our deck
doors. Odd, I thought. Wh... ...e back of the house
rather than the front door? ... ...eamed, "I need more
hose."

My husband and I both jumped up from our desks and dashed to open the door, curtained against the bright western sun. Smoke was now thick and undeniably close. In the country, neighbors rely on each other as the first line of defense as well as for friendship. Bill flew down the steps and ran to the vegetable garden to grab two hoses, shouting to me over his shoulder, "Grab the decking hose, and I'll meet you there." "There," of course, was the neighbor's home. Or so we thought.

I hurriedly pulled the hose off its reel, yanked and tugged at the gray duct tape that stubbornly held the faucet end in place. Almost without thinking, I took a few steps into the kitchen, grabbed scissors from the drawer and cut the unyielding tape. Finally, I began to unscrew the long green hose from the bib, cursing that I couldn't get the metal fastening to turn faster. Each turn I made slipped back half a turn while I tried to force the tangled hose to behave. Then I heard it. I heard it before I saw it.

The ominous popping, crackling noise caused me to turn. Out of the corner of my eye, and then full on, I saw and understood that the largest of our pine trees was exploding with yellow-red flames reaching 100 feet into the sky. I knew in that moment that our house would burn.

The fire on our property is seared into my brain's memory cells. Dramatic moments such as that August afternoon are not the exception. All waking moments, and even our dreams, are filled with and shaped by our five senses. Jill Bolte Taylor notes in the early pages of her memoir *My Stroke of Insight* that as a massive hemorrhage poured blood into the left hemisphere of her brain, she began to lose her ability to perceive the world through the five senses as one by one they ceased to work. As a neuroanatomist, she was able to understand and analyze the effect of the stroke as it slowly altered her perceptions. She realized that it is the five senses that keep us connected to the physical world.

...sensory information is the link between our physical world and our reader's mental world.

As writers, what does this mean to us? We can bring our readers into the world of our stories by using the same senses that enable us to function on a daily basis—sight, smell, sound, taste and touch. We want our readers to participate in the world we put on the page, and sensory information is the link between our physical world and our reader's mental world. The senses enable us to furnish the reader's mind.

Unless we have lost, or were born without, one or more of our senses, we experience each day through an ever-changing sea of sensory data. Consider this typical start to my day:

Better Description from In-Depth Understanding. Using the five senses in writing is a technique of both the fiction and non-fiction writer. But just knowing there are five senses and remembering to stick in a few sights or sounds or smells isn't the way you experience the world. It also doesn't let the reader enter the world in your story. In this chapter, we'll separately explore each of the senses with our goal being a clear understanding of the physical, biological and linguistic aspects that will enable you to use the senses in new and creative ways, moving you away from the trite and common. At the end of this chapter, I'll also recommend that you not only do a Deconstruction for the five senses, but that you Deconstruct five times, each time focusing on just one of the senses. As a result, you'll see your stories come to life in ways you may not have ever considered. The bonus is that thinking about the senses helps bring back additional memories.

The Sense of Sight

Brain research shows that through our eyes, we can register up to 36,000 visual messages each hour. Add to that statistic the finding that 80 percent of all information processed through the brain is visual, and you can see why we begin our exploration of the senses with sight.

Here are seven ways to consider the visual scene:

1. **The Big Picture:** Here you see everything, you see nothing. If you are standing in Zion National Park in your story, you might describe the sapphire blue sky, the dark, emerald green trees standing tall on the edge of the cliff, the waterfall tumbling down the sheer rock face culminating in a pool at its base, facets of diamond-like light dancing on the water and illuminating a rainbow of colors, deep shadows at the lowest level of the cliff with the profiles of dead trees standing in stark contrast to the corals and orange vermillion of the sandstone. When you describe this scene, you want the reader to be standing there with

you seeing what you see. No single element is central to your
story. You just want to share the big picture by taking into ac-
count everything that your eyes see.

2. **Focus *versus* Contrast:** Assume now that you've been climbing
in Zion National Park for several hours and have paused to rest.
Your eye goes to a lone pine tree growing out of a rock—not rich
soil but a rock. The first word that comes to mind is FOCUS.
You think the scene is about a single, scrawny tree struggling
to survive. You could even write a great description of the tree.
Perhaps, in recalling that moment of communing with nature,
you write:

> I stopped along side a lone fellow traveler for a few min-
> utes. The thin, stunted pine could not accompany me on
> my journey, held in place by its gnarled roots struggling
> to break through the dark shale to secure enough nutri-
> ents to survive. Walking on, I looked back and noted that
> although stuck in one place, the tree was noble with its
> yellow-green branches bathed in the morning's shaft of
> light. I take strength from the sight as I try to break through
> the difficult family relationships that are holding me back.
> Perhaps I also just might survive against the odds.

In your description, you may be misleading the reader if you
think this is just a matter of focus, of sharing one element with
the reader. You noticed the pine because of the sharp contrast
with the dark, flat rock and the brilliant sunlight on the tree. If
the same tree were in another setting, you might not even notice it. The background, although it seems to almost disappear,
creates the contrast that is responsible for letting us focus on
the tree.

There is no right or wrong description of this scene. It is
what you want your reader to see. You could use your visual
description to encompass the combination of the tree and sur-
rounding rock. You might only mention the rock in passing,
letting it be a backdrop for the tree. Or the nature of the rock
might become an important part of the story. The scene conveyed to the reader belongs to the individual writer's eye.

3. **Juxtaposition:** Sometimes a visual description becomes more
meaningful when one element is juxtaposed against a second

element. How do the two relate to each other? Think, for example, about describing a child. Then consider the description you might write of both the child and her mother. The juxtaposition will tell us more about each than a separate description focused just on one.

4. **Imagination and Color:** As a child, did you ever lie down on the grass in the summertime and look up as the clouds moved across the sky? Remember describing the shapes you saw? There's a train. Oh look. It's a bunny. I can see a horse with its tail wind blown. That was using your imagination. In something much more solid than a cloud, we can also use our imagination. We can see a shape that lets us describe the sight to someone who isn't there—to our readers. For example, John Updike, in *Seek My Face,* gives such a description in the phrase "pieces of snow visible in the woods like scattered laundry..." By using our imagination, we can sometimes better describe a scene than if we stick to a literal description.

My mother liked to find rocks, even twigs, that reminded her of something else. I still have a rock she gave me that if held one direction resembles a chicken sitting on her nest and if held from a different angle looks like the head of an elephant, complete with trunk. This is what she saw in this otherwise ordinary rock, and it is what I see thanks to her. I have it standing in a pot on my decking. Some days I turn it so that I see the elephant. Other days it is reversed and becomes the chicken.

Imagination provides you an efficient way to create a shared scene between the two strangers of the writer and the reader. Specifically, references to iconic shapes—using the familiar to describe the unique—enables someone to join you in your world with little effort. It is a lot easier to mention an elephant's head than it is to try to describe a series of angles, shapes, and protrusions of a rock.

5. **Color, Light and Shadow:** Sometimes what we see only seems to exist in the interplay of light and shadow through color. In trying to find words to convey an unusual image, it can be helpful to simply convey its hardness or softness as expressed through various colors. Or what about the ephemeral sunset? From our kitchen window, I saw the winter sun as it set behind El Toro in Morgan Hill, California. Before the last glow disap-

peared into darkness, I saw tangerine, blood orange, terracotta, plum and boysenberry sweeping across the horizon. What belongs in the scene you are writing that might be enhanced through a description of color combined with lights and shadows? A series of rapidly changing colors conveys the sense of a fleeting moment.

6. **Movement:** Motion is an aspect of sight that isn't usually mentioned. Yet, so many things that we want to describe are moving. Imagine you are sitting beside a river. As the water rapidly moves past you, it creates an altered perception. I remember an image taken by Skip McDonald, a photographer friend who teaches how the camera is a tool to help us understand ourselves, a tool of therapeutic practice. His photo of the Little Pigeon River in the Great Smoky Mountains National Park looks less like water and more like beautiful silk threads, white and translucent. It reminded me of the skeins of raw silk I had seen in the rural area of Petchboon, Thailand, a few years earlier. Consider what changes motion creates in the scene you are describing. For example, you should go beyond saying that you see a river flowing. Capture in words what that river looks like to you as it rushes by as if late for an appointment with a rock downstream.

7. **Mystery:** Our last dimension of sight is a fun one. When we initially consider describing a place or person, we immediately think we want to describe it as if it were all knowable. Sometimes sight can be used in a way that points to mystery, to the unknown and possibly the unknowable. When you are developing a description consider leaving a mystery to intrigue the reader and encourage her/him to continue with you on the journey through your story. You may want to save some aspects of the description that can be revealed later. Think about Chapter 3 on characters. You will want to describe a character as soon as he or she arrives in your memoir, but you don't have to tell everything at once. The same is true for sensory detail.

Now Get to Writing!

Take 10 minutes to write a description of two events, two scenes, two people or two places. Use the scene in your synopsis as one of the two. It doesn't matter whether you focus on events, settings, people or places as long as you have two and use each in juxtaposition to the other to tell us more than we would know if you provided two single descriptions. Here are a few points to consider:

1. In what ways are they visually similar? Think about the elements that you want to include. Perhaps your mother and you, the two people in the scene, both have red hair. Write about this.

2. In what ways are they visually dissimilar? What elements are you going to include? Be specific. Are the dissimilar elements different from the similar elements? Maybe your mother's hair is no longer naturally red and she now dyes it, while your hair looks like a maple tree in autumn.

3. Write 3 sentences describing similarities. What does the reader know at this point?

4. Write 3 sentences describing dissimilarities. What does the reader now know?

5. Are both similarities and dissimilarities needed to convey the complete description? Is one more effective than the other?

There are no correct or incorrect answers. Just answers that seem right for you.

Example of a visual description. Now that we've explored seven perspectives we might use to describe scenes visually, let's see what writers do when they use words to convey what the eyes see. My first example is from Virginia Woolf in *A Room of One's Own*. She writes:

> Here then was I...sitting on the banks of a river a week or two ago in fine October weather, lost in thought....To the right and left bushes of some sort, golden and crimson, glowed with the colour, even it seemed burnt with the heat, of fire. On the further bank the willows wept in perpetual lamentation, their hair about their shoulders. The river reflected whatever it chose of sky and bridge and burning tree, and when the undergraduate had oared his boat through the reflections they closed again, completely, as if he had never been. There one might have sat the clock round lost in thought. Thought--to call it by a prouder name than it deserved--had let its line down

into the stream. It swayed, minute after minute, hither and thither among the reflection and the weeds, letting the water lift it and sink it, until--you know the little tug--the sudden conglomeration of an idea at the end of one's line: and then the cautious hauling of it in, and the careful laying of it out?

In this excerpt, Virginia Woolf is using the descriptive power of her vision, but she does more with it than that. She uses the visual description to move the story along. It is not just there so that we know where she is sitting, although it also accomplishes that task. The description is there to advance her point, her perspective about finding a thought—an idea.

In order to Deconstruct our story into the five senses, we need to understand all the various aspects of this element. But when we use them, we want to do so in creative and effective ways to help us tell our stories. The visual description, therefore, is not to be used just as a decorative element, but to create a rich context for our story and, depending on where we are in the story, to move it forward, to guide us to another aspect of our story, to introduce a new place or person, to propel us on to the next chapter and more. In other words, use the details of sight to tell your story more effectively. Don't let description become an end in itself.

Let's return to the quote from Virginia Woolf. There are a few words in this passage that she uses to set the scene. She mentions October weather. Then as she describes the color of the bushes, we mentally see even more than she tells us because we have an experience base of autumn colors upon which to draw.

Consider some of the descriptions in this brief passage. For example, "the willows wept in perpetual lamentation, their hair about their shoulders." What a lovely example of imagination, one of our seven ways of using sight in your writing.

Now Get to Writing!

Close your eyes and recall the scene in your synopsis. Take 5 to 10 minutes to write a description of that scene, but just use color. Here are a few points to consider:

1. What are all the colors? Don't concern yourself with the who or the what. Just focus on the colors.

2. Consider the various shades of the same color. If you need help, imagine you are looking at color chips at the home improvement or paint store. Actually, the next time you are in a paint department, pick up several color charts. The way paint companies name their colors is creative and might be useful in your writing. Let me give you a quick example. I have three color cards from the paint store, each shows three related colors. Imagine the colors as you read the names. The first card shows Mother Earth, Desert Rouge and Earthen Red. The second includes Sunwashed, Bee Pollen and Autumn Wind. A third card has Ice Crystal, Lilac Glacier and Spa. Just seeing the names written on this page—not even seeing the color—gives you a good mental image of the colors.

3. Create a list of colors as you think about your chosen scene going visually from the left to the right.

In this exercise, you aren't writing a description in sentences. You are just writing about the colors. This lets you focus on one aspect and really explore it. Have fun with this—think of creative names for the colors.

A Color Bonus

Color is the first perception registered by a person. Therefore, it's not surprising that brain researchers, psychologists, marketers, artists and others have studied color extensively. While a lot is known about the effects of color, little has been written about the use of colors in writing to set a mood. This is a bonus discussion with two caveats:

- First, you need to be careful when using color as it is easy to overdue it and make the whole scene seem trite or contrived.
- Second, the association and symbolic meaning of colors is culturally determined. What I am writing is drawn from perceptions in western countries and is not equally true in all parts of the world.

Brain researchers have demonstrated that color generates electromagnetic radiation, similar to that produced by x-rays, infrared and even microwaves. Each color has its own wavelength and affects bodies and brains differently. Because we have memories associated with colors, writing about color can trigger reactions similar to those that occur when we physically see the color.

Color also affects emotions. Research shows, for example, that the color red tends to raise blood pressure and pulse rate while increasing respiration and perspiration. Blue, on the other hand, tends to lower blood pressure and pulse rate. Green also is a calming color, though less so than blue. Yellow is the first color that the brain is able to distinguish. Although it is associated with a certain degree of stress and apprehension, many shades of yellow create a sense of well being, happiness and optimism.

Through years of research and experimentation, scientists have found that bright colors are more likely to stimulate creativity and an increase in energy. Dark colors, on the other hand, are more likely to lower stress and create a sense of peace. Consider ways to take advantage of color research when you want to convey moods and emotional states to your readers.

The following is a list of 10 colors and descriptors that specify how the colors are typically interpreted by people. There are many more descriptors, but I have chosen these because they might be the most useful in your writing. Black, for example, implies seriousness and represents a somber state. Red, on the other hand, represents energy. Let's say that you are writing about a funeral. You might emphasize the blackness and grayness even if you are not describing the clothing of the mourners. Those colors have symbolic meaning for your readers, and the colors convey a mood that you want to create. In this scene, you probably wouldn't describe a woman who walks in wearing a red suit unless you are trying to jar the reader or to draw attention to the woman. Certainly her presence in a red suit changes the mood for the reader.

- **Purple:** The color of royalty and mystery.
- **Pink:** Love, beauty. Studies suggest that seeing a great deal of pink leads to physical weakness; it's been used in prisons. Pink is associated with sweet as in cotton candy. And then there's tickled pink.
- **Yellow:** This is the color of the sun, and gives us joy, happiness and energy. Yet there are phrases such as yellow-bellied coward.
- **Brown:** Earth, conventional. Brown stimulates appetite according to research. It's the color of stability, reliability (e.g., UPS has taken the slogan—Big Brown Machine).

- **Gold:** Wealth, prosperity, extravagance, wisdom. Remember "all that glitters is not gold."
- **Green:** Life, nature, well-being. Green can also mean jealous as in "green with envy." Because of the environmental movement we now talk about green buildings but do not mean that they are the color green. This is a good example of how a color carries connotations as well as specific visual elements.
- **Red:** Vitality, confidence, energy, courage. Think of *The Red Badge of Courage*, but don't forget "red herring" and "seeing red."
- **Blue:** Some shades suggest calmness and spirituality. Other shades are cold (e.g., ice blue). IBM's nickname is Big Blue.
- **White:** Purity, cleanliness, innocence.
- **Black:** Conservative, somber, stability, yet also sexy and sophisticated as in the Little Black Dress.

There are two uses of color. First, it is one aspect of visual description, and we try to accurately reflect those colors so that the reader sees what we see. Second, color can be used for the purpose of creating mood. Let's examine a paragraph in the memoir *Motiba's Tattoos* by Mira Kamdar:

> Motiba's ears offered physical evidence of the era when she had been rich and adorned. At the lobes were large holes, stretched long by the weight of the heavy gold earrings that had hung there for years. A line of smaller holes ran all the way up the outer edges of both ears, emptied now of the gold rings and studs set with precious stones that had once graced them. The left plane of her nose was pocked in the center by a hole that had held a magnificent ruby and pearl nose ring on her wedding day, replaced by a simple diamond solitaire she wore for years after. Motiba hadn't always been so plain. Once a luxuriant black mane of hair had flowed down her back to her knees, the rest of her person covered with gold and jewels.

One of the interesting points in this example is that instead of standing back and describing what her grandmother looks like, Kamdar starts with the small detail of the ear. Specifically, she starts with the ear lobe, not even the entire ear. She begins small, then lets us know a little more about the rest of the ear, the nose and finally her grandmother's hair. Yet we learn so much about her grand-mother—her previous life circumstance and her current one—in what seems to be a physical description through the use of sight. We learn that her life has changed, that she doesn't have the wealth she once did. It is only at the end of this paragraph that Kamdar says anything about the rest of her grandmother's body. Do you think this is an effective use of the sense of sight?

Now Get to Writing!

Read your synopsis again and imagine what the scene looks like. Then take 10 minutes to write a description, focusing on the visual impact that you want to convey to someone else.

For this example, don't worry about using the description to move a story forward. You are only writing the scene from the sense of sight. These four questions may help you:

1. What do you see that is unique?
2. Are colors important? If so, which ones? Is it more a matter of light or darkness than specific colors?
3. Are you going to focus on a few details or the big picture?
4. And finally, what unusual way can you convey your take on the scene using your sense of sight?

Remember, you are writing a description rather than a story. For this quick exercise, you can be as outlandish as you wish—exaggerating or thinking of wild comparisons. This should be fun—a kind of flexing of your verbal sight skills.

Sight and POV

There is one final thing to consider about the sense of sight, and that is point of view. In the previous discussion, it seemed as if the sense of sight was fairly clear cut with the assumption that you would describe a person or scene from your current perspective. However, think about what a scene looks like to a child. Then think about the adult looking at the same scene. Your height, your world knowledge, your vocabulary will all influence how you describe a person or place. Remember how big your elementary school seemed when you were in first grade? Did you ever go back years later only to discover the halls were narrower, the rooms smaller and the desks shorter? Or, if you have children, remember when you visited your child's classroom for parent-teacher conferences. The chairs that had seemed perfectly normal from your child's point of view caused your knees to almost touch your chin.

When I was a child, my mother took me to a store in Oklahoma City where I was fitted for a new pair of shoes each fall. I always sat in a special lion chair that seemed massive to me. It was exciting to be allowed to sit in it, and yes, a little bit scary. Two decades later, when I took my son there, I realized the lion was made of plywood and was a miniature chair, not the awesome throne I had remembered. The chair hadn't changed, just my point of view. Therefore, when you write be sure you remember the age of the person telling the story and craft your description to fit.

The Sense of Sound

Before moving into details of our sense of sound, I want to share three brief passages from Heather Summerhayes Cariou's memoir, *Sixtyfive Roses: A Sister's Memoir*. Pam, Cariou's sister, was diagnosed with Cystic Fibrosis at the age of four. Unable to pronounce the two words, Pam told people that she had *sixtyfive roses*, which eventually became the title of the memoir. See how sound surfaces in Cariou's writing:

> ...Her cough started deep inside the cave of her chest with a dark, wet rumble that rolled up and out of her like the sound of thunder with heavy rain. The sound poured into my ears, making me shiver....BOOM! The compressor in the basement started up and I was suddenly awake, gulping for air, shivering, hugging my knees to my chest, my covers kicked into a tangle at the end of the bed.... The compressor shut itself off. The tent hissed. The wind moaned. The house was still as a tomb. I strained my ears to hear if Pam was breathing. I was scared she would die in the night, without warning.

> ...Panting, I...threw myself on the ground, and let go the fierce tears that had been pushing at me from inside. The incessant knot of pain that sat in the well of my chest burned red up through my esophagus and screamed out along the path of my tongue. I sobbed and heaved against the pungent earth. My nostrils pressed to the dank soil,

I inhaled the sweet, piercing scent that soothed my hot head. The fallen leaves were damp and cool against my cheek.

When we use the senses in our writing, we rarely are purists; we mix and mingle them just as they are in life. Notice that in the third passage, Cariou has included sound as well as smell and touch. Before you begin Deconstruction for this sense, let's consider three ways to describe the sounds of a scene. These are:

1. **Proximity:** How close or how far are you from the sound? Imagine that you are taking a long walk in the country and have unexpectedly been caught in a downpour. You are in the midst of the storm without a protective structure to stand under. The wind-whipped raindrops swirl all around you. Notice how loud it is. The thunder, perhaps, makes the scene even more dramatic.

   Now mentally try backing off just a little from this story. Let's say you have a lovely deep veranda around your home in the country. The sun is shining but there has been a light rain all morning. No thunder in this scene. Just the gentle rain. You're sitting on the porch swing looking out on the rain. It's close but you are not in the midst of it. The sound is softer. Pause for a moment. Close your eyes and listen to the sounds.

   Step back even more. Image that you are in a restaurant, seated at a table by the window where you can look out on a torrential rainstorm. You're no longer in the rain. You're not on your porch looking at it. Yet, still, the rain is present, intruding into your sense of the evening. Perhaps the sound grows louder each time someone opens the door to come into the restaurant.

2. **Significance:** Independent of how close you are, some sounds are important while others remain as background noise. Let's consider the ocean. The water crashing into the beach or the cliff is a significant sound. You really can't ignore it. I try to get over to the coast at least every other month. Recently, I walked along the Aptos beach, listening to the sounds. When I got home, I tried to describe that sound. Here's my effort:

   Noisy waves crash into the narrow strip of sand the color of cafe au lait. But their forward progress meets an abrupt barrier in the steep, fossil-rich sandstone cliffs. Then, just as suddenly as the noise began, there follows a gentle hushing sound as the water pulls back across the tiny grains of sand as if retreating to a quieter place to re- gain its strength to try and storm the cliffs again.

While the ocean sound is all-enveloping, a bee's buzz has a point of focus and is peripheral rather than central to a scene. In assessing sounds in a scene decide what you should empha- size and what is minor. Of course, it's possible that the minor sound—be it the mosquito's Serenade in Whine Sharp—draws your full attention.

3. **Specificity:** A third way to bring readers into your scene is to move away from the generic to the particular. For example, when we think about describing a bird, there isn't one gen- eral sound. You don't get much muscle from your words by writing "a bird just flew by," or "I heard a bird in the tree yes- terday." Different birds have quite different sounds—a flock of geese heading south making their asynchronous squawking; a bluejay screeching, mad at the world; or a hummingbird click clicking as it makes its way from blossom nectar to blossom nectar.

Listen to the birds outside your window. Is it a chirping, a twittering, a honking, a cawing, a chattering sound? How many different sounds do you hear? If you live in a city and rarely hear birds, use the Internet to locate specific bird sounds and listen to the free mp3 files that are available on many websites.

I was fortunate to have mockingbirds just outside my study window when I lived in California. Most seasons I heard the songster soon after the sun began its daily trek across the sky. My mocker sat high on a telephone pole or sometimes on the top of a eucalyptus tree, always determined to be the highest bird around. A mockingbird is the master of improv, imitating other birds, even nearby sounds. The song changes all day long and seems only rarely to repeat. Learn something about the birds or other sounds in your story so that you represent them authentically.

Here are three sentences that create a scene complete with sounds that are memorable, in part, for their familiarity because we have experienced similar sounds. This is from Susan Allen Toth's memoir, *Blooming: A Small-Town Girlhood*:

Walking outside the stadium walls on Saturday afternoon, I could often hear the cheering rise and fall like a giant inarticulate voice. "OOOOOH," the voice cried, "AAAAAH." Then it would be silent, as though the giant had fallen back into his cave.

Of course, it is difficult to find examples of just one sense as writers mix them together. Hope Edelman brings the reader into the opening scene of her memoir, *The Possibility of Everything*, primarily through sound but also sight and touch. Of course, the intent of the scene is to begin our introduction to her 3-year-old daughter Maya.

The soft clinks of a metal spoon against stainless steel filters upstairs from the kitchen as Carmen prepares Maya's dinner. Tonight it's pasta with red sauce and a side dish of peas. Carmen hums as she cooks, low thrumming vibrations occasionally broken by a string of high-pitched la-la-la-las. I glance at the digital clock at the bottom of my computer screen....

The ceiling fan churns above my head in determined, repetitive circles. I pinch the fabric of my white cotton tank top away from my chest and angle an exhale between my breasts, trying to dry the thin film of sweat that's settled there. It's late September in southern California, our hottest month of the year, and heat rises precipitously in a house with a wall of windows downstairs....

I move my fingers across the keyboard faster, as if the speed of my fingers might stir up a breeze....

Downstairs, Carmen sets Maya's section plate and sippy cup on the dining table, the sound of plastic kissing wood. Then there's the scuff of a wooden chair being dragged back across the red tile floor.

http://womensmemoirs.com/sensation-1

A Twist on Sound

There are the sounds we hear and readily recognize but you can also use sound to describe something that most people don't usually think of as having a sound. The sound of a desk, the sound of you silently reading, the sound of a person sleeping (no, you can't cheat by having the person snoring). If we use a sound to describe something that doesn't have a sound, then our readers will become involved in a new way with our story. They won't skim past, but will linger over the description, first to understand what we're saying, and second to enjoy the new perspective. Consider this example that I've borrowed from Kendra's mother who was a commercial artist.

She created three drawings that were used for many years by Kellogg. Normally, when we think of a cereal, we think of taste and texture—sweet, dry, crunchy, chewy. Or we might think of smell (cinnamon, vanilla, even chocolate for General Mills Count Chocula). We might think of sight—the iconic O's in Cheerios. But we wouldn't think about sounds. Not until Kellogg created its well-known ad campaign.

Kendra's mother drew (actually reinvented the characters when Kellogg decided it wanted a new, younger look) three characters to represent sounds for its cereal—Snap! Crackle! and Pop! The characters Kellogg used, and still uses, to promote Rice Krispies.

In this case, the thought had been to find an unusual dimension or sense to describe a cereal—something that would distinguish Rice Krispies from other cereals—something that would make people focus on the one specific cereal and think about it in a different way. If Kellogg had just said that the cereal was delicious or that it smelled good or that it tasted wonderful, Rice Krispies would have seemed like all the other cereals. By giving Rice Krispies an unusual sense, the sense of sounds, Kellogg was able to create a distinctive cereal.

In our writing, we can make a person or an object come to life by giving it an unexpected sense.

Now Get to Writing!

Return to your synopsis. Can you recall any sounds associated with it? Close you eyes and listen. If the scene is outside, you might hear footsteps, voices, birds, wind. If the scene is inside, you might hear a refrigerator, running water, voices, feet running up the stairs, a door slamming, a television set detailing the day's news. Recall all the sounds that you can and write them down.

1. Think about how you are going to write about a sound. Perhaps you need to make up a word. You don't have to use existing words if nothing captures the particular sound, and that's acceptable as long as the word you've made up helps the reader experience the sound along with you. Maybe you want to use comparison sounds.

2. Think about how loud the sound is. How soft. Are you close to the sound or is it in the distance? Is it pleasing? Scary?

Sounds and Words

Consider two more dimensions—words with sounds and sounds with words. As you know, there are sounds in the words we use. This is a commingling of the sense we are writing about—sound—and the fact that the words we are using have their own sounds. The challenge is to get those two to work together.

There are five rhetorical devices that help us better understand ways we can make use of the sounds in the words we write with:

1. **Alliteration:** You might want to mention the sound of bees near you. By using alliteration, by putting a number of B's together, you can create the sound of those bees. *Big bees buzz near Betty's blooming bottlebrush bushes.* That sentence is way over the top, but it gives an idea of how words can be used to imitate a sound.

2. **Assonance:** Vowels, usually vowel combinations that rhyme, can be used to create an impression of a sound. *Did Sue chew too?* (eu/ew/oo)

3. **Consonance:** This is similar to assonance but we use the consonants rather than vowels. Consider this sentence: *All was harmonious—outside the pitter patter of rain, inside the chitter chatter of my twin daughters.* We have the same consonant/vowel combination *tter* and add either an *i* or an *a* in front of the combination. We've created a harmonious sound through our choice of words.

4. **Cacophony** and **Euphony:** In cacophony, we use raucous words, jarring words, words that when combined make a lot of noise, seeming to grate against us. They make us pay attention. They yell at us. If you are thinking of a sweet sound, then cacophony isn't for you. Here's an example: *A massive wave crashed onto jagged shards of granite and took revenge by clawing the sands with brutal force, sucking the beach into its open jaw.*

Euphony is the opposite. When you want to create a calm or peaceful description of a scene or situation, turn to words with pleasant sounds such as luxurious, sumptuous, blossom.

5. **Onomatopoeia:** These are words that sound like the sound they represent. Words like bang, cackle, crack, giggle, moo, oink, plop, screech, sizzle, staccato, yikes and zap. Those words become the sounds that move from the real world to the written world without losing any of their vitality.

Sounds don't occur in isolation; they are often layered

Until now, we've focused on individual sounds. But in the real world, sounds are layered. For example, if you are in a restaurant you may hear your dinner partner, multiple conversations at nearby tables, laughter across the room, voices of the table staff taking orders, dishes clattering, silverware clanking against plates, ice water being poured into glasses, chairs being moved, a car horn outside the window and more. It is a false reality to think there is only one sound at a time. We may choose to only mention a single sound, but we need to be aware that we are paying attention to that single sound to give it prominence. In all likelihood, it doesn't reflect all that is going on. When writing, consider when you may want to create this multi-layered sense of sound.

Even in a fairly simple scene there are multiple sounds. Here are the sounds and imagery found in a single sentence in *The Picture of Dorian Gray* by Oscar Wilde: "The sullen murmur of the bees shouldering their way through the long, unmown grass, or circling with monotonous insistence round the black-crocketed spires of the early June hollyhocks, seemed to make the stillness more oppressive, and the dim roar of London was like the bourdon note of a distant organ."

Is silence layered?

When we talk about using sounds, we imply noise of some kind—pleasing noises, loud noises, scary noises, complicated noises. But what about the absence of all of those sounds—silence? Might you want to write about silence? Is there one kind of silence? Is silence also multi-layered? Think about what silence means to you. Think about how you might want to convey a sense of silence in your writing. How would you do that?

As an example, think back to the Heather Summerhayes Cariou quote at the beginning of this section on sound. She wrote: "The house was still as a tomb. I strained my ears to hear if Pam was breathing. I was scared she would die in the night, without warning."

The Sense of Smell

As we begin to consider the third sense—smell—we can now see the important role that the senses play in our lives. That raises the question: Where in the brain is information from our senses received, processed and stored? From what regions in the brain are messages sent out to complete the sensory experience? All of the sensory information is localized in the part of the brain called the cerebral cortex. In rank order, sight occupies the most space, then sound, touch, smell and taste. In literature as in our brain, sight seems to be most frequently used. Touch is rarely used in literature, but is quite important in our lives. It helps us sense safe situations, dangerous situations, and in writing a memoir touch can be used in a similar way. I'll say more about that later. Taste is also infrequently used, but it can help our characters come to life.

The use of smell is found in literature, although probably not as much as sight or sound. However, it is useful to the writer in two ways. First, it serves as a trigger to help us remember scenes—important to memoir and fiction writers alike—and helps us bring our readers actively into our scenes. Mention a cup of hot chocolate or the scent of coffee in the air, and our readers are right there with us. No matter that smell occupies the second smallest amount of space in our cerebral cortex, we still need to find effective ways to use it in writing.

Science tells us that smell was the first sense to evolve, making it our most primitive sense. It is intertwined in the brain with the center for our emotions, behavior and long-term memory. That's why smelling something often triggers memories.

An Example of Scent and Memory. In her book, *The Scent of Desire*, Rachel Herz illustrates the intimate link between smell and memory in a series of personal stories. In one of my favorites, Herz relates an incident involving her cousin. Amanda was visiting friends who had invited her for dinner and to stay with them while she was in town. Amanda wanted to do something for her hosts after the lovely dinner and insisted that she help with the cleanup. Picture Amanda in the kitchen washing the dishes. She begins to cry. This isn't a little sniffle with moist eyes. This is a full blown, tears streaming down the cheeks, kind of bawl. Her host says, "Amanda, what's the matter, what's going on?" Amanda tells her that the smell is the same as the dish soap that her grandmother used to use. Here is Amanda's quote: "I can see my grandmother perfectly. We're in the kitchen on the last Thanksgiving we had together. I'm helping her do the dishes. I can't believe how much I feel her. I miss her so much." This is a perfect example of how a single smell, because of the way it is linked intricately with our emotions and memories, can evoke a long-past scene and bring it into the present.

Memoir writers create more effective scenes when they utilize smells both to trigger scenes they have known and to convey these scenes to the reader. Yet it is easy to leave smell out of our writing because we don't have a good vocabulary for smells.

How Do We Know What a Smell Smells Like?

Smells are learned; they are learned by association. Recently I read a case study of a man who had complete amnesia and the medical staff investigated his ability to identify smells. The patient could not describe anything that he smelled. He was capable of smelling but did not know how to describe the scents. He could label intensity and would respond, "That is strong. This is weak." But other than intensity, he could not describe what he smelled. The researchers concluded that because labeling smells is a learned response, he would continue to be unable to describe smells as long as his amnesia lasted.

The Absence of Smell

What happens when you lose the capability to smell? I'm not talking about when you have a cold, although remembering what happens to your ability to smell when you're sick may be useful to you as you write. Here I'm focusing on what we can learn about smell when it disappears. The medical condition *anosmia* means smell blindness. I have a friend who has anosmia. She completely lost her ability to smell as a side effect of a flu. She consulted several doctors as well as a neurologist, and they all say this is a permanent loss. Now, several years later, she rarely cooks. She worries that she may burn the food and not realize it. Obviously, it also creates a fear that if her house were to catch on fire, she would not be aware of it. Just before she lost her sense of smell, she was preparing to replace her electric stove with a gas one. Then she realized it would not be a good idea because she could not detect a gas leak.

Smell is involved in almost every aspect of our lives. It tells us of pleasure and of danger. When we can't smell, we have lost an important part of the texture of our life. Similarly, the absence of smell in our writing removes part of the possible texture of a story.

Here's Something for You to Try. The next time you are cooking, pay special attention to the scents in the air. Then hold your nose for five minutes, breathing through your mouth. Think of the contrast between the previous five minutes full of sensory detail and the five minutes without the ability to smell.

Your Challenge. I'd like to give you a writer's challenge. I want you to think of your readers as individuals who have anosmia. You are the only person who can give them back their sense of smell. When they first open your book, they cannot smell. Then, page after page, you give them back their ability to smell. You can bring them into your freshly painted room, into your garden with its bed of fragrant star jasmine planted next to gardenias, into your trip through the desert in springtime when wild flowers have just come into bloom, into your mother's hug just after she showered with lavender soap by giving them back their sense of smell. Without using smells in our writing, it is as if we have bestowed anosmia on our readers. And that's not a nice thing to do.

Shakespeare Was Wrong, Sort of

> What's in a name? That which we call a rose
> By any other name would smell as sweet;

What Juliet is saying, of course, is that what something *is* matters, not what it is called. Yet, in learning about the language of smell, we need to remember that since we know smells through an association with specific words, the name does matter. We can't be casual when we describe a smell if we want the other person to share our remembered experience or the scene we are creating. We need to use words that others also associate with the smell. This lets us create common points of reference.

"This smells just like the zanthuiw flower." Does this bring any scent to mind? Of course not. I made up the word *zanthuiw* so the word cannot evoke a smell in you memory bank. We have to be careful to find the right words in order to convey what the smell is like. I would have been much more successful if I'd said, "This smells just like the gardenia corsage James gave me for my first date."

The Language of Smell
There is no technical or colloquial language for smells that is separate from the shared or learned memory of the source of the smell. However, we can look at two content areas that require precision in smell—perfumes and wines. An interesting study of perfumes was conducted several years ago in France, the home of the perfume industry. Sixty consumers were asked to smell various scents and to distinguish them by using words that they thought appropriate. The researchers took the words and content analyzed them. Here are their findings:

- 50 percent of all the descriptions identified the smell by mentioning the source of the scent. For example: *This smells like a lemon. This smells like a rose.*
- 19 percent of the descriptions used words that are borrowed from the sense of touch. For example: *This scent is heavy. This scent is warm.*
- 15 percent of the descriptions used words that were borrowed from the sense of taste. For example: *This scent is sweet. This scent is salty.*
- 8 percent of the descriptions used words of intensity. For example: *This is a strong smell. This is a powerful smell.*
- 4 percent of the descriptions used words of acceptability. For example: *This one is pleasant. This is stinking. This scent is disgusting.*

- The last 4 percent of the descriptions were categorized as miscellaneous. For example: *This smells expensive. This smells feminine.*

You can use these findings to help guide you in your search for just the right words that might help in a descriptive passage. If you choose to compare something to a scent that is familiar or if you use words that rely on the sense of touch or taste, you'll probably connect with most readers.

Wines, too, can teach us about the language of smell. As a multi-billion dollar industry, we can imagine that vintners have done a great deal of research into the scent of wines. Le Nez du Vin offers a series of instructional books and kits for learning about the scents related to wine; the most expensive of these kits sells for around $400 and includes corked vials with individual scents to be learned. Note the operative phrase *to be learned.* These scents can only be identified because they are specifically learned. In this top-of-the-line kit, there are 54 different aromas or smells. They are divided into the following categories:

- 23 distinctive fruit aromas including: lemon, grapefruit, orange, pineapple, banana, melon, apple, pear, quince, strawberry, raspberry, red currant, black currant (notice that there is enough difference between red and black current scents that they can be learned), blackberry, cherry, apricot, peach, almond and prune.
- 6 distinctive floral aromas including: acacia, honey, rose and violet.
- 15 distinctive vegetal aromas including: green pepper, mushroom, truffle, yeast, cedar, pine, licorice, cut hay, thyme, vanilla, cinnamon, clove, pepper and saffron.
- 3 animal-related aromas: leather, musk and butter.
- And, finally, 7 grilled aromas: toasted bread, roasted almond, roasted hazelnuts, caramel, coffee, dark chocolate and smoked.

These are not the only distinctions to be made in the categorization of scents, but they may help you begin to make your own distinctions when you begin to use smells in your writing.

Go Smelling

Enough of sitting, reading and writing. Mark where you are in this book and stand up. Go smell something. Go into the kitchen and take out one spice. Open it and smell. Or go into your garden. If nothing is in bloom right now, take a leaf, crumple it between your fingers to release its scent and smell—even a dried winter leaf. Get yourself, your nose, your mind thinking about smells. If you happen to have rosemary growing in your garden, as I do, pick a sprig, rub it between your fingers and smell the scent as it wafts through the air. If no fresh rosemary is available, you might have some of the dried herb in your spice drawer, or perhaps thyme, cinnamon, or nutmeg. Don't just try to recall the scent. Open the jar and smell it, or sprinkle a little into the palm of your hand, close you hand to let the spice warm, then open to release its scent and inhale.

An herb you might have in your kitchen is mint. I grow mint in pots just outside my kitchen door to use in salads and teas. If you don't have fresh mint, you might have mint tea bags. Take the tea bag and rub it between your fingers. Then smell the bag. I want you to not just think about scents intellectually but to experience them.

In Linda Kaplan's memoir *My First Crush: Misadventures in Wine Country*, she describes cooking massive amounts of food for the large number of people who come to harvest and sort the grapes. She has a problem the first time she cooks for the helpers, and I need to mention this because she uses the word "tundra" in connection with turkeys. Kaplan had purchased three huge frozen turkeys. She put them next to each other in the refrigerator to thaw before cooking. However, they were so cold they created what she called a "tundra" and wouldn't thaw:

> I began with two turkeys at three hundred fifty degrees. Many hours later, the little rascals browned up and cooked through. After carving turkeys one and two and returning them to the tundra, I slipped number three in the oven. Later that afternoon, I ran to the grocery store to stock up on ever more provisions. While I waited at the deli counter, another shopper came up behind me....
>
> "I'm going to have some of that turkey. It smells delicious," she said.
>
> "We don't have turkey," announced the clerk. "Vegetarian lasagna, meat loaf, or fried chicken. That's it."

Less cordial now, the customer impatiently shoved her bracelet up her arm and readjusted her paisley shawl....

"I can smell the turkey," she insisted.

As subtly as I could, I sniffed the arm of my sweatshirt. It was then I realized the exhaust from my oven had permeated my clothes and hung like a cloud in my hair. Embarrassed, [I] grabbed [my] cheese and ran.

You've probably cooked a turkey or been in a home or restaurant where it was cooking. It's a distinctive smell most of us know. Even in writing about it now, I can begin to sniff it in the air. By using the smell of the turkey as a reference, the author evokes the scent for the reader. This is a good example of making a reference to smells that everyone can remember. We don't have to describe what the smell is like because we all know. We all have a mental reference point. This simplifies layering the scent onto the page.

Now Get to Writing!

1. Once again consider the scene in your synopsis. Close your eyes and take yourself back to that place. What do you smell? If you are outside, you might smell flowers or newly mowed grass. If it's the 1960s or earlier and you are in an office building, you might smell stale cigarette smoke. If you are in the house you might smell the last whiff of yesterday's burnt toast or this morning's coffee.

2. Remember that using smell will help the reader better understand your unique sense of the scene. Go back to the earlier writer's challenge that I gave you. Assume your reader has anosmia and cannot smell. It is up to you to help him smell all the scents in your story.

3. You might also try to give the sense of smell a twist. Think of an unusual way that the scene or the mood of the scene might be described through smell. Maybe the scent is the simile or metaphor for describing something else. You might even attribute a smell to an object that we don't usually think has a smell.

See where the exercise takes you. Be willing to explore creative ways to use smell in your writing.

The Sense of Taste

What do you know about the word "sense?" It can be traced back to the 1300s and comes from the Latin word *sensus*, which means sensation, feeling and understanding. As a verb, sense means to detect, find, discover, notice or observe. I especially like those last three concepts: discover, notice, observe.

As writers, we use the five senses to help our readers *discover* the world we know and share what we have *noticed* and *observed*. As a bonus, you'll find that sharpening your awareness of the five senses to use in your writing helps you become more mindful of your surroundings on a daily basis. It becomes a positive spiral and enhances both your writing and your enjoyment of life.

Taste, as you remember, occupies the least amount of space in the cerebral cortex. And although recent findings in the human genome research project have shown that individual molecules can provoke a response in a single cell and transmit that information to the brain, we still find that language makes it difficult to express taste. This influences the way we use taste in our writing.

1,000,000 taste cells

Let's start first with where we taste. Not surprisingly, the tongue is our primary area for taste. There are additional taste buds along the lining of the check and the roof of the mouth. But the main action takes places on the tongue, which has over 10,000 taste buds and each of these buds has about 100 taste cells.

What we commonly know as taste is actually a combination of chemical sensors in our taste buds. When we add texture, temperature and smell, we have a perception of flavor.

Four Tastes, No, Five Tastes, Well, Maybe Seven

There are only four basic tastes: *sweet*, *sour*, *salty* and *bitter*. Sometimes it is difficult to think about a bitter taste. Try this experiment—take a sip of coffee, hold it for a few minutes on your tongue, then swallow. That is the taste of bitter. Also, if you have ever eaten dandelion greens or mustard greens, you've experienced a bitter taste.

There are only four basic tastes...

In 2002, a fifth official taste was added to our list. It is called *umami*. It is our ability to taste the chemical glutamic acid, which is often found in fermented or aged foods. It is what we think of as a meaty or savory flavor. The name *umami* was given by a Japanese chemist Kikunae Ikeda, about 100 years ago. It is the Japanese word for "yummy" or "delicious"—that satisfying taste we get from savory foods.

The last two tastes, *pungent* and *astringent,* come to us from Eastern traditions and are not considered official tastes. They can be distinguished and therefore may be helpful as we try to expand our language of taste. Pungent is associated with the taste of cardamom and cinnamon. Astringent is a difficult one to explain. But if you have ever bitten into an unripe persimmon, you know the taste. Your mouth puckers. Have you ever tasted sage? I grow it in my garden and sometimes make a sage tea. It also has an astringent taste.

With taste, as with smell, we turn to the field of wine for assistance on language that may be helpful in our descriptions. We've selected the following words and phrases from numerous sources. Think of this as a departure point. You may be inspired to add others:

1. Acidity
2. Robustness
3. Body (consistency, density)
4. Complexity
5. Crispness/Briskness
6. Finish/Aftertaste (taste lingers after swallowing)
7. Grassy (herbaceous flavor)
8. Life (invigorating sensation on the palate)
9. Lushness (soft feel)
10. Silkiness (smoothness)
11. Texture (thin, viscous, grainy, coarse, gritty)

Consider These Examples

Following are four examples to help you consider how you might use words from the previous list.

- If you are describing the taste of an apple, the word *crisp* conveys more than *sweetness,* which probably we would use if we were confined to the basic four tastes.

- I grew olive trees on my property in California. When we picked and crushed olives in the fall, the taste of the new oil is *grassy*, even the color has a green tint to it.
- *Life* may seem like the oddest one on this list. Think of a carbonated drink that creates both a taste and a sensation on the tongue.
- A true story: A few days after the wedding, I thought I'd make a cake for my new husband. All was fine until it was time for the frosting. The recipe in a wedding-present cookbook called for confectioners' sugar. I'd never heard that term. I knew about sugar and powdered sugar. I assumed confectioner's sugar must refer to ordinary sugar, otherwise it would be called powdered sugar. You guessed it, the *texture* of the frosting was *gritty*. You'd have thought I added sand.

Taste and Color

When I was a Girl Scout, I remember working on my cooking badge. For dinner one night, I took over making the mashed potatoes. Being a creative child, I thought it would be great to put blue food dye in the potatoes. Trust me, this is an experiment you don't want to repeat. It was almost impossible for any of us to eat those blue mashed potatoes because the unexpected color interfered with the taste. The eye confused the brain. The sense of sight was more powerful than the sense of taste. When you write, be aware of the effect on the reader of your use of colors when talking about taste.

Lost: One Sense of Taste

In the discussion of smell, I mentioned the medical condition anosmia or scent blindness. There is a parallel condition, *ageusia*, that means taste blindness. Previously, I told you about my friend who has anosmia. Actually, she has both anosmia and ageusia. She can only distinguish texture in foods—crispness, softness, smoothness and such. Fortunately, she remembers taste and can rely on memories to enjoy, for example, a chocolate mousse. All she can really tell is that it feels smooth in the mouth.

I'd like you to think of a reader as a person who has the condition of ageusia and only you can give her back her sense of taste. You will do this by the way that you describe food in your writing. In Laura Esquivel's *Like Water for Chocolate*, she writes:

When nobody eats the last chile on the plate, it's because none of them wants to look like a glutton, so even though they'd really like to devour it, they don't have the nerve to take it. It was as if they were rejecting that stuffed pepper, which contains every imaginable flavor: sweet as candied citron, juicy as a pomegranate, with the bit of pepper and the subtlety of walnuts, that marvelous chile in walnut sauce.

This is a luxurious use of taste. I can easily sense the complexity and richness of flavors in the chile. Can you? This is what you want to give your readers.

Go ahead and indulge yourself. Consider this exercise a required part of your education on the senses. Get a piece of chocolate, preferably still in its wrapper. Take a deep breath and physically hold your nose closed before you unwrap and bite into the chocolate. What do you taste? If you have a milk chocolate candy, you may only taste sweetness. But if you have a dark chocolate candy, you will taste sweetness and bitterness—two of the four basic tastes. You will not taste chocolate because that sensation comes from the smell.

Now Get to Writing!

1. This is the fourth Deconstruction of the scenes in your synopsis. If there is any taste associated with the scene, write about it. Try to remember the obvious such as food. However, you may not have any taste in the scene. Therefore consider use of taste with a twist. For example, a sweet person, a sour personality, a bitter experience.

2. If after considering your scene, you can't find any way to work in taste, I'd still like for you to get experience with describing taste since it is likely to come into your memoir at some point. Therefore, find and then taste several food samples (chocolate, almond, coffee, lemon slice, dill pickle) or recall a favorite taste. Then take 5 to 10 minutes and write a description that includes one of the items you tasted. Work the taste into a situation that includes a place or person or event. Here are two points to consider:

• What do you taste that is unique? In other words, bring your own perspective to what you write.

- Is it sweet? Sour? Bitter? Salty? Savory? Pungent? Astringent? Umami?

An Author's Experiment

I'd like to bring in the author Isabel Allende again. She has written about attending a conference where a guru of wisdom was speaking. He gave each person in the audience one grape and told them to eat it, but in no less than 20 minutes. She writes: "During those interminable 20 minutes, I touched, look at, smelled, turned over in my mouth with excruciating slowness, and finally, sweating, swallowed the famous grape. Ten years later, I can describe its shape, its texture, its temperature, its taste, and smell."

Let's extrapolate from her experience. When you are ready to write about taste, don't just take a bite of the substance, swallow and then write. Take a bite, chew slowly, savor it, consider the aftertaste. Even if it is a drink, keep the liquid in your mouth, swirl it around and then swallow. Think of this as an exercise in mindfulness so that you are fully experiencing the taste.

The Sense of Touch

The classification system of the five senses is attributed to Aristotle as he first discussed them in *De Anima* (*On the Soul*). Even before there was adequate information about how our senses work, it became clear that we acquire a great deal of knowledge through our five senses. As writers, it is easy to understand that when we want to share that knowledge, we can use the senses to connect with readers.

As we learn more about the fifth sense, touch, you may want to keep in mind that deep emotions and feelings are often described as *touching*, as in "you touched my heart." Touch seems to be the most direct and least intellectually mediated sense. As you recall, the sense of smell requires learning to distinguish aromas. Such is not the case with touch. Not surprisingly, Aristotle named touch as the first sense.

Two thousand years later, research has proven Aristotle's point. Touch is the first sense to develop and the last to leave. It is an active sense even in the womb. And, when we are dying, even when we have lost other senses, we can still feel touch.

Touch's organ, the skin, is the largest organ of any of the five senses. It covers our entire body, even our eyelids, our ears and our nose—three of the organs of other senses. So not only does the touch sense organ have its own independent role, it also serves to protect three of our other senses.

Perhaps the importance of touch is best acknowledged by the vital role it plays in human development. Babies that do not have an adequate amount of affectionate touch often fail to thrive in one or more of three critical areas—physically, mentally, emotionally. The need for touch seems even more important than the need for food as demonstrated by the psychologist Harry Harlow in the 1950s. He studied infant monkeys separated from all other monkeys at birth. He introduced two surrogate mothers—one was made of wire and had a bottle of milk while the other was made of wood that had been covered in a soft cloth. The baby monkeys hugged the cloth surrogates for hours, long after hunger should have been the dominant need.

...importance of touch is best acknowledged by the vital role it plays in human development.

The type of touch—*discriminative* or *protective*—matters in human development as well as in the way we incorporate touch in our writing. A discriminative touch is one that lets us determine if the object or surface is rough or smooth, soft or hard. The second type of touch functions to protect us, allowing us to quickly remove a hand if the stove is hot, for example.

Sight, sound, smell and taste all have their receptors near the brain. Touch has its discriminative and protective receptors in our skin, which can be a long distance from the brain. Still that information needs to get to the brain quickly. And it does, transmitted to the brain via the spinal cord. Each of these two receptor types has its own tracts of nerve cell bundles.

The following example of the use of touch in literature illustrates a friendly touch. Of course, while touch can convey love and compassion, it can also convey hate, frustration, abuse. In *Paper Daughter: A Memoir* by M. Elaine Mar, the author writes:

> For a long time, I was afraid that Father would disappear if I didn't stay by his side. So like Mary's little lamb, I followed him. Every so often I touched him--his arm, his sleeve, his face--to reassure myself of his presence....

Then one night Father didn't come home at all. I felt his absence as soon as I awoke. Our house was so small that he couldn't have slipped in without my knowledge. Any human presence there was palpable, each new body pressing the air tighter around my skin. I sat up and reached for my glasses.

"You don't need to look," Mother said. "He's not here."

Consider if you want to use touch to move your story forward (a goal orientation) or to express tenderness, appreciation, understanding (a process orientation).

An individual has four major touch receptors:

- **Mechanoreceptors.** Sensitive to pressure, vibrations (such as from a cell phone).
- **Thermal receptors.** Sensitive to hot and cold.
- **Kinesthetic receptors.** Sensitive to where are limbs are at any given moment.
- **Pain receptors.** Sensitive to what is harmful and, to the extent we have control over the situation, reminding us to remove ourselves from the situation.

By touching we can change what we have touched. This is not true of the other senses. We can look at a balloon, and the vision remains unchanged. We can hear a bird, and the sound stays the same. We can smell a flower, and the scent is just the same as before we smelled it. We can taste a piece of chocolate and the rest of the chocolate, in the package tastes just the same. However, when we touch, we can change what we touch. If we push down a piece of bread dough with our hands, then the shape of the dough has been changed. It is now flat instead of round.

Remember Mr. Whipple? For years, on television commercials, he told us to not squeeze the Charmin. Of course, even he did. His touch, at least briefly, changed the shape of the rolls. So once again, we note that touch has different characteristics than the other four senses. This gets us to thinking about how we can use touch in our writing. It is "just another sense" and yet it is quite different from the other four. And, although all of our skin is involved with touch, some areas are more sensitive than others—the finger tips, the face, the back of the neck, the chest, the upper arms, and soles of the feet.

There are a number of words we can use to describe touch. The language of touch is not as restricted as in some of the other senses. A few examples of touch words are: rough, smooth, bumpy, gritty, sticky. You will come up with many more words to use when including the sense of touch in your writing.

Now Get to Writing!

Back to the scene in your synopsis for one final Deconstruction for the senses. This time, focus on just touch. Do you or the person in the scene touch anything? If the person is touched, the touch doesn't have to be by or to another person. If you live in the south, you might rub against the rough bark of a Loblolly Pine or the smooth bark of the PawPaw tree. If you live in California, your skirt might brush the Star Jasmine (touch) and release its sweet scent (smell). Take 5 to 10 minutes to write a description. Here are three points to consider as you write:

1. What do you feel? Think of three different ways to describe what you feel and try to make at least one of these unique to you.
2. Write about the texture. Is it smooth? Rough? Pebbly?
3. Think how using touch helps the reader better understand your perception of a place, person or event that is featured in the scene in your synopsis.

The Five Senses and the Fire

Knowing now more about the five senses, you can perhaps better understand why and how the fire on our property is permanently seared into my memory. Looking back, the sound of that pine tree exploding 100 feet into the air wasn't so much deafening as scary. Suddenly, the thick, smoky air burning my eyes became ominous.

When I saw the forceful fingers of the flames reaching up as if to burn the sky, I dropped the recalcitrant hose and ran back into the house. The well-practiced internal list of 50 things to take in the case of a fire became limited to my computer (where portions of this book resided) and my husband's computer and external hard drive (where 800 pages of his manuscript were stored). No time to think about anything else, not even the family photo albums that we keep in plastic buckets precisely in case we needed to grab them should there be a fire.

Picture this. With adrenaline-fueled action, I pull computers off their power cords and tuck them in my arms, dash out the front door and begin running toward the open field across from our home. I figured that area would be safe even if our house went. I didn't know where my husband was. My thought was I had to secure the computers and then go find him. Two computers in a field frequently shared with cattle and deer? It seemed logical at the time.

Fortunately, my husband showed up at that moment, looking for me. He had briefly used the hose, but the fire was too big, too hot, too close. We took the computers and jumped in the car to leave. We live on a cul-de-sac and knew to get out while we could. As we backed our car onto the asphalt, the first of what became eight fire engines roared up our hill, soon followed by 10 support vehicles and about as many police cars. At almost the same moment that we saw the fire engine, we heard the whine of the first of two California Department of Forestry twin-engine planes.

We were barely down the hill, when the planes began dumping orange fire retardant on our home and the rapidly racing fire. We had to imagine losing everything and found that we could and still be fine. Perhaps ten minutes later, a flatbed truck had offloaded a tractor, which was slowly crawling up the hill and pushing the grasses and soil to the side in an effort to stop the widening burn area.

I found myself shouting at the plane, "Dump it. Dump it now. Now. Now. Now." I plaintively urged the tractor, "Faster. Faster."

Thanks to the incredible efforts of the ground and air crews, our home didn't burn nor did the homes of our neighbors. We did lose 15 trees—pines, redwoods and olives—plus the enclosed flower garden that enabled me to keep my ollalieberry vines and roses away from the deer with their voracious appetites. Four additional olive trees looked dead, their brown, scorched leaves hanging bravely to the branches. No signs of green, but we agreed to wait another season to see if they would come back. With true American determination, we decided to make the burned area better than before. We cut down the charred tree remains, cleared the area and built a decking. We surrounded the area with pink-blossomed oleanders, believing them to be more resistant to fire than large resinous pines.

On the mantle in my study, I kept four blackened pine cones as the outward reminder of the inner memory. But I didn't really need them to see the flames, hear my rapidly beating heart as I raced to grab our computers, smell the acrid air, taste the bitterness of fear in my mouth or touch the comfort of the front door knob when we finally returned, more than three hours later, to find our home safe, dirty with the oily film of fire retardant, but safe.

What's Next?

As we leave our examination of the five senses, let's put it all in perspective. Your multiple Deconstructions have given you a level of detail that you never imagined possible. When you get to the Construction phase (Chapter 8), you will see that the details are there not for their own sake but to move the story forward and to bring your reader into your story. As a poetic and beautiful example, read how Molly Peacock used sensory detail to tell us about her parents in her memoir *Paradise: Piece By Piece*. In the scene, Molly is about five years old and doesn't know how to write. In order to send her grandmother a note, she has her mother write the letters to several words for her. Molly struggles to replicate the right letters to form the words and has just shown her mother the note:

> The writing drew a smile from those straight, slightly purplish lips whose carmine lipstick had disappeared to find a better home on the filter tips of cigarette butts in a square glass ashtray, an ashtray so heavy that when my father let it fly against the wall in an argument it didn't even break.

By now you see how your story can be Deconstructed for the people, their emotions, their conversations, and their sensory-rich world. But when and where does your story happen? The final element of time and place may be background or context for your story, or it may take center stage. How do you examine time? Is it subjective or objective? What does it contribute? What is meant by place? Is it geography? Is it internal or external? Or, is it lifespace, a concept from the social sciences? In the following chapter, we'll guide you through techniques and methodologies that will give you non-obvious ways to Deconstruct the time and place of your scene.

References and Resources

Allende, Isabel. *Aphrodite: A Memoir of the Senses*. New York: Harper Perennial, 1999.

Cariou, Heather Summerhayes. *Sixtyfive Roses: A Sister's Memoir.* Toronto: McArthur & Company, 2008.

Edelman, Hope. *The Possibility of Everything: A Memoir.* New York: Ballantine Books, 2010.

Esquivel, Laura. *Like Water for Chocolate.* New York: Anchor Books, 1995.

Herz, Rachel. *The Scent of Desire: Discovering Our Enigmatic Sense of Smell.* New York: William Morrow, 2007.

Kidder, Tracy. "Field Drafts to Full Notes." In Kramer, Mark and Call, Wendy, Eds. *Telling True Stories: A Nonfiction Writers' Guide from the Nieman Foundation at Harvard University.* New York: Plume, 2007.

Kamdar, Mira. *Motiba's Tattoos.* New York: Plume, 2001.

Mar, Elaine M. *Paper Daughter: A Memoir.* New York: Harper Perennial, 2000.

Peacock, Molly. *Paradise: Piece by Piece.* New York: Riverhead Books, 1998.

Taylor, Jill Bolte. *My Stroke of Insight.* New York: Viking, 2006.

Toth, Susan Allen. *Blooming: A Small-Town Girlhood.* New York: Ballantine Books, 1998.

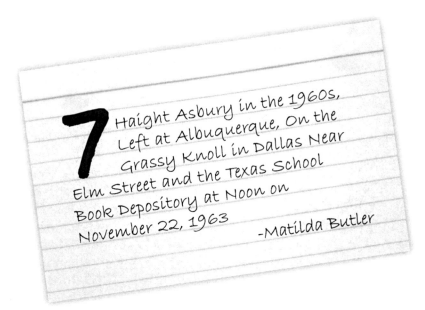

7 Haight Asbury in the 1960s, Left at Albuquerque, On the Grassy Knoll in Dallas Near Elm Street and the Texas School Book Depository at Noon on November 22, 1963
    —Matilda Butler

The Element of Time and Place

A Personal Sense of Time and Place

In 1997, we sold our Palo Alto home of 25 years and moved to the countryside—in a town located just inside the last few miles before Santa Clara county becomes San Benito county—about 30 minutes south of San Jose. The most productive crop on our 10-acre slice of hillside was lava. When the Spanish wild oats were tall, I occasionally tripped on pieces of lava, unable to see them protruding from the ground. When we needed to dig a ditch, we spent most of our time using a peavey (a tool I'd never seen before moving there) to pry out huge boulders.

When we added a guest cottage, the massive auger that drilled into our mixture of clay soil and lava to create the required 12-inch by 12-foot piers sheered in half. The replacement fee was $250. The first drilling company's driver left the job site, saying, "The task ain't possible." The boulders temporarily won the battle between human and rock. The specs we negotiated with the next drilling company were for 24-inch by 8-foot piers. One day, the tractor slid partway down the hillside and scared that driver. Another driver worked for several weeks and eventually got through enough rocks to create the required number of piers, but not before finding he had to dig some of the large boulders out of the earth as nothing would go through them. Later we had a bulldozer contractor, more artist than driver, move four of the largest unearthed boulders to create what we fondly called our Stonehenge. Actually, with our guidance, he positioned them so that the largest one became a picnic table and three others were turned into benches. We often sat at that rock table and looked across the Santa Clara valley with its fields of peppers, tomatoes and corn.

"What crop other than rocks can we plant here?" I asked my life partner. We looked at produce grown in countries rich in volcanic rock—Greece, Italy, Spain—and found that they shared in common tens of thousands of acres of olive trees. Drawing on their knowledge and ancient wisdom about the land, we planted Maurino, Coratina, Frantoio and Leccino olives—delivered to us by Samantha Dorsey who had propagated them from a stock of 1000 trees Nan McEvoy brought from Italy to her new ranch in Peta-luma. This was in the days before Dorsey became too busy to handle deliveries herself, before she became Nursery and Vineyard Manager of the 30,000-tree McEvoy Nursery. Along the way, Nan McEvoy became one of my role models. She started as a reporter at her grandfather's *San Francisco Chronicle* newspaper and eventually became Chair of the Board from 1981 until 1995 when she was forcibly retired during a bitter rift among board members on the family-owned newspaper. While other 72 year olds might have gone quietly home, Nan McEvoy bought a 550-acre dairy farm, researched olive trees and soon had a producing olive ranch that is now famous for its award-winning oils. Only a few years later, we had her trees on our tiny property.

"What crop other than rocks can we plant here?"

Even before we purchased 154 olive trees, before we dug holes to plant them, before we moved still more huge lava boulders, my curiosity about this land that I walked on and worked in caused me to want to understand its rocks. We had no volcano nearby so where did the lava come from? None of our neighbors knew the history of our rocks; most had no interest and merely accepted them as part of the land. Our closest neighbors sold their property six months after purchasing it; they despised the presence of lava everywhere. Their original thought had been to remove all of them. You can imagine the outcome of that match up.

Through research I discovered that our lava had originally been thrown about 50 miles from an erupting volcano near the current town of Lancaster in southern California nearly 23 million years ago. In the intervening years, the San Andreas fault split the volcano and moved half of it 195 miles north to what is now the Pinnacles National Monument. Our boulders moved along with the Pinnacles volcano and we resided with them in Gilroy. It's no wonder we couldn't find a volcano source. We hadn't thought to look 50 miles from us and most assuredly had not thought to look at their original location 245 miles to the south.

This connection to the land and its history changed me. I grew up in Oklahoma City and always lived in cities—Washington, D.C., Boston, just outside Chicago in Evanston and Palo Alto. True, these weren't all mega-cities, but none were rural. Then came our 10 acres in the countryside, across from a 2000-acre county park with cougar, wild boar, deer, turkeys and rattlesnakes, just outside Gilroy with its population of 51,000. Almost daily walks on the land transformed me, integrating my soul with this place. I picked up small pieces of lava and examined them, thrilled when I occasionally found a small shell cupped in a volcanic bubble. I ran my fingers over the fine-grained rhyolite and wondered what rock it had touched while cooling in order to create the stretch mark I saw. I lugged hundreds of medium-sized pieces to line paths throughout the property. I created natural sculptures out of fairly large boulders, displaying them on custom-made steel bases as if they were fine art. Never before had I thought about the land beneath my feet, about the occasional stones I handled, or even the seasonal changes in the constellations above me. All of that changed, beginning late the first night on the land when we walked outside.

This connection to the land and its history changed me.

"The sky looks hazy, must be fog from the coast."

"That's the Milky Way," my partner said.

Sharing Knowledge of Time and Place with Readers

Time and place are frequently woven together in storytelling, just as I did in writing about the land where I lived until a recent move brought us to Corvallis, Oregon, where the constellations regularly disappear behind massive cloud cover.

Let's consider a different example. If you begin a story or a chapter with you waking up one November morning, the reader probably thinks you are indicating a season, a time of the year. If you add that you've just opened your eyes in a hotel room on November 22, 1963, then the reader thinks you might be traveling on business or for pleasure and is alerted to the specificity of what is to happen. This isn't just any day, however, but a singular day. Until this point, time is the detail being revealed.

If you go to breakfast and read the newspaper, the reader learns nothing more. However, if you open the *Dallas Morning News*, then readers of a certain age or with specific knowledge of events will know this is the day that President John Fitzgerald Kennedy will be assassinated and may begin to wonder how your story will overlap with history.

At this point, time and place have commingled with your story. We combine them in this fifth element because they nourish each other. The places we write about were only like that at a certain point in time. And the time, even the times we write about influence our feelings about place. Although time and place often homestead the same space in a story, let's look at them separately to better understand their meaning to us as writers and to discuss points you will want to consider when you Deconstruct your story for them.

http://womensmemoirs.com/time-place-1

Perspectives on Place

A well-crafted description of place gives us a visual sense as well as insights beyond the simple listing of what is seen. Take, for example, the following passage in Dana Stabenow's *Play with Fire*, a Kate Shugak Mystery that takes place in Alaska:

> The drive to the borough school administration offices took Kate through the abomination of south Fairbanks,

an echoing expanse of pavement divided into four lanes and two frontage roads. One strip mall was succeeded by another and one parking lot rolled into the next with occasional fast food restaurant interruptions, Kentucky Fried Chicken, McDonald's, Denny's. There was even a Super 8 Motel next to Denny's. Progress. It looked like Dimond Boulevard in Anchorage, except Dimond had the single saving grace of the Chugach Mountains in the background.

Why do people allow this to happen in the places they live? she wondered...

Maybe, Kate thought, warming to her topic, maybe the Fairbanks city planners thought the only way to control ugliness like this was to pick up the town by the northern border, shake it fiercely and confine all the junk that fell into the southern half behind chain link, the better to guard against it ever spilling over into the real world.

A few years ago, I gave a presentation about a sense of place to a group of writers. I split my talk into two symmetrical halves—objective geography, or writing from the outside in, and subjective geography, writing from the inside out. I thought that encompassed the topic rather well. Now, I see that the split was too tidy and want to share a more complex, and much richer, way to understand place.

Since that presentation, I've been influenced by Wendell Berry's well-known quote: "If you don't know where you are, you don't know who you are." When Pulitzer-prize-winning author Wallace Stegner explained those words, he wrote that Barry was "talking about the knowledge of place that comes from working in it in all weathers, making a living from it, suffering from its catastrophes, loving its mornings or evenings or hot noons, valuing it for the profound investment of labor and feeling that you, your parents and grandparents, your all-but-unknown ancestors have put into it. [Berry] is talking about the knowing that poets specialize in."

There are many writers who make place the cornerstone of their writing. Here is Peter Mayle's description of the setting for his book, *A Year in*

Many writers make place the cornerstone of their writing.

Provence, that contributes to our knowledge of both the *who* and the *where* of the story.

> We saw it [the house] one afternoon and had mentally moved in by dinner.
>
> It was set above the country road that runs between the two medieval hill villages of Menerbes and Bonnieux, at the end of a dirt track through cherry trees and vines. It was a *mas*, or farmhouse, built from local stone which two hundred years of wind and sun had weathered to a colour somewhere between pale honey and pale grey. It had started life in the eighteenth century as one room and, in the haphazard manner of agricultural buildings, had spread to accommodate children, grandmothers, goats and farm implements until it had become an irregular three-story house. Everything about it was solid. The spiral staircase which rose from the wipe cave to the top floor was cut from massive slabs of stone. The walls, some of them a metre thick, were built to keep out the winds of the Mistral which, they say, can blow the ears off a donkey. Attached to the back of the house was an enclosed courtyard, and beyond that a bleached white stone swimming pool. There were three wells, there were established shade trees and slim green cypresses, hedges of rosemary, a giant almond tree. In the afternoon sun, with the wooden shutters half-closed like sleepy eyelids, it was irresistible.

The Sense of Place

Since we're memoir writers considering place, let's begin with the understanding that place primarily exists because we give meaning to it. *Space* becomes *place* because we bond with it emotionally, cognitively and behaviorally. And each of these ways of linking ourselves to place is bound up with our relationships to other individuals, to our needs and to the elements of the environment that help create our unique perception of place.

Now I know it seems that I've changed the character of place in a radical way. I'm suggesting that place is really about relationships and needs rather than a simple physical reality. Before we go down that path, let's work our way to this notion through the more familiar concept of place. Let's start with this: Imagine, if you will, that place is a character in your memoir.

[handwritten margin note: Place is a character in memoir.]

Physical description (unbuilt, mostly)

Just as if you are writing about a person in your memoir, you can describe the objective place where your story takes place. This might include its geology, as I did in the opening to this chapter. It might include the climate, the people, the economics of the area and its history. Will all of this make it into your memoir? It's unlikely, but only when you immerse yourself in place will you begin to understand its true influence on your story.

For example, by now you're aware that I was raised in Oklahoma City. I am the person I am today because I grew up there. The flat plains seemed to stretch forever. I saw the rain coming long before it arrived. The wind that swept across that flat land, its progress unimpeded by mountains, often caused me to tug at my scarf, securing it tightly to protect my hair.

I remember the story of a French couture designer who said upon arriving in town for a fashion show, "Women in Oklahoma look terrible. The scarves they wear make them look frumpy." A few days later, a reporter caught up with him and asked what he thought of Oklahoma. He responded, "Now I understand why women here wear scarves. The wind never stops."

So while I endured the wind (actually, much like a fish not knowing its environment is wet, I didn't realize how windy it was until years later after I married and moved to Boston), I also was inhaling the pioneer spirit and the enthusiasms of a state opened by The Run of 1889.

I grew up knowing about Boomers (those who promoted the opening of the state) and Sooners (those who sneaked across the line before the official gun was fired to start The Run, to secure some of the best land). My elementary school teachers emphasized the youthfulness of the state, and I took away the notion that I could do anything I wanted as I didn't have to worry about long-held traditions that would limit me. As sixth graders, we even reenacted The Oklahoma Run. I played the role of a mother in our family unit, probably because I volunteered to bring my Radio Flyer wagon, complete with an arched cover that my father helped me configure from metal hoops and a worn-out white sheet. My doll Hannah was the stand in as my baby, and my duck (in a cage for safety) was part of our household.

To this day, the land of Oklahoma lives on in my psyche. I don't like twisty roads, feeling most comfortable on a flat straight road just like the section lines I was raised on. Once, on our way to look at a possible home in the California hills, I realized how much the road curved this way and that. Partway there, I suggested I could never live on a road like that. We turned around and never bothered to see the property.

> *...the land of Oklahoma lives on in my psyche.*

Sometimes a memoir writer brings a sense of place to center stage. Susan Wittig Albert—bestselling author of multiple series including the China Bayles herbal mysteries, Cottage Tales of Beatrix Potter and her newest The Darling Dahlias—is an author who carefully crafts her story. In her memoir, she reaches out to the land around her, touches it and brings it into her story to show the reader its influence on her. Yet how do we tame the land so that it becomes personal? One way is through our use of names and the appropriate descriptive vocabulary. Albert writes in her memoir *Together, Alone: A Memoir of Marriage and Place*:

> Naming connects us to the places that have significance for us, places that tell our stories. How do we know where in the world we are if we can't place ourselves in the landscape? How can we describe a natural setting if we don't have a vocabulary that defines its features?

Physical description (built, mostly)

But is place always a state? Always land? Of course not. Place might be a city, a neighborhood, a block, a house, an office, even a room. I had one student who lived with her family on the second floor flat of her German grandmother's home. As she came to class and shared her chapters, week after week, we all began to see the house as a character in her story. We knew what it looked like, where the rooms were located, the lighting in the hallways, the carpet on the stairs. We saw it from the perspective of its vegetable garden and from the perspective of a little girl scampering up and down the stairs inside.

[handwritten: endow the place w/a personality of its own through description.]

Robert Levine, author of *A Geography of Time*, writes:

> ...places, like people, have their own personalities. I fully concur with sociologist Anselm Strauss that "the entire complex of urban life can be thought of as a person rather than a distinctive place, and the city can be endowed with a personality of its own.

There are multiple *places* in your story. Don't feel overwhelmed by the notion of describing all of them at once. Start with the scene in the synopsis you are using while you go through the exercises in *Writing Alchemy*.

Now Get to Writing!

First you need to imagine the place and how much that place influenced you and your story. You may not really know about the influence until you dig deep during the Deconstruction. Hold the place in your mind. Look around. Look in front of you and behind you. To the right and to the left. If you can, imagine yourself slowly turning around. Walk through the place. For example, even though I no longer live on the property I described at the opening of this chapter, I can still close my eyes and walk across its land. When I do, I find myself putting each foot down carefully if I'm in a patch of tall wild oats. I don't want to stumble on a lava boulder and I definitely don't want to scare a rattlesnake.

1. **Use Your Memories.** Write everything that you see in your mind's eye. Describe the place so that someone else can see it with you, even though they are separated by hundreds or thousands of miles. If you have a hard time, imagine a good friend is talking to you on your cell phone. You want to let him know what you are seeing. Write what you are saying. Remember to describe the place of your scene whether a built or an unbuilt environment. Provide as many physical details as you can.

2. **Use Research.** At this point, you may want to do some research on place. On the Internet you can find a wealth of information. Some may surprise you. For one class, I wanted to talk about the downtown of Oklahoma City when I was a child. I found penny postcards of buildings that no longer exist. This helped me fill in details. If you are writing

[handwritten margin notes: Homestead area: • sagebrush • no water source • no roads • how land was acquired]

[handwritten bottom note: Dad told Jay, "If the land will grow sage brush, it will grow crops."]

about a childhood home, you or family members may have
photos that will facilitate your memory. Or, you might want
to have conversations with others about your home. The
research may include the geology of the land, the history
of its people, its settlement pattern, its economic condition, or other aspects of land that will help you to understand the place. If the focus of place is a neighborhood, research will help you determine when the homes were built
in that area, what happened on the land before structures
went up, and just perhaps explain that apricot tree in your
backyard (from a once-large orchard). Open yourself to the
information and to possible surprises. Don't feel you have
to go down a rabbit hole, just investigate enough to anchor
yourself in place.

Physical Place and History Intertwined

I remember going to Arkansas to find the land that my great-
grandparents homesteaded. The people who live there now still call
it the Ol' Calderhead Place, the name passed down for more than
a century. They showed me the large pile of stones, all that is left of
the original home. My great-grandfather, John Bishop Calderhead,
was a stone mason in Scotland before he came to the United States.
With pride, he added a stone fireplace and chimney to the small
home he built for his family. Years later, when he was sitting with
his wife and two daughters in the main room of the house, lightning
flashed down that chimney instantly killing my great-grandmother
and one of their daughters. My great-grandfather died three days
later from the burns he sustained. I hefted one of the stones
in my left hand and touched its smooth surface with
the other. In my mind, I could see that stormy afternoon, which ended the lives of three members of
my family.

In my mind, I could see that stormy afternoon...

Several years prior to that fatal day, my grandfather and his new bride settled on the 160 acres
adjacent to his parents. Because they lived there for
five years, built a small home and grew crops, President
Taft signed a document granting them the land under the Homestead Act. My mother was conceived on that land and was born in
the nearby town. My grandparents' land stayed in the family until a

few years ago when I sold it. But not before visiting it to secure my own sense of place.

Jid Lee, in her book *To Kill a Tiger: A Memoir of Korea*, does a masterful job of combining physical place and history to reveal her personal story in relation to the suppression of women in a country that does not value them. Lee's own story is heightened when we understand the place and the odds she was fighting against.

Emotional or Psychological Description

Although we don't want to go too far into anthropomorphizing place, a location can have an emotional description as well as a physical one. The emotion of the place might be love or hate, hope or fear, joy or sadness. Place might seem enchanting or frightening to a child as if the land is actually that way.

http://womensmemoirs.com/time-place-2

But more often, emotional description means the way we feel about a place. For many years, I'd heard Gertrude Stein's description of Oakland on her return from Paris. She wrote in *Everybody's Autobiography*, "...there is no there there." What did she mean? I always figured that Oakland—a city I knew well from my four decades of living in the Bay Area and Stein's childhood home—paled in comparison with the beauty and history of Paris. Later I learned that upon a return visit, Stein found all of her emotional touchstones of place—her home and the park where she played—no longer existed. In their place were a row of craftsman-style bungalows.

Understanding this interpretation of Stein's words was comforting to me because the Palo Alto home where we lived for 25 years and raised our children was torn down by the family who bought it from us. After living for a few years in that caffe-latte, two-story, traditional building we called home, they decided to demolish it and erect a modern-style home painted pumpkin. All the special touches—double-etched glass in the kitchen window rescued from the Palo Alto Hyatt just days before the wrecking ball showed up, a massive front door made for us by a friend using old redwood reclaimed from a California barn and orchard walnut that he'd cut and cured for a year, the brick patio laid in a basket-weave pattern by my teenaged son—gone. Thelma, a long-time, Palo Alto friend phoned me to say that she drove by our old house one day on a whim. Her father was a carpenter and had installed our custom front door so she felt a special fondness for the place, even after we had moved. She called, her voice still shaky, to tell me the house that had been our home was gone. Just gone. There was only a massive hole in the ground. She sat there for more than an hour crying, mourning the place that wasn't there.

Yes, we have strong emotions about place.

To create an emotional portrayal of place, you need to feel its heartbeat. Anne Hull, journalist for the *Washington Post* and 2008 Pulitzer Prize winner for her stories about the scandalous conditions at Walter Reed Army Hospital, urges us to give heart to place (from her article in *Telling True Stories: A Nonfiction Writers' Guide from the Nieman Foundation at Harvard University*): "A story needs to have a geographical heart....Push that information through a creative sieve. This is the hardest part. You want to weave a sense of place, not just give a laundry list of details."

Now Get to Writing!

In the first exercise, you focused on a physical description of place. While important, those details can become overly analytical. This second description takes you through an analysis of your emotions concerning the place.

1. Take a piece of paper and draw a rectangular box in the middle of the page. Jot notes into it that convey the physical description of place. You can take this from your previous exercise.

2. Then consider all the positive emotions you feel about the place. Create a list that includes the positive emotions and then a statement explaining why you feel each emotion.

3. Finally, consider the negative emotions you feel about the place. Create a list of the negative emotions along with a brief statement about why you feel that way.

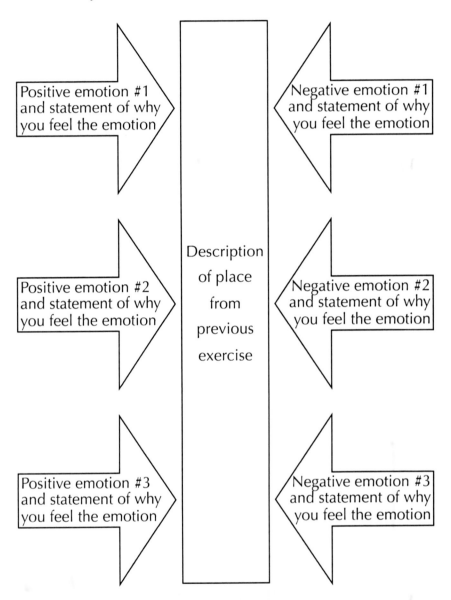

Positive emotion #1
and statement of why
you feel the emotion

Negative emotion #1
and statement of why
you feel the emotion

Description
of place
from
previous
exercise

Positive emotion #2
and statement of why
you feel the emotion

Negative emotion #2
and statement of why
you feel the emotion

Positive emotion #3
and statement of why
you feel the emotion

Negative emotion #3
and statement of why
you feel the emotion

Sensory Description

The previous chapter examined the use of our five senses in writing. Without going into that same level of detail, we do want to show that sensory information can help bring a place to life. Consider this example from Angela Gerst's first novel, *A Crack in Everything*:

I kicked off my shoes, tucked myself into an armchair and listened to the sounds of Odette's snug home. In the kitchen, the freezer chunked ice into a tray. The dishwasher volleyed water down the drain. Somewhere behind me, an air-conditioner hummed. House harmony, I thought, in a melancholy minor mode.

What I especially like in this description is that Gerst uses sounds to give character to the home. Not only is this evident in her choice of details but also when she attributes the sounds to "house harmony."

Let's go back to Anne Hull, who speaks with the voice of a journalist, but who offers advice that is just as relevant to memoir writers. This is from an interview with Matt Thompson:

> ...As a reporter, be physically present to witness and absorb, if even for three hours. Have all your sensory pistons firing: seeing, hearing, smelling, etc. In trying to convey the nuances of a culture or neighborhood, the drama is in the small observed or spoken exchanges, and one needs to be there to see it unfold.

Hull then concludes her conversation with Thompson with a question she poses to herself on a read-through of what she has written:

> ...As the newsroom clock is ticking, read over what you've written and ask yourself, Did I take readers somewhere or does this piece read like I never left the office? Go back and re-infuse it with sights, sounds, smells, bits of dialogue.

As memoir writers, we have been physically present in the places we write about. That's not our problem. Instead, much like the question Hull raises, we need to ask ourselves, "Have I conveyed the essence of this place to my readers? If they haven't been there, will they sense it as I do?"

Here's another way to think about senses and place. Several years ago, I read an article by Jason Logan, entitled "Scents of the City," that appeared in *The New York Times*. Logan walked through numerous neighborhoods, paying attention only to smells. Here's a bit from that piece:

As my nostrils led me from Manhattan's northernmost end to its southern tip, some prosaic scents recurred (cigarette butts; suntan lotion; fried foods); some were singular and sublime (a delicate trail of flowers mingling with Indian curry around 34th Street); while others proved revoltingly unique (the garbage outside a nail salon). Some smells reminded me of other places, and some will forever remind me of New York.

His city explorations remind us that a place may be given depth through its scents as well as its physical description, history and emotions.

Do you know Michael Shapiro's book, *A Sense of Place: Great Travel Writers Talk about Nature Writing*? The author explains that he "wanted to learn from the masters," and he did traveling to and interviewing Simon Winchester, Frances Mayes, Bill Bryson, Isabel Allende and 14 other authors who craft their stories around place. When Shapiro asked Allende, "What do you think is most important to create that sense of place?" she replied: "I describe the smell, the color, the temperature, the texture, how you feel time because time varies in every place."

How will you create your sense of place through the senses?

Now Get to Writing!

1. From the two previous exercises, you have physical and emotional Deconstructions of place. This time, mentally go back to the place of your scene and consider the senses—especially smells and sounds but others that seem appropriate as well. Write with as much detail as you can.

2. Now consider the essence of the place, both the ordinary and the extraordinary, and see how senses can be used to show the essence.

Guidance to Our Understanding of Place as Relationships

Before getting into a social science perspective on place, let's consider the work of a renowned writer on place and an architect concerned with environment to see how they discuss place and relationships, the concept I brought up earlier in this chapter.

All Place is Personal

National Book Award winner Barry Lopez has more than 15 published books to his credit as well as numerous essays and articles that have appeared in *Harper's*, *National Geographic* and other major magazines. His special interest across both fiction and nonfiction is the importance of place. I've extracted a brief passage from his often republished essay "Landscape and Narrative" to give you a feel for the way he looks at the relationship of place and person:

> I think of two landscapes--one outside the self, the other within. The external landscape is the one we see--not only the line and color of the land and its shading at different times of the day, but also its plants and animals in season, its weather, its geology, the record of its climate and evolution....One learns a landscape finally not by knowing the name or identity of everything in it, but by perceiving the relationships in it...The difference between the relationships and the elements is the same as that between written history and a catalog of events.

Lopez's words help us to see that when we write about place, the task is larger than naming a city or describing its flora or fauna. We need to move past a catalog of what is seen and heard, although that is a good place to begin, and consider the relationships among the elements. Next Lopez describes what he calls the "second landscape."

> The second landscape I think of is an interior one, a kind of projection within a person of a part of the exterior landscape. Relationships in the exterior landscape include those that are named and discernible...The shape and character of these relationships in a person's thinking,...are deeply influenced by where on this earth one goes, what one touches, the patterns one observes in nature...These thoughts are arranged, further, according to the thread of one's moral, intellectual, and spiritual development. The interior landscape responds to the character and subtlety of an exterior landscape; the shape of the individual mind is affected by land as it is by genes.

Changing Places, Changing People

David Seamon, also sees the relationship between people and place. A professor of architecture and an environment-behavior researcher at Kansas State University, Seamon has written about place through an analysis he described in "Place, Placelessness, Insideness, and Outsideness in John Sayles' *Sunshine State*." Seamon notes that independent filmmaker John Sayle has set *Sunshine State*:

> ...in Plantation Island, Florida, where large-scale corporate development is transforming two communities—one black, the other white—into upscale winter resorts. Sayles' film probes the place experience of some sixteen vividly drawn characters and illuminates how the same physical place, for different individuals and groups, can evoke a broad spectrum of situations, meanings, and potential futures. One of Sayles' conclusions is that people cannot escape the place in which they find themselves. They can, however, learn from that place and thereby decide whether and in what ways they will offer that place commitment or not.

Let's leave Lopez and Seamon for now and move to *person and place*, my earlier theme that place is really about relationships. While Lopez talks about relationships within place, here I am referring to our relationships with others, objects, emotions and the physical environment, an approach more similar to Seamon when he writes about how place has a unique impact on each individual. We might call this the social-emotional-geographic environment that influences, and in some cases even determines, part of our behavior. Sometimes place is just, well, a place. But place becomes an integral part of our story when we explore its relationship to our behaviors.

In Chapter 3 on character, we learned the many ways to understand and describe personal characteristics. We now see that place is another element that shapes the person. This is why place matters. It isn't just backdrop or context for our story. It isn't just the stage set in front of which we act. I have a friend who lived for most of 45 years in and around Bar Harbor, Maine, the town where she was born. She

...place is another element that shapes the person.

loved that place. All of her family lived there. When her husband was transferred to Scottsdale, Arizona, she of course went along. He even built them a beautiful new home on a lovely piece of land. But she went into a multi-year depression, often finding it difficult to get out of bed. She made few friends. Place conspired to change her behavior. So, yes, place is a piece of our story because it influences our behavior and the behavior of others. And since each individual perceives the same place differently—some more positively, some more negatively, some as a goal enhancer, some as a goal distractor—we need to weave our unique perceptions of place into our stories to help others see and understand us and our behaviors. This social-emotional-geographic environment is similar to what social scientist Kurt Lewin called lifespace (usually spelled as a single word, but occasionally you may find it as two).

A Social Scientist on Place, Lifespace and Our Behavior

Gestalt, a German word meaning a coherent whole...

Let me back up a moment and introduce Kurt Lewin. Lewin was born in Prussia and moved with his family to Berlin when he was 15. At the university, he studied medicine and biology before eventually taking his Ph.D. in philosophy, during which time he studied with the founders of Gestalt psychology. Gestalt, a German word meaning a *coherent whole*, became an important way to understand behavior as Lewin investigated how people interpret their environment at the same time the environment and its forces are influencing them. We struggle for balance in our lives and do that within the negative and positive aspects of our personal world—our personal lifespace.

Although a rising star in the German academic world, Lewin found it necessary to gather up his family and leave for America in 1933 when Hitler became Chancellor and Lewin imagined what the future would be for him. Fortunately, Lewin had previously taught at Stanford University as an invited lecturer and knew he could make a place for himself in the United States. His significant work on field theory with its positive and negative forces eventually caused him to be considered the father of modern psychology. True, for Lewin lifespace did not include the physical world, but it is easy for us to extend his work out one ring beyond psychological reality to include physical reality since that is the original source of the positive and negative forces on the individual.

Let me give an example of Lewin's field theory as we can use it in our writing. His theory states *human behavior is a function of both the person's characteristics and the environment with its positive and negative forces.* In the following fictional story (although loosely based on a true story once told to me by an uncle), I put a (-) when a negative force and a (+) when a positive force is mentioned. The negatives and positives are perceived ones and might not be true for another person. In other words, this is one person's construct of reality:

Assume you are in a canoe on Red Lake in northern Minnesota on a sunny fall day when a storm suddenly comes up. You don't normally go out by yourself but your partner cancelled because of an unexpected business meeting. When 288,000 acres of water are whipped up, a canoe has little chance of maintaining its balance. You tip over and find yourself in the turbulent water. While you struggle in the icy temperature, the unexpected waves carry the canoe away from you. You look all around trying to figure out what to do. Could you swim to land? No, it is much too far (-). As the canoe bobs in the water, ever farther away, you imagine it turning over, filling with water and possibly sinking before you can reach it. At about that time, you hear a voice and twist yourself around in the water where you see a man in a rowboat. He waves for you to swim toward him and throws a life ring into the water to encourage you. Your goal, of course, is to live through this experience. You glance over at your canoe, which is closer to you than the rowboat, but you are concerned about the canoe's constant movement and your loss of the paddle. The closeness is appealing (+). Quickly though, you decide to swim the longer distance to the man, even though you are already losing your energy (-), because once you are there you will have help (+). You struggle in the water until you reach the line, and the old man begins to pull you in. But the stress and physical exertion is too much for him and he collapses while you are still in the frigid water. You use the line to reach the boat and manage to pull yourself in over the gunwale. With your heart racing and your hands trembling, you touch the semi-conscious man and guess that he has had a heart attack. The storm has brought rain, high waves, and now an early darkness. How will you get to land and can you get there soon enough to save the man's life, the man who wanted to save yours?

Using Lewin's concepts we begin to understand that for the person in this situation, there is a *gestalt*, a wholeness to this place. It is more than water, a storm, two boats, a man and you. Your idea of distance to your canoe, whether accurate or not, is part of the construct of this scene reflecting your perceived positives and negatives of the factors in the environment. Your willingness to try to swim the longer distance to the rowboat is reinforced in your mind by knowing you'll have someone else to get you back to land. Like many situations, the individual elements can't explain this place and your behavior. You have taken all the factors and created your own construct of reality—of what was there, what mattered and what you should do.

In our everyday world, not just when we are in crisis mode, we are influenced by the forces in our environment, including the physical place and the perceived reality we create out of what actually exists. Remember my friend that I previously mentioned? She had a perceived reality of the place where she moved. To someone else, the new place, the new landscape would be exciting and filled with opportunities to meet new people and learn about a new environment. Therefore, consider that when your writing engages the reader in your social-emotional-geographical environment, then you will be able to reveal more about yourself and your story. Place is all about the complex nature of these relationships.

A Memoir Writer's Guide to Using Lifespace in Writing about Place

To help you apply Lewin's concepts to your memoir, I've created a list of five points for your consideration:

- Remember that place is a personal construct, and for the reader to understand it, you need to include all that is relevant.
- Include in place its positive and negative influences on your *behavior* as well as the behavior of others.
- Consider not only physical places, but the people, the events and your feelings associated with place.

- Conjure with indirect places—places that live in your mind through the media or friendships. These places may also lead to a better understanding of *behavior* in a scene.
- Anticipate not just "where you are now" but where you are in your head. Your actions and behaviors may be influenced not by your current surroundings but where you know you will soon be or where you just were.

Wyoming will always be home.

Now Get to Writing!

In this exercise, you are going to draw your lifespace on paper. Have fun. Let your creativity take over. You never have to show the result to anyone so enjoy the process and see what develops.

1. Get a piece of paper (the nearest one may mean grabbing a sheet out of the printer drawer).
2. If possible fish out any crayons or colored pencils that you have around, even some pushed to the back of a drawer. Nothing like this nearby? Then use your imagination to find some drawing tools. At a minimum, you should be able to find a pencil (that will do for dark gray), a black pen and a blue pen. Perhaps you have a yellow highlighter. Assemble as many different colors as you can.
3. Draw yourself in the middle of the page. I have zero drawing talent so I just make a stick figure. You will probably do much better than I can.
4. Now recall the place in the synopsis that you are using for your Deconstruction.
5. Draw your lifespace on a sheet of paper. Begin with the outer physical space—trees or mountains or ocean or playground or neighborhood homes or your house or your room or place of work. Whatever is the place in your synopsized story, draw it on your paper. If any element is more salient to you, draw that larger. The result should show your feelings; actual size is quite irrelevant. Don't worry if your Steiff Teddy Bear is larger than the house when the animal was your best childhood friend and confidant.
6. Continue by adding your relationships with people in this place. Show these other people close to the center if you

perceive them as important in the story of this place or near the edge if they are insignificant.

7. Label people, places and behaviors with single words or short phrases. This is mainly a picture of the lifespace but identifications can also be helpful to you later as you write about place.

8. Draw the positive and negative forces on you in this place. If you can think of a shape for them, use that. A heart if you were in love. Clouds if you were depressed. Use your imagination. Otherwise, if shapes don't work for you, use words.

9. Now step back from your drawing, even putting it away for a day. Then come back to it and see what you have learned about the positive and negative forces on you in this lifespace.

Before Leaving Place Behind: a Social Scientist on Internal Responses to Place

In the exercise above, you drew objects in the physical environment from your *perception* of salience rather than worrying about actual size. A tree that didn't matter might be quite small while the one with your much-loved treehouse refuge might be oversized. Why? Why include this in the exercise?

To answer that question, let me describe the research of Jerome Bruner. A thumbnail synopsis of Bruner informs us that he was born in 1915, educated at Duke and Harvard, taught as a professor of psychology at Harvard before and then again after World War II (served as a social psychologist working with the US Army Intelligence during the war) and is currently (as of 2012) a senior research fellow at New York University's Law School. Yes, your math is correct. At the age of 96, Bruner is still teaching, now with a focus on how psychology affects the legal profession.

In the years after the war, Bruner focused on moving psychology away from the strict stimulus-response paradigm of the experimental branch. He introduced a more nuanced understanding of the role of cognitions in which a response to a stimulus is also internally interpreted. He became one of the significant research voices that helped establish the branch of cognitive psychology. And although Bruner didn't explain it this way, we can say that the positive and negative force fields that we learned about from Kurt Lewin apply here. Places that are positive for us evoke a different internal response than negative ones.

In a landmark study, Bruner asked 10 year olds to estimate the size of five coins—penny, nickel, dime, quarter and half dollar. At first, the children used their memory of the coins. Then they were shown the coins, one at a time, and asked to again estimate the size. For the experiment, each child was seated in front of a box with a knob that enabled her or him to change the size of a circle of light until it was the estimated size of the specific coin. The question Bruner was exploring focused on the *perceived value* of coins and how that perception might cause children to over-estimate the size of each coin, even when they saw the actual coin in the hand of a researcher.

The results were published in 1947 (that was a long time ago, but it is relevant to the point), and it turns out that all of the children over-estimated the size of the coins—whether the coin was present or absent. In what might seem to be a surprise twist, the children over-estimated sizes to an even greater extent when the coins were held near them at the time of size estimation. It seems that the actual coin reminded the children of its monetary value and they unknowingly showed the *perceived value* by increasing the estimated size.

What makes this study interesting to us as writers is that half of these children were from wealthy families while the other half were from a slum area in Boston. When Bruner examined the study results separately for the wealthy and poor children, he found that the former created light circles that were significantly closer to the true coin size (+10% - +22%) than the poor children who over-estimated the coin size to a much larger extent (+22% - +52%).

We can extend this finding to help us understand place. The places we value, and yet do not have around us routinely, are likely to seem larger in our thoughts because we perceive a significant value to them. These places will be over-estimated. Let me return to my friend who became depressed after her move. Her former home, imbued with the charm of childhood memories, with much-loved family and friends, writ large in her mind. The new home with its lack of familiarity and friends became insignificant and off-putting in comparison.

Or let me give you a personal example. I love going to Hawaii and yet get to do so infrequently. Some years pass without a visit, and other years I may only get a few days there. Yet, if you were to ask me to describe it, Hawaii would be bigger than life—the flowers sweeter, the ocean warmer, the beaches cleaner, the rainbows more plentiful, the birds more exotic, the people friendlier. If I lived in Hawaii, I'm sure that my perceptions of the place would be closer to reality.

So when you write of place, be sure to include the *physical* description, the *emotional* description and the *sensory* description. And then with that strong foundation, also examine both the social-emotional-geographical environment of lifespace and your internal response to a place with high (or low) value to you.

Time On Its Own

We know, of course, that time and place are often linked. However, let's focus on just time in this section beginning with... *What is time?* It's not as easy a question to answer as we might think. Around 397 AD, Saint Augustine wrote in what may be the first recorded auto-biography, *Confessions*: "What, then, is time? I know well enough what it is, provided that nobody asks me; but if I am asked what it is and try to explain, I am baffled."

We do know through literature and history that time, while once thought by the early Greeks to be circular, is now considered to be linear. Contrary to movies like *Back to the Future*, we can't revisit a past time nor investigate a future one. And according to the philosopher Heraclitus (535 BCE), "You could not step twice in the same river; for other waters are ever flowing on to you." So although I have returned to Yosemite National Park and stood at the same place in the icy Merced River multiple times, I'm not re-ally in the same river. The melted snows of the high country that flowed through the courseway of the Merced the first time I was there were soon in the ocean, never to be stood in again. Repeated experiences don't take us back in time for each is different in the seeming reenactment.

Time's precise measurement awaited the beginnings of science.

Time's precise measurement awaited the beginnings of science, and the concept of small increments of time identified by the individual only happened after the development of pocket watches, a fairly modern concept. Remember the first portable timepiece was only invented in 1504.

William Faulkner, in his novel *The Sound and the Fury*, gives us an anti-clock perspective when Quentin, the eldest son in a southern family now in decline, repeats his father's words, "clocks slay time...time is dead as long as it is being clicked off by little wheels; only when the clock stops does time come to life." Quentin recalls those words on the day he tries to escape time and finally realizes his only release from time is suicide.

Christina Haag offers us an interesting perspective on time. Haag is author of *Come to the Edge: A Love Story*, a memoir about her college friendship and eventual five-year romance with John F. Kennedy, Jr. in the 1980s. She wrote in the January 14, 2012, *Wall Street Journal* about her understanding of time for a memoir writer:

> In the early days, my diaries felt like they held the secret. But while they invaluably shaped a timeline, and provided a wealth of detail and dialogue, a diary is not memoir. In the latter, time becomes a character, and the reader is part of the equation....
>
> Accuracy of time and place was important. I did research, read and traveled, half-expecting to find the heart of the story at a turn in the road. But after a trip to Martha's Vineyard, where several chapters take place, I realized that the past would not be found in the places or in the people as they were now. It was alive in the recalling, in the act of writing.

Today our lives are for the most part controlled by and measured in time. If we don't wear a watch, we check our cell phones or computers for the current time. We keep a calendar, digital or analog, to remind ourselves of appointments. We get up when an alarm tells us to and retire when a clock says it is time.

But what if we consider the question, *whose clock?* Have you heard of the Clock of the Long Now? Danny Hillis, its inventor, provides this description: "I want to build a clock that ticks once a year. The century hand advances every 100 years, and the cuckoo comes out on the millennium. I want the cuckoo to come out every millennium for the next 10,000 years."

Danny Hillis, Stewart Brand, Brian Eno and others participate in the funding and implementation of this major undertaking to draw attention to our obsession with time, with compressed time that only considers the next five minutes, five days, five weeks, five months but that ignores the next five years, 50 years, 5000 years.

Time and the Memoirist

What does this mean for the memoirist? Our lives—the events we write about, the people who populate our stories, the places where we have been—happened in a specific time. To share our stories, we use time in multiple ways. For example:

1. *Time may be a marker, a turning point, in a story.* For instance, in Wilma Mankiller's memoir, *Mankiller: A Chief and Her People*, she describes an accident in which a car was passing on a hill and crashed headlong into her car just as she got to the rise. Once Mankiller was out of the coma and recovering from serious injuries, she wondered why her best friend didn't come to the hospital to visit her. Finally, her family told her what happened. Her friend was the driver in the other car and died in the crash. Mankiller writes that from then on, she always talked about "the time before" and "the time after."

   ... "the time before" and "the time after."

2. *Time may be subjective or objective.* An event might take place over a month but seem to last for only a day. Or a major life change might take place in five minutes but seem to go on for an hour. This is subjective time and reveals our perceptions. It is up to the writer to understand the stretching or compression of time and to convey that to the reader. In objective time, personal events stand in the midst of history: a woman walking out of the doctor's office in downtown Boston, beaming with the exciting news that she is pregnant only to learn from the cab driver that President Kennedy had just been assassinated—or a grandmother picking up the phone to learn that a grandson has just been born, thirty minutes before turning on the television and seeing a plane fly into the World Trade Center. Economic boom or bust times, war times, social movement times, almost all times are part of a story even if they are the small part. Sharing what is going on behind or around a story is the

writer's responsibility. You may decide that the objective time-frame isn't important, but you won't know that until you have considered it. Understanding "the times" may help the reader to understand your actions while it seems quite obvious to you. Remember, it's always about the reader.

3. ***Time may be evoked by your age when the events took place.*** If you are writing about your childhood using the point of view of a 10 year old, then your knowledge, attitudes and behaviors and language ability at that time will influence the way the story is told.

4. ***Time and its reflections may organize the memoir even in non-linear ways.*** Sven Birkerts in *The Art of Time in Memoir: Then, Again* mentions a number of memoirs including Annie Dillard's *An American Childhood*, Eva Hoffman's *Lost in Translation*, Jo Ann Beard's *The Boys of My Youth*, Tobias Wolff's *This Boy's Life* and Mary Karr's *The Liars' Club*, and then explains the double use of time this way:

> Apart from whatever painful or disturbing events [the memoir writers of the books mentioned above] recount, their deeper ulterior purpose is to discover the nonsequential connections that allow those experiences to make larger sense; they are about circumstance becoming meaningful when seen from a certain remove. They all, to greater or lesser degree, use the vantage point of the present to gain access to what might be called the hidden narrative of the past. Each is in its own way an account of detection, a realized effort to assemble the puzzle of what happened in the light of subsequent realization.

Now Get to Writing!

Write about the relevance of time in the vignette or scene you are Deconstructing for the exercises in this book. After you have written about time for 5 or 10 minutes, ask yourself the following questions:

1. Is time a marker for my life story?
2. Am I using time subjectively or objectively? Why? How?
3. What age was I in the story and am I writing in the voice of a person of that age? If not, what is the age of the person in the scene?

4. Given Birkerts's description, am I looking back at my life from my current perspective in order to make sense of my life (a sense-making that is probably not linear but uses time to analyze and reflect on multiple previous time points)? If so, in what way?

Social Science and Time

Let's turn now to research that can provide new insights into time and how we might use it more effectively when we write. The psychologist Marilyn Dapkus (Chapman) at the University of Tennessee conducted the first of our studies of interest. She wanted to know how adults experience or think about time. She then content-analyzed her interviews and found three major categories:

real time? (handwritten margin note)

1. Time as a way to represent change and continuity—a kind of "becoming" in time
2. Time used to show limits and choices—considered "doing" in time
3. Time expressing the tempo—considered "pacing" in time

Now Get to Writing!

In Kendra's chapter on dialogue, she showed you how to turn that element into a power tool. The same is true with time. Consider how you will use it in your memoir.

1. Examine your scene or chapter from the perspective of each of the three categories Marilyn Dapkus identified. Can you use time to show change and/or continuity? Can you use time to illustrate how you made decisions? Can you use time as a way to move your story along—to pace it?
2. Write for five or ten minutes from at least one of these three categories.

Working Time into the Narrative: How Might You Do This?

Bruce DeSilva, after 40 years as a journalist, became an award-winning crime writer. In the chapter called "Handling Time," from the book *Telling True Stories*, DeSilva helps us see how we can work time into the narrative. If you use time to show change, for

(handwritten margin notes: winter, ice, skating, stories)

example, you might consider letting external indications of time such as the mention of newly hatched birds or the arrival of snow to help the reader also see your internal change. It really depends on what you are trying to accomplish in the scene. If you want to move the story along—to speed it up, then reflections on changes in nature can help the reader know how much time is passing. DeSilva notes that only when the exact time is critical should you resort to a time stamp—explicitly giving the time or date. Of course, there are a number of circumstances when that is relevant so you shouldn't shy away from it. Just make sure you don't bore the reader with too many times and dates if not pivotal to the story. When in doubt, ask yourself if the reader would understand the story just as well if you left out time and date.

Time is a Marker of Cultures

Your life and how you treat time are intertwined. Are you usually just a little late when you show up for appointments as well as parties? Or do you prefer to arrive early, even if it means waiting in the car until the appropriate time? Your attitude toward time is one marker of you. The behavior of individuals also gets summed within cultures and subcultures so that each has a "unique temporal fingerprint" according to Robert V. Levine in his book *A Geography of Time: On Tempo, Culture and the Pace of Life*. My own copy of this book bears an earlier subtitle, *The Temporal Misadventures of a Social Psychologist*, suggesting the concept that we can all get caught up in time assumptions and their accompanying behaviors.

Levine studied how time is treated in 31 countries using a number of unobtrusive measures including the average walking speed over a fixed distance, the amount of time postal clerks take to fulfill a standardized request for stamps, the accuracy of publicly displayed bank clocks in downtown areas and others. Levin found, for example: hotter places have a slower pace; bigger cities, places with healthy economies, developed countries and places or cultures that emphasize individualism over collectivism tend to have a faster pace.

In other words, time isn't just clock time. It is culturally determined and can influence our behavior. Do you have a friend who maintains an internal time that is outside the boundary of the culture you both live in? I do. After many years, I've learned to tell him an earlier time for the beginning of a party since I know he will still be late, just not as late. Besides, if he suddenly changed his behavior, I don't want him to be too early. This different time perception probably influences my relationship with him as well since I'm always aware that I need to maintain this small deception.

There is more than clock time.

But there is more than *clock time*. Levin describes *natural time* and *event time*. At one point in history, people were under the influence of *natural time*. When it was dark outside, work ceased and a person was most likely to sleep. And although we now have considerable control over natural time, we are still influenced by it. As a fairly new arrival in Oregon, I've learned the importance of taking extra Vitamin D. I have friends who use light therapy or light boxes to help ease their Seasonal Affective Disorder (SAD). Natural time may influence your behaviors in how you use time and how you feel.

Event time is cultural. It is a perception of time that is not bound to a clock or to nature but to the completion of a task. For example, if clock time is dominant and you agree to study with a friend at 8 p.m. for two hours, then that's what is likely to happen. If event time is dominant, then the start and end times are not relevant. You'll start when you both happen to get together and keep going until you feel you have mastered the material. Event time isn't dominant in American culture but you might have encountered it if you lived in another country. If you are writing about your experiences while traveling or living abroad, then time may be an important element in your recollections.

Time and Writing

With your greater understanding of the personal and cultural meaning and use of time, you can incorporate in your writing Robert Levine's 10 situations in which time enables us to evaluate ourselves and others: 1) concern with clock time, 2) speech patterns, 3) eating habits, 4) walking speed, 5) driving style, 6) schedules, 7) list-making habits, 8) nervous energy, 9) waiting behaviors and 10) alerts (what others say to you).

Now Get to Writing!

1. This first exercise helps you understand yourself and what time means to you. For each of Robert Levine's 10 time in-

dicators, write how you behave under most circumstances. For example, do you frequently check what time it is? Are you a fast or a slow walker? Do you have a lot of nervous energy? Each of the different indicators will help you find ways to *show* rather than *tell* how you treat time.

2. Come back to the scene in your synopsis. Write behaviors that show how you handle the relevant Levine's time indicators in this specific scene. You may behave in a way that is unusual for you. For example, you might enjoy walking at a leisurely pace most of the time, but find yourself almost running to catch up with a friend who's feelings you have hurt. Your change from your usual pace would show how important this is to you.

3. Once you have examined your behaviors for each of the 10 time indicators, do the same thing for the second most important person in your scene.

What Time Type Are You?

You may remember the 1974 popular book by Meyer Friedman and Ray Rosenman called *Type A Behavior and Your Heart*. The authors shared a cardiology practice and tried to understand the significant increase in heart attacks among men, believing that cholesterol levels and diet had not changed nearly as much as the rate of coronary disease. Noticing that the front edge of the chairs in the waiting room kept wearing out, the two physicians eventually developed studies of what they called Type A and Type B behaviors. Type A/ Type B became a popular thesis and other books followed from these authors, including *Treating Type A Behavior and Your Heart* (1984) and *Type A Behavior: Its Diagnosis and Treatment* (1996); they all focused on a set of behaviors in which time impatience and the anger it engendered led, they believed, to increased heart attacks. Type A behaviors included a strong sense of time urgency and time consciousness, multi-tasking, anger when kept waiting and the like. Many researchers have faulted the studies, but the concept continues to be a popular one.

I certainly remember labeling friends as either Type A or Type B, and while these are not personality types, they are behaviors that can help a writer create a person's sense or use of time. You might want to think about people in your memoir: does a person walk rapidly, eat quickly, exercise and read at the same time, interrupt your sentences if you seem to be dragging out a story? That's your classic Type A.

In your memoir, consider how the time-related behavior of a person in a scene can change its impact. For example, during a dialogue do you just have the conversation politely alternate between two people who seem suspended in time or does one person pace back and forth or interrupt frequently?

A Measure of Your Sense of Time

If the concept of personal use of time still seems vague to you, I suggest you take the Jenkins Activity Survey, which measures speed and impatience. This is a 20-question test that will take you about 10 minutes to complete (unless you are a real speed demon, in which case you will be finished in 5 minutes.) Although designed for college students, you can easily generalize the questions and will find them helpful in understanding how you treat time. The range of scores is between 35 and 380. I have taken the test twice, separated by about six months. My scores were quite consistent. It is with some embarrassment that I confess my two scores are 270 and 300.

Try This: Use this link to get to the Jenkins Activity Survey: http://www.psych.uncc.edu/pagoolka/typea-b-intro.html You will be asked for a name, but no email address so you won't be contacted by the site.

Now Get to Writing!

1. After taking the Jenkins Activity Survey (JAS), note your score and write about some of your behaviors that make you either a person who is relaxed or frantic about time. The JAS will give you ideas about settings where your behaviors may come to light.

2. Do any of the behaviors you wrote about relate to the scene you are working on? If so, write about them. Otherwise, save this material for use when you are writing other scenes.

A Famous Social Scientist Gives Us a Clue about Time

You may remember the name of Phil Zimbardo from the early 1970s when he became famous (or infamous, depending on your perspective) for the1971 Stanford Prisoner Experiment. His exploration of situational ("everyone else was doing it so I thought it was okay") versus dispositional ("I've always been a defiant person so that's just how I behaved") determinants of behavior are not my focus here but you may wish to read more about it—especially if you feel that there have been times in your life when you or someone else in your life took actions based on one or the other of these factors. For this chapter, I want to highlight Zimbardo's 2009 book called *The Time Paradox: The New Psychology of Time That Will Change Your Life*. Zimbardo and co-author John Boyd (Research Director for Yahoo!) summarize much of the research on time perspectives and conclude that people gravitate toward any of six possible outlooks—all of which are variations on Past, Present and Future. Outlooks on the Past are either positive or negative. In the Present, people either subscribe to fatalism or hedonism. And when considering the Future, they either envision a plain future or a transcendental orientation.

Which is your time perspective? What about others in your memoir? Zimbardo's six time orientations provide insight into how you remember your past, what you do now and how your beliefs about the future partially determine what you do in the present. Zimbardo has two tests you can take to gain insight into your own attitudes and behaviors related to time. The first is called the Zimbardo Time Perspective Inventory (ZTPI).

Try This: Go to: http://www.thetimeparadox.com/surveys. The ZTPI measures Past (negative and positive), Present (fatalism and hedonism) and Future. There are 56 items that will probably take you about 10 minutes to complete online. You are asked for age, gender and religion, but you don't need to give any personal identification. At the end of responding to the items, you get your scores on each of the five time perspectives. There is a visual chart you can use to compare yourself with others as well as with an "ideal" charted in red.

But what about Transcendental Future? It is measured in its own Transcendental-Future Time Perspective Inventory (TTPI), the second test available from the same website http://www.thetimeparadox.com/surveys. There are only 10 items so go ahead and complete it and then you can compare all of your scores to the visual chart.

When I took both of these tests, I felt the scores were an accurate reflection of how I feel about as well as how I use time. But don't be misled. Zimbardo and Boyd don't just want you to be aware of your personal perspective on time, they want you to understand that time is under your control and that you can be more proactive in your use of it.

Now Get to Writing!

1. Take the two Zimbardo inventory tests. Write your six scores and compare your scores to the overall scores of others who have taken the test as well as idealized scores. Now go back in time to the scene you are working on. Vividly imagine yourself at that age. What actions or decisions did you make during that scene that exemplify your behaviors in relation to time? Write about them. Does this help you see the situation differently?

2. Take the two Zimbardo tests again, this time in the role of the other major person in the scene. To what extent do you think the actions or words in this scene reflect the other person's perception of the role of time in a life? What's interesting, of course, is that we don't usually think about time in this way.

3. After you have taken the Zimbardo inventory tests, you may want to watch two YouTube videos of Zimbardo's work. One is an animated version of his presentation (http://www.youtube.com/watch?v=A3oIiH7BLmg) and the other is his TED talk (http://www.youtube.com/watch?v=bo4HiVetBd0). The content overlaps but each has original material that will help you consider a non-obvious way that time is important in your memoir.

Of Marshmallows and Money

This discussion of Zimbardo takes me back to an early study on delayed gratification (a highly related topic) that also took place on the Stanford campus. Walter Mischel, a psychologist, worked with children at the Bing Nursery School in the late 1960s. In Zimbardo's TED talk, you noticed that he mentions this study. Each child came into a room where Mischel introduced himself and sat at a small table with the child. The child was given a marshmallow and told that because Mischel had "to go do something right now," he or she could eat the marshmallow now or wait until Mischel came back into the room (in 15 minutes). The child was told that if he or she waited, there would be a bonus marshmallow so the child would have two instead of one. Then each child was videotaped while Mischel was out of the room. About one-third of the children ate the marshmallow immediately while the others used various techniques (turning away, sitting on their hands, licking the marshmallow, etc.) to delay.

The real surprise of the study was when Mischel interviewed these children many years later. Children who were willing to wait 15 minutes to have two marshmallows rather than one immediately had higher SAT scores and were more successful later in life. In other words, delaying gratification is a behavior that affects life outcomes. The way people use time in relation to perceived rewards affects both current and future behaviors.

George Ainslie, in his book *Picoeconomics*, reports on similar experiments with adults. For example, when offered $50 now versus $100 in a year, most people opt for the immediate reward of $50. However, when the choice is between $50 in five years and $100 in six years, most people are willing to wait the extra year. In other words, there is a time discount that goes on. Waiting a year beginning now seems like a long time and not worth the wait for only an extra $50. However, if the person can hold off for six years instead of five years, then it seems worth the wait to get the extra money.

Time, Place and Memoir

The way we use time and our attitudes about time influences our lives and, therefore, the stories we write about. But now it is appropriate to go back to time and place, intertwined as they often are.

Susan Tweit orients herself and her readers early in her memoir, *Walking Nature Home: A Life's Journey*, when she describes the importance of the constellations in her life, a life eventually shattered by news of an illness that was expected to end her life in two to five years. A plant ecologist, Tweit takes us into nature and stories of love of the natural world and of family that bring about healing.

> I fell asleep that long-ago night hearing [my mother's] voice telling the stories the stars drew in the sky. Orion, seeming to stride through the heavens with complete con-

fidence, was the one that captured my dreams. Since that night, I've looked to the heavens to orient myself, both literally and metaphorically. Whenever I go outdoors after dark, I turn my gaze upward, checking the view of the stars to gauge the weather, and to remind myself of where I am in the year, since the apparent movements of the stars and planets chart the passing of the seasons, and where I am in physical space, since the view is different from different parts of the globe. Looking at the heavens places me in time and space—and beyond them.

http://womensmemoirs.com/time-place-3

A Personal Time and Place Example

In my final example, I've brought time and place back together, sharing with you a special memory that illustrates this close relationship.

It's almost noon when I look up from my math lesson. A glance out the window confirms what I had guessed—what I had smelled. Across the playing fields of Linwood Elementary School, I see the dark Oklahoma storm clouds racing across the flat midwestern plains toward us. The rain is coming, the rain is coming.

The first large raindrops splash on the windowsill. Miss Lightfoot dashes to close the classroom window, her thick, low-heeled black shoes clomping on the wooden floor. I had smelled the rain coming—willing it to come. For me, rain means a special chili dinner.

I smell chili, garlic, cumin, oregano and onion in the air...

Today, almost six decades later, I watch rain falling gently outside my study. Suddenly I smell chili, garlic, cumin, oregano and onion in the air, although I haven't even started dinner. If the years weren't enough of a separation from these childhood scents, there is also distance, more than 2000 miles if I were to drive the familiar roads of Oregon, California, Arizona, New Mexico and Texas.

Although I lived in California for 40 years, I now live in Oregon where the land yields 99 percent of America's supply of hazelnuts rather than Oklahoma City where the land yields oil from under the state capitol itself. Do I still have time today to start a batch of chili?

Rain, especially winter rain in my childhood, brought the likelihood that we would enjoy a spicy, fragrant chili either at El Charrito or at home. A meal out was a rare treat when I was growing up in the 50s. The rain-borne expectation of a restaurant meal was enchanting. Looking back, I realize that El Charrito was doubly unusual. First, it was housed in an Art Deco building in the Paseo District that eventually became an Oklahoma City landmark, an unlikely exterior for a Mexican restaurant. Second, the owners had helped to invent Tex-Mex cuisine. Maria Cuellar Alvarado, born in Texas, and her husband Luis Alvarado, born in Mexico, brought together their favorite recipes and unique spices from both sides of the border to create distinctive dishes for the family restaurant they opened in the late 1930s, years before we named a cuisine Tex-Mex and decades before it became trendy in the 1970s.

I fondly remember one wet March evening in 1953 when my father asked the purpose of a sign-up sheet on a battered clipboard next to the cash register. Luis Alvarado told him, "When I left my small village in Mexico, I swore to all my friends that I would not return until I could come back with a fleet of Cadillacs. They laughed at me."

"I guess they didn't know what a fine cook you were," my father said.

"Now, I'm taking some of my customers on an auto tour of Mexico. We will make many stops and eat wonderful food. But you can only sign up if you drive a Cadillac. I will enter my village at the head of a long procession of Cadillacs."

My father was intrigued and always willing to test the limits. He responded, "I have a good friend who would like to go, but he drives a Mercedes. Can he sign up?"

"No," said Alvarado, "only if he drives a Cadillac." My father, a farm boy and villager himself, liked to tell that story over and over.

Meanwhile, my mother was perfecting her chili. The Depression made her forever economical in her grocery purchases, so a cheap chuck roast, coarsely ground for her by the butcher, was a favorite starting point for the chili recipe. When the beef was well rendered in her worn cast iron skillet, the same one I use today, my mother began to add the tomatoes and seasoning. She always soaked and cooked her own pinto beans, which became the final ingredient. When I married in 1962, she gave me her chili recipe in a small set of recipe cards with the note, "These will help you entertain well and cheaply."

Later, Mother alternated making her own recipe with Lady Bird Johnson's Pedernales River Chili. Recently, I found the newspaper version of the recipe that she had carefully cut out and tucked into a cookbook. I treasure the pair as I now see how she changed Lady Bird's ingredients to reflect her own changing tastes—less chili powder, basil instead of oregano, and on the back, a comment to add beans. Always the beans. Always soaked overnight. Always slow-cooked. Never canned beans as she thought them too expensive.

Recently, I computerized all my recipes, adding a brief story to most. Printed copies, a fun Christmas present, are in the hands of my sons. Hopefully they will mean as much to them in the future as having Mother's recipes mean to me now. Even though I've included her recipes along with my own, I still love handling Mother's handwritten recipe cards.

Twenty years ago, in an unexpected twist, I became a vegan. Imagine a rare-beef-eating Oklahoman becoming a vegan. At first I thought I'd have to give up a large number of my favorite childhood dishes. Over time, I've found great pleasure in veganizing those recipes, including Mother's chili. Just as Mother once taught me, chili is again a convivial meal in our household. What can be more satisfying on a rainy day than filling the kitchen with the scents of chili, garlic, cumin, oregano and onion?

"Matilda. Matilda."

My food reverie vanishes. "Yes, Miss Lightfoot?"

"Will you please pick up the math papers and bring them to my desk? Then everyone is released for lunch. Please stay inside today. It's raining."

Chili tonight. Maria always treats me to a little scoop of vanilla ice cream.

"And One More Thing..."

With a nod to Lieutenant Colombo, I want to give you one more thing—an additional framework for your consideration. *Mindfulness.* This concept, an important element of Buddhist teachings, is reflected in the sentence: Be here now. The first two words refer to *place* and the third to *time.*

When you focus on time and place, when you mentally transport yourself to the time and place of your vignette, when you are mindful, you:

- Remember more details,
- Anchor the narrative, and
- Ensure your reader shares the experience with you because she or he understands the where and the when as well as their impact on you psychologically and behaviorally.

What's Next?

You now have your scene's Deconstructions for each of the five elements of Writing Alchemy—Character, Emotion, Dialogue, Senses and Time/Place. What will you do with all of your notes, paragraphs, lists and dialogue? You've gone much deeper into the scene than you previously thought possible. You've written material faster than you thought because you had Deconstruction steps to follow. Of course, you want to tell your story but you seem to have it spread out in pieces. Interesting pieces, but pieces nonetheless. In Chapter 1, we gave you a Head Start approach of what to do, but what you've been waiting for is in the next and final chapter: Construction. We'll show you how to benefit from your work and turn yourself into a Purposeful Writer who can tell a story powerfully, connecting with your readers whether family or the general public. Let's get started.

Put the decon-structed pieces together to construct the story.

References and Resources

Ainsley, George. *Picoeconomics: The Strategic Interaction of Successive Motivational States within the Person.* Cambridge: Cambridge University Press, 1992, 2010.

Albert, Susan Wittig. *Together, Alone: A Memoir of Marriage and Place.* Austin: University of Texas Press, 2011.

Birkerts, Sven. *The Art of Time in Memoir: Then, Again*. Saint Paul, MN: Graywolf Press, 2008.

Bruner, Jerome S. and Goodman, Cecile C. "Value and Need as Organizing Factors in Perception" in *Journal of Abnormal and Social Psychology*, 1947, 42, 33-44.

Dapkus, Marilyn A. "A Thematic Analysis of the Experience of Time" in *Journal of Personality and Social Psychology*, Vol. 49 (2), August 1985, 408-419.

DeSilva, Bruce. "Handling Time" in Kramer, Mark and Call, Wendy (eds). *Telling True Stories: A Nonfiction Writers' Guide from the Nieman Foundation at Harvard University*. New York: Plume, 2007.

Ehrlich, Gretel. *A Match to the Heart: One Woman's Story of Being Struck by Lightning*. New York: Penguin Books, 1995.

Friedman, Meyer. *Type A Behavior: Its Diagnosis and Treatment*. New York: Plenum Press, 1996.

Gallagher, Winifred. *The Power of Place: How Our Surroundings Shape Our Thoughts, Emotions, and Actions*. New York: Harper Perennial, 1994 (Reissued 2007).

Gerst, Angela. *A Crack in Everything*. Scottsdale, AZ: Poisoned Pen Press, 2011.

Gussow, Alan. *A Sense of Place: The Artist and The American Land*. Washington, DC: Island Press, 1997.

Hull, Anne. "Being There." In Kramer, Mark and Call, Wendy (eds). *Telling True Stories: A Nonfiction Writers' Guide from the Nieman Foundation at Harvard University*. New York: Plume, 2007.

Hull, Anne. Matt Thompson interview, *The Invisible Reporter: Q&A with Anne Hull*, October 8 2003, updated March 2, 2011 (www.Poynter.org).

Jackson, J.B. *A Sense of Place, A Sense of Time*. New Haven: Yale University Press, 1996.

Lamb, David. *A Sense of Place: Listening to Americans*. New York: Crown, 1993.

Langer, Ellen J. *Mindfulness*. Reading, MA: Addison-Wesley, 1989.

Lee, Jid, *To Kill a Tiger: A Memoir of Korea*. NY: The Overlook Press, 2010.

Levine, Robert V. *A Geography of Time: On Tempo, Culture and the Pace of Life*. New York: Basic Books, 1997.

Logan, Jason. "Scents of the City." *The New York Times*, August 29, 2009.

Lopez, Barry. "Landscape and Narrative," in *Crossing Open Ground*. New York: Vintage, 1989.

Mayle, Peter. *A Year in Provence*. New York: Vintage Books, 1989.

Seamon, David. "Place, Placelessness, Insideness, and Outsideness in John Sayles' *Sunshine State*" in *Aether: The Journal of Media Geography*, vol 3 (June 2008), pp. 1-19.

Shapiro, Michael. *A Sense of Place: Great Travel Writers Talk About Their Craft, Lives, and Inspiration*. Palo Alto: Travelers' Tales, 2004.

Stegner, Wallace. "The Sense of Place," in *Where the Bluebird Sings to the Lemonade Springs: Living and Writing in the West* (Reprint Edition). New York: Modern Library, 2002.

Tall, Deborah. "The Where of Writing: Hemingway's Sense of Place." *The Southern Review*, March 1999.

Tweit, Susan. *Walking Nature Home: A Life's Journey*. Austin: University of Texas Press, 2009.

Wallis, Michael and Mankiller, Wilma. *Mankiller: A Chief and Her People*. New York: St. Martin's Press, 1993.

Zimbardo, Phillip and Boyd, John. *The Time Paradox: The New Psychology of Time That Will Change Your Life*. New York: Simon & Schuster, 2009.

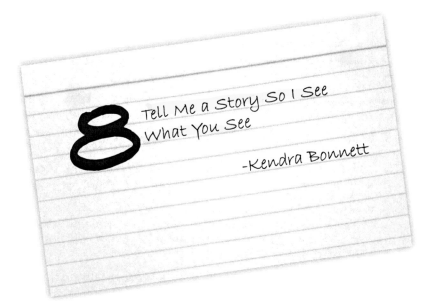

Constructing with the Five Essential Elements of Writing

You're sitting at your computer. Staring at a blank screen. Make that a blank screen with the word "the" shining in luminescent pixels... it's your way of denying the power of the blankness. Your mouth is dry, but that's all right because your palms are compensating. Feel the cold dampness of your fingertips as they barely brush the keys. Your hands are poised and waiting...for words, for ideas, for inspiration. You're ready to write, and panic is setting in.

CUT!

That's the old scenario. That's the opportunistic writer trying to pull the elements of her story together in real time and in any order.

Assuming you've followed this book and performed your Deconstructions chapter-by-chapter for each of the five essential elements of writing, then you've already written your story. Yes, technically, you've written it five times. No, not in perfect prose. Maybe not even in complete sentences. But you have captured the essence of your story from five perspectives.

From here out, you're not so much writing your story as Constructing it. You've plumbed the depths of your memory for details. You've listened to your inner ear and reconstructed scenes in dialogue. You've put your people through Jungian-type analysis, allowing them to open their personalities and motivations to you. You've sent your inner writer back in time and revisited the places where your memoir is set. You have more than context; you understand your relationship to time and place. You've shut your eyes to the distractions around you in order to connect with the sensory world of every scene. And you've tracked the course of your emotional roller coaster—yours and that of every major character.

You've told your story in terms of each essential element of writing and you've written it down. You've made timelines, lists, notes, even written out the scene in dialogue. Through your *pre*-writing, you've built the bones of your story. You've been composing—treating each element as if it were the harmony, the melody or the underlying beat.

In one sense, the hard part is over. You've thought through your story—channeled it through each of the essential elements. As you prepare now to Construct, you sit with fresh ideas, elaborate character developments and colorful details spread out in front of you. That trumps a blank screen and a prayer that inspiration will find you. You've got a palette of words and ideas at your fingertips just waiting for you to apply.

Let me tell you a story.

Before we get into the finer details of Construction, let me tell you a story. Actually let me tell you three stories as my way of instilling in you the power of Writing Alchemy. For I fear you are still at risk of Writing Alchemy's fatal flaw: Internalizing and intellectualizing everything in this book without getting hands-on, then reverting to your traditional writing ways. Matilda and I have seen it happen more than once. We've had students take our class then try to fool us by performing their Deconstructions *after* writing their stories—as if Deconstruction was just some exercise they needed to finish to satisfy their teachers.

They never fool us. We can spot the post-Deconstructionists every time. Not because we're clever or have x-ray eyes but because the quality of their writing gives them away. Oh the sheepish admissions we get when we ask, "Did you write your story first?"

"Why, y-yes," one stammered, eyes averted. "How'd you know? You mean this stuff really works?"

It does work...if you'll just follow the steps. Do the Deconstructions *before* you Construct. *Writing Alchemy* represents a multi-year investment in our many students', and now your, writing success. For that reason, I'm going to do what I can to get you to more than trust the process. I want you to find the fun in it and fall in love with words and ideas again. This is your opportunity to take control of your writing and become a purposeful writer.

...become a purposeful writer.

Construction Lessons

My First Lesson Story

Being the oldest of three children has its challenges; it also has (or had) its perks. My mother, an avid reader, wanted to instill in me her love of stories, and with only my father and me to feed and care for in the early years, she had time to read to me most afternoons. By the time my sister and brother came along, she was cooking for five, cleaning a much larger house, driving to three different schools, grocery shopping at multiple stores and more. I got stories; my sister and brother got a taxi service that could cook.

But while my mother read to me by day, Daddy was in charge of my bedtime stories. Perhaps it was a first-time-parent experiment in bonding. Maybe it was his downtime after a long day at the hospital. Whatever it was, I delighted in our time together. We lived in a garden apartment in town until I was five, and one of my best memories is of Daddy setting up my crib cage (I told you about that in Chapter 2) and then saying, "Now, Kendra, what do you want me to read tonight?"

"Cactus, Daddy. Read cactus again." There was no *Stuart Little*, no *Maple Sugar for Windy Foot* for my father. He only read from *Encyclopædia Britannica*, and cactus was my favorite entry. Years later, I looked up cactus and I'm convinced he was not actually reading the entry but telling me a story about the cactus and showing me photos while he read the discussion of cactus morphology and phylogeny to himself. If that's the case, he wove a wonderful story about barrel cacti, organ pipe cacti, saguaro, ocotillo, beaver tail, prickly pear and cholla. I learned them all; I could recognize each on sight--a skill for which I had no immediate need as I lived in cosmo-politan Greenwich, Connecticut. And I learned some great cactus trivia. As you know, the cell structure enables a cactus to store water like a sponge, which makes it possible both for the plants to survive desert droughts and for someone stranded in the desert to cut open a cactus and find enough water to stay alive until rescued.

Flash forward about two years. I was five and a half, and Daddy had a patient who each Christmas gave him a brightly colored, hand-painted, ceramic planter filled with tiny cactus and jade plants. The first time Daddy brought one of these planters home he mentioned to me that jade is a member of the cactus family.

That's all I needed to hear. This was my opportunity to put Daddy's bedtime story into practice. I was going to find life-sustaining waters in that tiny succulent. I set the little planter in my bathroom. I watered the jade every few weeks, and then I'd test the plant for water. I'd bite one of the thick, rubbery leaves. No water; just a bitter aftertaste. But I never gave up. I'd wait a few weeks and try again. And so it went each Christmas when the same patient gave us a new planter full of cactus and jade. As my sister and brother grew old enough to understand, I passed along the magic lore of cactus. For the next 10 years we had jade plants in our bathroom, and every single leaf bore the scars of little teeth marks from one of the three of us testing for water.

Construction Lesson #1

So here's your takeaway. When you have all your details and facts from your Deconstructions laid out in front of you, remember that it represents much more material than you can possibly use to make a strong story. It's also more than readers will ever find interesting. Consider all your options but use *only* the elements that best make your story.

My father didn't bore the 3-year-old me with a lot of science. He focused on the colorful cacti names, the photographs and the plants' most remarkable capacity to sustain life. He connected so well with his audience that I never forgot my cactus lessons...even though to this day and after five years of living in Arizona I have yet to suck so much as a thimble full of water from a barrel cactus. But if I see a jade plant in anyone's home, I'm tempted ever so slightly to bite into a leaf when no one's looking.

It's not about amassing every fact. It's about perspective—your perspective. That's what makes it your story. Keep both your story objectives and audience in mind when selecting details from your Deconstructions to Construct your story.

My Second Lesson Story

If you were a girl in the 50s or 60s, you couldn't go to a slumber party without someone pulling out a pad of Mad Libs. Let's look in on my friend Gail's sleepover party:

"Give me a time and a noun...a piece of clothing," Annie says, pencil poised and Tootsie Pop stick hanging from her lip like a gangster moll's smoke. Ellie hugs her pillow and plush dog as she curls up on the braided rug next to Annie. Laura, a yellow down comforter draped cape-like over her shoulders and Mason Pearson boar bristle hair brush in hand, moves next to Ellie and starts brushing her tight curls. Gail's just been talking with her mom out in the hall; she's wearing her favorite pink plaid shortie pajamas and fluffy pink slippers. She doesn't want to miss the fun and begins picking her way among the bodies in her bedroom, stooping twice to snag first a marshmallow Circus Peanut and then a Bit O Honey candy off the carpet. Someone must have knocked over Sandy's bag of penny candy because it's everywhere under foot. Finally Gail plops herself directly in front of Annie.

"Okay," Annie continues, "now give me a number, a plural noun and a verb." Peetsie suggests horses; she's a rider on the school hunt team.

"Throw," says Audrey. "Use throw as your verb."

And so it continues until Annie has all her words. By this time, everyone's either huddled around Annie or working their way into the circle. Nowell's busy blending chocolate sauce with her vanilla ice cream. Mary, for one brief moment, has stopped talking long enough to listen. She leans over to Gail's nightstand and turns down WABC radio. As for me, I have emerged from the bathroom barefoot and wearing my fire-engine-red flannel PJs from LL Bean. In keeping with my red theme and forgetting about the fact that I have just brushed my teeth, I'm sucking on a giant Atomic fireball jawbreaker. I'm not thinking about the possibility of cavities. All I want is to be in time to hear Annie tell us how to walk a cat. And now I've found my place on a blanket, sitting between my two best friends Sandy and Audrey. Find a comfortable spot and listen in to the cat outing from hell:

> Wait until just before **bedtime**, then put the **raincoat** on your cat. You should be able to comfortably slip **six horses** between the **raincoat** and her skin. **Throw** her a **disgusting** meal treat and **ignore** her. Let her wear the **tee shirt** around the **bathroom**. If it seems to bother her, distract her with a **rotten apple**. When your cat seems to be accustomed to the **dress**, take it off. Continue this routine for at least a **decade**. Next, attach the leash to the **dress** and let kitty walk around the house, dragging the **dog**. Praise her for being such a **vile** cat, and give her some **horrible Easter eggs**. Do this every day for about 100 days. When the cat accepts the **nightgown** and leash, you're ready to pick up your end of the leash and **dance** as she wanders. Keep the tension slack, so as not to restrict her movement. Practice this for several **lightyears**. Now you're ready to teach kitty to follow you by **cooking** her in a **belligerent** manner and **gruesomely sawing** on the lead. Don't fight her. Leash-training should be a **turquoise** experience for the cat and owner.

Yes, I know, even I have trouble recalling why these Mad Libs stories were so funny to us. But we were 10, and we'd roll on the floor laughing at our clever creations. We also made shoebox homes for Lucky Troll dolls, complete with scraps of wallpaper and wall-to-wall carpeting. I rest my case.

When it came to picking adjectives, nouns and other parts of speech, we'd try to out-do each other with the silliest, most bizarre and disgusting words we could think to suggest. Bathroom humor was the order of the day. But other than encouraging us to use adverbs, Mad Libs probably were good for our storytelling skills. In my case, I know they showed me that writing could be fun. My mother would only occasionally buy us a Mad Libs book. The rest of the time I wrote my own Mad Libs stories.

Construction Lesson #2

I hated writing my Monday-morning themes, "What I Did on the Weekend," but I loved crafting Mad Libs stories where I was free to be as outrageous as I pleased. I drew on my creativity and inner writer. I pulled from everything I knew at the age of 10. It was just about the most fun I had writing as a kid.

If you did Mad Libs as a child, recall the giggles you had and never lose touch with the pleasure that's possible when you're crafting with your words and ideas. Your pre-writing Deconstructions took you inward to your inner writer for the details. Now, with those words and ideas at hand, you're free to develop your own natural style. You don't have to affect a style to impress. Be yourself.

Construction is about clearness of expression. Write with clarity and rely on the details and memories you discovered during Deconstruction to provide the connection to the reader.

My Third Lesson Story

When I was about eight, I invented a game called Editor and Reporters that I played with my little sister and brother. Even though they couldn't read or write, they knew the alphabet and could copy words, and that's all I required of them. I equipped them both with small pads of paper, freshly sharpened pencils and a couple of Daddy's old felt fedoras. They were my reporters, and it was their job to search for "news." Not events but words, and whenever they found them—an ad in a magazine, the title of a book, a recipe, a listing in a phone book or a piece of junk mail lying on the kitchen counter—they had to write it down. They'd bring me the slips of paper filled with their eclectic and unrelated collection of words and phrases, which I'd assemble into a story. We'd entertain ourselves for hours, and I had an excuse to play with Daddy's old manual Smith-Corona typewriter. The metal chassis was painted black and scarred from years of use. The keys were flat and cold to the touch; there was nothing ergonomic about their position or angle. The rubber platen was old and hard, and the ribbon equally dry. I just loved that old typewriter.

Construction Lesson #3

Yes even a goofy game like Editor and Reporters has a lesson for you. Sitting at my father's desk those many years ago, I would lay out the dozens of little slips of paper so that I could see all the words and phrases I had at my disposal. As a story idea took shape in my mind, I shuffled the papers. I'd circle something on one page. I'd move another to the bottom of the stack. I'd sometimes tear a sheet in half and put part of it near the beginning and the other half in the middle. I did all this before starting my two-finger hen pecking on that old portable.

I was looking for the ideal way to tell my story. I used these words and phrases to *my* advantage. I cut them, I moved them, I never let them control me. These were my creative materials—my paints, my musical notes, my ingredients—and I was the artist, the maestro, the chef rolled into one. Whether or not the words resulted in anything worthwhile was entirely up to me. My "reporters" had Deconstructed the story by selecting the words and phrases they felt had value and meaning. But I Constructed, I orchestrated the final story.

As you Construct your story using your Deconstructions, pull the best out of your words and ideas. Discard the weak or irrelevant. You don't have to use them all. You're looking for the best way to tell your story.

Three Metaphors for Construction

Throughout this book, we've used metaphors for our Writing Alchemy system of Deconstruction and Construction. Matilda and I both like using metaphors because it helps make something different seem a little less abstract. A metaphor makes the new more familiar. Matilda likes to use cooking references, and in workshops she often talks about how three ingredients (flour, water and yeast) are brought together (Constructed) to make a loaf of French bread. What's magical is that when we bite into a freshly baked baguette, we don't taste flour, water and yeast. We taste this artful creation that is crusty and brown on the outside and steamy hot and soft inside. It's a perfect treat, and it all started with flour, water and yeast in the hands of an artist.

Here are the three metaphors I like to use:

Building

"If you have built castles in the air, your work need not be lost; that is where they should be. Now put the foundations under them." So wrote Henry David Thoreau in *Walden* more than 150 years ago, and it applies to Deconstruction/Construction today. Think of your Deconstructions as your castles in the air. This is where you dream and imagine and consider every possibility—gingerbread detail, winding stairways, decorative moulding, load-bearing walls, casement windows and great solid oak doors. When it comes to your story, if you think it and if it falls under the purview of one of the five essential elements of writing, write it down as part of your Deconstruction.

Then, when you Construct your story, you will build a solid foundation for your essential elements. Just as you stack your bricks, you'll establish a context—a time and place—for your story. Just as you frame a house, you'll reveal characters to readers. Just as you trim and paint the finished structure, you'll bring your story to life with sensory detail.

Music

If you were a musician instead of a writer, your Deconstructions—instead of character developments, dialogues, emotions, sensory details and context—would be notes, chords, rhythms, tunes and melody. And you would have written from different perspectives, different voices or instruments. If each essential element of writing is a solo instrument, then you would have written the score for each instrument.

Now what you must do is orchestrate; the step we call Construction. The musician works with elements and makes decisions about timbre (tone color), time and key signatures, tempo and chorus. Will he introduce a rondo? A canon? Counterpoint? Will she create harmony or dissonance? In the end, all the decisions, all the selections, all the artful blending will create an orchestration that works in the whole. Audiences will hear only how everything works together.

Example: Take five minutes and listen to John Williams' classical quartet *Air and Simple Gifts*, which he composed and arranged for the 2009 Presidential Inaugural. Here's one link to it on YouTube: http://www.youtube.com/watch?v=9k6h48Kcxe8. (If for some reason this file is no longer available, search YouTube for *Air and Simple Gifts*; you'll find several recordings.) You will hear Joseph Brackett's classic 1848 Shaker hymn, *Simple Gifts*, come in about midway through and you'll hear each instrument separately and together. This is a beautiful orchestration.

Now, for comparison, listen to this version of *Simple Gifts* played on an acoustic guitar: http://www.youtube.com/watch?v=CkANiY7sdX0. *Simple Gifts* played on a single instrument is comparable to one element in your Deconstruction. When you decide how to introduce aspects of your characters' physical attributes and personality, when you determine a scene that is best presented through dialogue, when you select sensory details that bring a scene to life, you too are orchestrating.

Gardening

Do you like to garden? I've never been interested in tending flowers, but this last summer I decided to try raised-box vegetable gardening. I love it. I totally embrace the sense of accomplishment that comes with growing one's own food, and I'm already working on my plans for an expanded garden this year. I pour through the plant and seed catalogs looking for organic and heirloom plants whenever possible. I've put together a list of about eight different tomatoes—Pruden's Purple, Black Prince, Green Zebra, Cherokee Purple, Paul Robeson, Rose de Berne, German Johnson, Soldacki; six lettuce varieties—Della Catalogna, Rouge d'Hiver, Pan di Zucchero Chicory, Green Deer Tongue, Yu Mai Tsai, Antares; carrots—Oxhart; turnips—Gilfeather is the one my neighbor recommends; cauliflower—Graffiti (a name any writer would choose); two varieties of cantaloupe—Petit Gris de Rennes Muskmelon and Passport; three types of peppers—Bulgarian Carrot Chile, Thai Hot and Sweet Pimiento; and two onions—Borrettana Cipollini and Red Marble. But I have just six raised boxes. I have choices to make.

I can only handle three types of tomatoes; the other five don't make the cut. I can try to get an early start and squeeze in two plantings this season. That takes planning: Which plants are the hardiest? Which have the shortest growing cycle? When I'm done, I'll have a complete garden that works. My plants are Deconstructions. How I make them work together to form a garden that flourishes and produces the best vegetables, the most vegetables, that is my Construction.

...you are in full creative control.

Whatever the metaphor you wish to use, you are in full creative control. You are telling your story. More importantly, you are telling your story with all the heart, all the power, all the emotion you can muster. With your five Deconstructions or prewrites close at hand for referral, you can concentrate on telling your story without worrying that all your best writing instincts and great ideas will escape. You have them on paper. Now you must decide how they work together to create the perfect loaf of bread...the architectural masterpiece...beautiful music...a garden full of sustenance...a memoir only you can write. You are in control. You have the power to write your best story ever.

Begin Constructing Your Story

According to a *New York Times* survey, 81 percent of people in this country think they have a book in them and should write it. This statistic is bandied about on the Internet—Google it and you'll see—although I can't find an original source from the *Times*. If the number is true, then I find this disturbing because 81 percent translates into more than 200 million people in the United States. Yet in any given year only something around 300,000 new titles and editions are published. If we attribute each publication to a different person—and that's not the case—then less than a quarter of one percent, closer to only 0.15 percent, of the population that think they have a book in them actually finishes and publishes a book.

Why so few?

Matilda and I feel that several issues are at play: First, a large number of wannabe writers will never get started; they're talkers not doers. However, many will start only to be derailed at some point by their lack of focus, frustration with the writing, ineffective organization, unworkable scope of project and no plan for moving from ideas to putting words on a page...page after page. Each of these hindrances is like a snowball careening down a mountain, picking up more problems along the way and growing out of proportion until a once-enthusiastic writer gives up and shelves her or his book project.

Fewer than 0.15 percent of people who think they have a book in them actually finishes it. I want you to keep that statistic in mind because as you apply our Writing Alchemy system of Deconstruction and Construction to your memoir you are increasing your chances of being among the finishers. You have everything you need to write and finish your memoir and to go from aspiring writer to author.

You are a writer. Your memoir is the one story that only you can tell.

Let's Construct.

Step 1: Get the Big Picture from Your Deconstructions

Now here's the magic (the alchemy, if you will) that comes from De-construction. When you are ready to write (Construct), you'll start by studying the notes, details and insights you have created. You'll start to discover natural strengths in the material. You might, for example, realize that the dialogue between characters is so powerful that a certain scene is best told through their conversation rather than narrative.

It's possible that one person's personality may shine through. You may discover that she had more influence on your life and your decisions than you first thought...so much so that you decide to change your perspective and elevate that person's prominence in the book.

Your knowledge of emotional states and behaviors may show a much more fluid scene than you originally thought. With this new-found information, you may choose to emphasize the emotional highs and lows of the scene so as to bring your reader into your story in a way that you never imaged.

Similarly, your in-depth focus and analysis of both the place and the time of the scene may have changed your understanding of how important these elements are in terms of direct or indirect influence. Without Deconstruction, time and place may have been ignored instead of given center stage.

And since you've taken time to really process all the five senses, reviewing your notes will put you in the scene—the same effect it's going to have on readers.

You'll come away from this overview review with a sense of your scene and eventually your entire book. You will identify the power-ful elements you can use to breathe life into your story and tighten your bond with readers.

Step 2: Finalize Your Theme and Message

Often when Matilda and I ask students why they want to write the story they have in mind, they'll say, "Oh, because it's a good story and it captures my life." That's when we have to ask, "That sounds in-teresting, but tell us in a couple of sentences exactly how this story captures your life. In other words, what's your theme, what's your message, what's your point?" And that's when we get the blank stare.

It's not really their fault. If you read much about theme and message, you'll find that the two terms often are used interchangeably. I find this regrettable because having a clear vision of one's theme AND message can help keep a writer focused. So let me clarify: With theme, we identify the fundamental and often universal, overarching idea behind our writing; we then use the specifics of our story to share our personal understanding and/or expression (our message, in other words) of the universal theme.

For example, two of my favorite books are *This Side of Paradise* by F. Scott Fitzgerald (1920) and *The Catcher in the Rye* by J.D. Salinger (1951). Both are coming-of-age novels about young men in the years after a world war. That is the theme, and there the similarity ends. It is in the message that we find the different stories: In *This Side of Paradise,* Amory Blaine strives to throw off nonconformity and become more like everyone else. When he finally achieves his goal and feels he fits in with his crowd, he discovers just how meaningless and empty conformity is.

At the ripe old age of 16, *The Catcher in the Rye's* Holden Caulfield is thoroughly jaded by modern society and alienated from peers and adults alike. Unable to find meaningful communication and interaction, his separation and seclusion become ever more palpable. Where Amory ultimately found comfort in the nonconformity of his lost generation, Holden finds only the loneliness of an outsider in an age of conformity and envy for the simple naiveté of innocent youth.

One theme. Two very different messages.

It is through your message that you will tell the story that only you can write. By delving into characters and introducing descriptive detail, you give veracity to your message and connect with readers. For example, you may share the theme of overcoming illness with Jill Bolte Taylor (*My Stroke of Insight: A Brain Scientist's Personal Journey*), but your journey of recovery is your personal message. Perhaps you connect with Sue William Silverman (*Because I Remember Terror, Father, I Remember You*) in her writing about childhood sexual abuse, but readers want your unique perspective on this terrible crime against children. Finally, like Mary Karr (*Lit: A Memoir*) you may decide to inspire readers with your story of survival and overcoming addiction, but no one else can tell your story; it's a personal journey.

Refer to the synopsis you wrote back just before beginning the Deconstruction process. We suggested then that you ARTICU-LATE the point of your scene. This was to get you thinking about your reason for writing. Now you need to revisit your purpose and finalize both your theme and message.

Step 3: Review Your Character Deconstructions

As you study your character deconstructions, look for physical attributes you want to play up. If your sister is in her 70s and still has hair that flows down her back almost to her waist, that is a unique characteristic. It says something about your sister beyond just the length of her hair. Is she vain? Is she carefree? Does she maintain a special connection with the past? This is probably something that needs to be developed as the story unfolds, but only if it adds to readers' understanding of your sister.

Take aspects of personality and motivation for each of your characters and start blocking out how, when and where you'll reveal their behavior. Just as in life you get to know about a person over time, some things will reinforce a picture that is taking shape; other things may distort the picture or cause you to rethink what you believe about a person. In either case, make sure you get the effect *you* want in your writing. You're in charge. The revealing process is not an opportunistic accident; it's a purposeful path to creating multi-dimensional characters. What you want to reveal across the entire memoir will help you choose the specific scenes you need to include and which stories/details get dumped as just fun anecdotes that don't contribute.

Step 4: Review Your Emotions Deconstructions

Understanding and tracking the emotions in a scene is going to help you plot your story because emotions come out in both words and actions. Try making a timeline of the emotional changes, then as you review your Deconstructions for dialogue and the senses, look for conversations and sensory details that help you, the artist, reinforce the mood in subtle ways.

For example: The year is 1969. It's a Saturday afternoon and you and your 6-year-old brother are building a massive card house on the rug in your parents' living room. Your father is sitting in his favorite chair--the one with grease stains on the arm rests and stuffing beginning to pop through two worn spots on the seat cushion--listening to a baseball game on a Zenith Royal 500 transistor radio. Your mother is darning a pair of your little brother's socks although she doesn't sit for long. She's watching the ham she has baking in the oven. The scene is quiet, save an occasional shout from your dad when his team bats in a run.

This peaceful, domestic scene, however, is about to change. Your 17-year-old sister bursts into the room swinging an oversized shoulder bag that she carries as a purse. She blows in like a small cyclone, and your eight-story card tower flutters to the floor in a heap. Just as you are ready to complain to your mother, Sally announces she's going to drive up to the Woodstock music fair in upstate New York with a bunch of friends. For one brief moment, the room is suspended in time. No one moves. No one speaks. And then your father says, "The hell you are." And the scene erupts. Everyone is talking and screaming at once.

Now what can you find in your Deconstructions to capture and reinforce these emotions? I mentioned the card house falling down. That's a visual cue for the change when Sally enters the room. Glass is a molten material that becomes frozen in time and space when cool. Maybe there's a glass vase that serves as a lens to capture that moment of suspended time. Is the mantel clock the only sound? Solid, steady, enduring?

Red is the color of anger. Is there anything red you can use... besides your dad's flushed face? Perhaps an angry red sunset? You're not making up details, just culling your Deconstructions for details that help set the mood. Turns out the clock wasn't the only background noise. The ballgame's playing. Can you hear the crowd screaming with your family's screaming layered on top? Is your little brother crying? Are your parents so caught up in the argument that your mother forgets to check the ham until everyone smells the burning meat? Use your emotional timetable to help you select the details that add the most to your story.

Step 5: Review Your Dialogue Deconstructions

I'll carry the above example over to dialogue. This is the type of scene that you should have tried writing entirely in dialogue as part of your Deconstruction. Look for powerful exchanges between Sally and your parents. Do their words capture the drama and emotion better than narrative ever could? You may have found a whole scene that begs to be told in short, powerful exchanges with lots of interruptions and incomplete sentences.

While the opportunistic writer may throw in a couple of lines of dialogue because he thinks it's expected every few pages, the purposeful writer (you) will use dialogue because it is the best way to present the scene. You want to use dialogue to capture emotion, move a scene along and let the characters express themselves, show their personalities, in their own words.

Remember, however, you're writing a memoir, not a screenplay. Although some scenes, perhaps even many scenes, may be told primarily in dialogue, you need to blend your dialogue with narrative across the entire memoir.

Step 6: Review Your Sensory Deconstructions

As you start going through the five senses, you're going to have more detail than you can possibly use. Circle the thoughts, ideas and phrases that you most definitely want to include in your writing. Make a list of these creative bits...an outline of sorts. What do you see?

We're back in your parents' living room again. What details help readers connect your living room with their own memories? Maybe it's the big green glass ashtray on the coffee table...most adults smoked in 1969. Maybe it's the Danish-style furniture in teak and walnut. Is your father sipping a cold beer? What's the brand? If he's listening to the game on an AM station, is the announcer often drowned out by static? The smallest details can speak volumes to a reader.

But what's different about your living room and this scene in 1969? What was unique to your family? Maybe it was the fact that your parents had a taste for the avant-garde. While most of your friends lived in colonials, capes and ranch-style homes, your father built a Frank Lloyd Wright-inspired home with cathedral ceilings, redwood walls and terracotta-colored terrazzo floors.

The details you choose to use need to advance your storytelling by connecting with a reader's memories, reinforcing an emotional scene, suggesting something iconic of the times. Remember, when you decide to leave something out, it will be because you KNOW you don't need it...not because you forgot.

Step 7: Review Your Time and Place Deconstructions

Time and place are sometimes about context and sometimes an important driver of the story. After your time and place Deconstructions, you'll know just how important these elements are and what emphasis they deserve in your memoir. If you're writing about an aunt who in 1902 decided never to marry and chose to travel to Colorado and start a cattle ranch all by herself, time and place are going to be very important. How did her Boston Brahmin parents react to the news that she preferred raising Brahman bulls? Maybe your family has always marched to a different drummer. You can begin to see how time and place is not only relevant, but sometimes everything.

If your memoir is about the terrible auto accident one snowy night in Cleveland that landed you in a hospital for two years, place may not be particularly important to your story. One hospital is much like another, and the icy street could just as easily have been in New Hampshire.

So while we include time and place among the five essential elements of writing, and we urge you to complete theit Deconstruction, you'll have to decide during the Construction phase just how prominent a role you want to give them. There is no right or wrong answer here. It comes down to what you want to get across to readers. What is best for your story. Is your theme about the universal journey to recovery? Then time and place may not be important. Now, if your accident occurred while on vacation in the Congo in 1948, time and place may be integral.

Plotting Your Story

I've mentioned theme and message and how critical they are to helping you focus your story. Plotting is equally important but not the focus on this book. I'm including Martha Alderson's *The Plot Whisperer* in the reading list at the end of this chapter. She provides a useful way to visually plot out your story. A second book that will help you with plot is Tristine Rainer's *Your Life as Story*, especially her section on "The Nine Essential Story Elements."

I mention these books because Matilda and I have had students get so completely caught up in Deconstruction and Construction that they forget they're writing a story. Ever so briefly, character developments, snippets of dialogue, tracking emotions, sensory details and understanding the role of time and place rule their thoughts. And then it hits them. They have a story to tell. So here's a quick reminder of the three universal components of plot:

- **Beginning:** This is where you introduce characters, set the stage and initiate a few elements of plot (story). Maybe you choose to start the backstory or foreshadow the story to come. Toward the end of the Beginning, you can set up the problem or change that is to occur and will be the focus of the Middle. You can also introduce a flashback during the Beginning.

- **Middle:** This is the heart of your story where protagonists and antagonists struggle. If there is to be a journey of any kind, it is played out in the Middle. Most of your backstory appears here as well.

- **End:** This is where you resolve all issues, expound on lessons learned and share your message for the reader. Although relatively short, it's critical. I had a teacher once who put weak conclusions on par with letting the air out of a tire. Don't let your endings go flat.

Memoir Writing and Journaling

Before getting into the important topic of memoir and truth that we touched on briefly in Chapter 5, let's consider the role of journaling as a resource for your Deconstructions. A large number of authors have gone back through their journals in order to reconnect themselves with their story, to bring out details long since forgotten, and even to quote what they wrote in the moment— sometimes comparing those early statements with their current reflections.

http://womensmemoirs.com/construction-2

Such well-known authors as Virginia Woolf and Sylvia Plath were avid and faithful journalers. Woolf wrote in her diary during

April 1919: "The habit of writing for my eye only is good practice. It loosens the ligaments." Plath's journals, it turns out, were not for her eye only. They have been published and give us a glimpse into the level of detail that some people record. Following is a brief excerpt from Plath, an entry dated March 29 - Thursday, published exactly as she wrote it, including misspellings:

> Some people have to have silence and peace when they write. I am in a bad position, looking at writing from the point of view of celestial inspiration. My fat fleshy grandmother sits in the corner, breathing loudly, sewing on the coat I will wear tomorrow. The ice box clicks and whirrs. From the downstairs bathroom comes the bristly sound of my brother brushing his teeth. If I were going to be realistic, I would not say much more than "It looks like an add of the middle-middle class home." Yet somehow I don't give a damn about the srcaped place on the yellowed and finger spotted wallpaper. I don't care too much that the rug in the dining room is blueflowered and has the threads showing when the chairs are scraped across it, or that the chair seats, once shining maroon with satin stripe, are now darkened and greasy with food stains. I can almost ignore the room grammy loves so much--with its unbelievable color combination--pale blue wall paper with sprays of pink and white pussy-willows, dusty rose bedspreads, maroon rugs, and an off-blue and pink flowered chair. It's funny, but now I'm home, and no matter how many mansions I will see, I won't care about the shabbiness of this dear little house. For I feel a great equanimity about peoples opinions, now.

If you were doing your Deconstruction for the five senses and had such a detailed journal, you can imagine how the rich source material would help you. Writers such as Susan Wittig Albert based her two memoirs on her journals. The first, *Together, Alone*, we mentioned in the previous chapter because it is a memoir of place. The second, *An Extraordinary Year of Ordinary Days*, is based on one year's worth of journaling.

Journaling is also vital to author Diana Raab and was an important resource of her first memoir, the award-winning *Regina's*

Closet: Finding My Grandmother's Secret Journal. In her second memoir, *Healing with Words: A Writer's Cancer Journey,* Raab urges readers to keep their own journal and gives them 12 benefits of doing so. She says the notebook:

- Is a companion and best friend,
- Is a place to record and remember events,
- Nurtures the creative spirit,
- Increases awareness,
- Clears the mind,
- Builds self-confidence,
- Allows self-expression,
- Is a safe place to vent bottled-up emotions,
- Connects us with our inner voices,
- Encourages reflection,
- Invites imagination, and
- Is an emotional release.

http://womensmemoirs.com/construction-2

Raab plumbs her own journals and extracts quotes that she uses in her memoir. From her, we can easily see that a journal is not a memoir, but it can provide insights and details.

Similarly, Madeline Sharples used journaling, as a tool that she calls "an obsession and a balm" to get through the years after her son was diagnosed with bipolar disorder and then more importantly to somehow survive her son's suicide. Her journals became source documents when she wrote *Leaving the Hall Light On: A Mother's Memoir of Living with Her Son's Bipolar and Surviving His Suicide.*

And, of course, we can't conclude this section about the usefulness of journaling both as resource material for Deconstruction and also as instrument of healing without mentioning acclaimed author Louise DeSalvo's *Writing as a Way of Healing.* If you are not familiar with her three memoirs--*Crazy in the Kitchen, Vertigo* and *Adultery*--you'll want to add them to your reading list.

Not everyone keeps a journal. Should you worry? Feel you can't write? Of course not. The tools we have given you in *Writing Alchemy* are designed to help you recall important factors and details.

Writing Truth

Although you can use *Writing Alchemy* with virtually all your writing, this particular edition is for the memoir writer. As such, I have a few thoughts about memoir I'd like to share with you. Between our blog WomensMemoirs.com and our Women's Memoirs Group on LinkedIn, Matilda and I are in constant contact with memoirists. Through our online and in-person classes and conference workshops, we get to know some memoir writers quite well. Some are published, some aspiring and many just starting out.

Among the writers just starting out, there is discussion about what they should be writing and the scope of that work. What usually comes out is they want to know if they should write the chronological story of their lives or pick a theme. I've already shared with you our thoughts about theme and message so let me raise another aspect of this question. It has to do with the difference between autobiography and memoir. The former is the chronological story of a life, and it's usually written by a public figure late in life. In its purest form, autobiography is NOT memoir. And autobiography is not what readers of the memoir genre want from you.

In memoir, they want to be inspired, educated and encouraged by the stories of men and women who have faced the challenges of life and overcome them; they want to be charmed by memoirists who paint a picture of an extraordinary event or time...or an ordinary event or time that the writer captures and expresses with incredible clarity of word and thought. You're never too young to write a memoir, and many professional memoir writers write several memoirs in their lifetime. Poet, novelist and memoirist May Sarton was born in Belgium in 1912. She died in New England in 1995. In her 83 years, she wrote dozens of books of poetry, children's fiction and adult novels; she also chronicled her life through memoir:

- *I Knew a Phoenix: Sketches for an Autobiography* (1959)
- *Plant Dreaming Deep* (1968)
- *Journal of a Solitude* (1973)
- *A World of Light* (1976)

- *The House by the Sea* (1977)
- *Recovering: A Journal* (1980)
- *At Seventy: A Journal* (1984)
- *After the Stroke* (1988)
- *Encore: A Journal of the Eightieth Year* (1993)
- *At Eighty-Two* (1995)

There are many reasons you can feel compelled to write your memoir, and two you should reject. Here are a few of the reasons to write:

- Pass along your legacy
- Experience healing
- Inspire others
- Honor those who helped shape you
- Make sense of your life
- Share what you've learned through a life fully lived and examined

Don't write memoir, however, to make money. It may happen, but it takes a lot of work and a dedication to marketing—especially these days. And don't write to get even with people for past wrongs. Go ahead and write about terrible things that have happened in your life and how you resolved them and have been able to move forward. Use your writing to learn and heal, just don't make it about vendetta.

Libel, Another Aspect of Truth

Libel and truth are two related, yet separate, topics that I'll mention briefly. It is possible, even without going on the attack, to libel someone in your memoir. That said, you have several easy ways to limit the chances of anyone coming after you with a lawsuit. But before I suggest a few of the things you can do, I need to tell you that Matilda and I are not attorneys; we are not giving you legal advice. If you have any questions about what you're writing and whether or not you're at risk for a lawsuit, speak with an attorney. *If you think your memoir might result in a lawsuit,* here are a few ways to reduce the chances of being sued for libel:

- Speak to everyone living and to the relatives of people not living whom you write about in your memoir. Tell them what you are doing. If you think it is necessary, get their approval in writing.

You may be surprised that although the story is not pleasant, the people involved will agree you have a right to tell it. You don't need to do this before you write, especially if you think it will restrict or curtail you ability to tell an honest story.

• Let everyone included in your memoir read the book before going to print. If someone has a problem, try to resolve it without destroying the integrity of the story. Change the person's name. Sometimes that will be satisfactory to the person even when the person is a close relative.

• Change everyone's name and write under a pseudonym. It's done all the time. But don't change the facts, since you are still writing a memoir.

• Present your true story, your memoir, as fiction and, of course, change all the names. Even, then you may need to get advice from a lawyer. Some of these points are covered in Robin Hemley's book, *Turning Life into Fiction*.

Finally, there's the matter of truth in memoir. This is often a subject of heated discussion among memoirists. What is truth? In his 1987 book *Inventing the Truth: The Art and Craft of Memoir*, William Zinsser described the process of writing memoir as "imposing a narrative pattern and an organizing idea on a mass of half-remembered events." Yes, without audio and video footage of every scene in your life, the story you tell will be, in part, based on half-remembered events. I think this is one of the reasons many memoirists shy away from dialogue because they know they have to make it up. However, restating the same words originally used does not necessarily mean you have arrived at a greater truth than the one you recall now, looking back. Zinsser, in the 30th Anniversary edition of *On Writing Well* helps us look not for truth in specific words but for universal truths:

> Look for small self-contained incidents that are still vivid in your memory. If you still remember them it's because they contain a universal truth that your readers will recognize from their own life.

Maureen Murdock, author of several books of interest to writers brings us a Toni Morrison quote (thanks to William Zinsser, again) that opens up another element of truth:

they contain a universal truth

In an interview with William Zinsser, Toni Morrison made a great distinction between fact and truth, which I think applies here: "Fact can exist without human intelligence but truth cannot." Anyone can write facts; not everyone has the courage to write the truth, particularly about herself.

Matilda and I have always found a quote from Mark Doty useful when working with students. Doty has written four memoirs, and was asked about a poet's approach to memoir in an article in *Poets & Writers* magazine. Several of his points are worth considering:

> Memoir's an active, dynamic force, not just a recording one, over the course of a life, as perspective shifts, we keep moving into different relationships to the past, reconsidering, so that *what happened* turns out to be nothing stable, but a scribbled-over field of revisions, rife with questions, half its content hidden....What you're writing is not about "what happened," its about the experience of happening.

Anne Lamott makes a similar point in her book *Bird by Bird: Some Instructions on Writing and Life*:

> Becoming a writer is about becoming conscious. When you're conscious and writing from a place of insight and simplicity and real caring about the truth, you have the ability to throw the lights on for your reader. He or she will recognize his or her life and truth in what you say, in the pictures you have painted...

Becoming a writer is about becoming conscious.

Matilda and I have read, thought, and discussed truth in memoir for years. Here's our belief: As long as you are as true to the circumstances—to the emotions, to the gist of the conversations, to the behaviors and motivations, to the scenes—as possible and you don't deliberately change the story to fit the outcome you want or to put someone in a negative light then you are telling your truth. It's the honesty with which you approach the task that matters. You're not out to remake your life and events out of whole cloth, and memory may fail to recapture every detail, every word of conversation. But the impact on you, this is what you can recall from the perspective of time and an understanding unique to you. Your memoir is your lens into a world and a set of events; it's going to be your vision no matter how hard you labor to get the details exactly right.

If I had to simplify this message down to one sentence, I'd say, When writing memoir, it's more important to write with integrity than truth. As memoirist Susan M. Tiberghien wrote in *One Year to a Writing Life*, "Memory and imagination hold hands in writing memoir."

Before closing this section on truth, I want to mention one other important resource. Judith Barrington's *Writing the Memoir: From Truth to Art* has something relevant to say on every page. However, I've chosen one quote because it picks up the other end of the truth stick:

> I should say here that truth alone does not make for good writing. You may have read, as I have, some pieces of writing that are painfully truthful but nevertheless boring, embarrassing, or annoying. And you may have heard their authors, on hearing mild criticism, defend themselves with an indignant "but it's *the truth*," as if that alone guarantees literary excellence. If the writer is more interested in writing to humiliate someone from the past than in working her story into a form that transcends her desire for revenge, no amount of factual truth will save it. It is that unique blend of truth and art--a blend that may take years of practice to achieve--that can touch a reader's heart with immediate sorrow or lift a reader's spirits in a flash of recognition.

In your desire to write the truth, do not stop your quest there. Writing the truth still needs the careful crafting of story that brings your message to light. That's where we have found Writing Alchemy can come to your assistance.

Alternate Forms of Memoirs

If I say the word memoir, you think of a book or perhaps an ebook. And while most memoirs are written, there are other forms possible. For example, Janet Grace Riehl wrote *Sightlines: A Poet's Diary* to tell her family's story of love, loss and healing. She followed it with a CD version, *Sightlines: A Family Love Story in Poetry and Music*, that included storypoems and music that were read and performed by both Riehl and her father, enabling her to capture more than she could in the written volume.

Rather than (or in addition to) printing your memoir or turning it into an ebook format, you could choose to read it. Audios need production and post-production effort, but might be the right choice for you and your story. If you go this route, there is information on the Internet to help you find your way. In Chapter 3, we mentioned Betty Auchard's memoir, *Dancing in My Nightgown: The Rhythms of Widowhood*. After its initial success and awards, she decided to create an audio version using her own voice. Why? Many people enjoy listening to a book while commuting or exercising. It seems that we all have more air time that can be multi-tasked than dedicated seat time.

If your story is fairly brief, you could consider a video. Again, there are inexpensive tools to let you edit your video if you decide to do this on your own. Seeing you tell your story could be an added treasure for your family. Maybe a relative would volunteer to help you. If not, and you don't want to take on the task yourself, there are professional videographer services dedicated specifically to capturing memoirs.

I want to point you to a memoir performance that I feel captures both the essence of a person's life and the value of using the five essential elements of writing. The film is called *The Life of Reilly*, and it's a one-man show about the life of actor, comedian, director and drama teacher Charles Nelson Reilly. Yes, I'm talking the man who was a fixture on game shows in the 1970s. But suspend all your objections, you're in for a treat and a lesson in writing memoir. If you have a Netflix membership, you can watch *The Life of Reilly* as a digital download. It's also available for free on YouTube (http:// www.youtube.com/user/LifeOfReillyMovie) where it's been divided into 28 parts. Apparently, this one-man show, this memoir, came out of a series of lectures Reilly gave to college theater students. The original theater production was called "Save It For the Stage: The Life of Reilly," and in 2006 his stage performance was recorded. It's the last time Reilly ever performed.

Now Get to Writing!

1. As you watch *The Life of Reilly*, keep a running list of examples of character development, emotion, dialogue, sensory

detail and time and place and note how effectively Reilly uses each to tell his story. It's 84 minutes of pure perfection. Toward the end of the film, Reilly says, "All of those people are the roots of what I do." That single sentence, I think, captures his message.

2. Go back through your list and circle the ones that are most effective. Then consider how this Construction can help you write your story.

Now Get to Writing, Really!

Matilda and I use the phrase "Now Get to Writing!" to encourage both our students and ourselves. If you've read straight through this book looking for ideas and inspiration that you hope to make part of your writing process but didn't follow through with the writing to actually Deconstruct a scene or vignette, then I urge you to return to the beginning and make *Writing Alchemy* work for you.

In talking about her personal discovery that she was not going about her writing in the best way, writer, editor and teacher of writing Brenda Ueland wrote in *If You Want to Write*:

> I learned from [my students] that inspiration does not come like a bolt, nor is it kinetic, energetic striving, but it comes into us slowly and quietly and all the time, though we must regularly and every day give it a little chance to start flowing, prime it with a little solitude and idleness. I learned that you should feel when writing, not like Lord Byron on a mountain top, but like a child stringing beads in kindergarten—happy, absorbed and quietly putting one bead on after another.

Fun. Joy. Happiness. Work. And Alchemy.

Have fun with your Deconstructions. Find joy in seeking details. Above all, like Brenda Ueland said, be happy. Matilda and I have given you ideas and step-by-step instructions for using Deconstruction and Construction. Yes, we want this to be a hands-on process for you, but how you actually employ the lessons of *Writing Alchemy* is up to you. Our hope is that you'll move away from opportunistic writing and take control of your words and ideas through this process.

Writing, of course, is work. It takes time and determination and perseverance. To develop the creative habit of Deconstruction, you need to systematically follow through with each of the five elements for each story segment (scene, vignette or chapter). We don't live in the sci-fi world of the movie *The Matrix* where the hero Neo, played by Keanu Reeves, has information downloaded from a computer directly to his brain. After his brain receives the program for kung fu, he says, "I know kung fu!" Our lives are not this easy. So while, you won't instantly know Writing Alchemy, it is a system that takes you step by step so that you can write fast and deep.

As you Construct, give yourself time to truly create. And remember, Construction is not a literal translation of everything you wrote down. It's about using the best of everything...to your advantage and purpose. This is how you become a purposeful writer. And when you are finished, the elements you have chosen to use should blend together as smoothly and imperceptibly as the flour, water and yeast used to make a hot loaf of crusty bread, fresh from the oven, its yeasty fragrance filling the air.

In the end, I guess it really is alchemy.

References and Resources

Albert, Susan Wittig. *An Extraordinary Year of Ordinary Days.* Austin: University of Texas Press, 2010.

Alderson, Martha. *The Plot Whisperer: Secrets of Story Structure Any Writer Can Master.* Avon, MA: Adams Media, 2011.

Barrington, Judith. *Writing the Memoir: From Truth to Art.* Portland, OR: The Eighth Mount Press, 2002.

DeSalvo, Louise. *Writing as a Way of Healing: How Telling Our Stories Transforms Our Lives.* Boston: Beacon Press, 1999.

Doty, Mark. "Bride in Beige: A Poet's Approach to Memoir." In: *Poets & Writers,* March/April, 2008, pp. 33-36.

Goldberg, Natalie. *Writing Down the Bones: Freeing the Writer Within.* Second Edition. Boston: Shambhala Publications, Inc., 2005.

Hemley, Robin. *Turning Life into Fiction: Finding Character, Plot, Setting and Other Elements of Novel and Short Story Writing in the Everyday World.* Cincinnati: Story Press, 1994.

Karr, Mary. *Lit: A Memoir.* New York: HarperCollins, 2009.

Lamott, Anne. *Bird by Bird: Some Instructions on Writing and Life.* New York: Anchor Books, 1995.

Lippincott, Sharon. *The Heart and Craft of Lifestory Writing: How to Transform Memories into Meaningful Stories.* Pittsburgh, PA: Lighthouse Point Press, 2007.

Murdock, Maureen. *Unreliable Truth: On Memoir and Memory.* New York: Seal Press, 2003.

Plath, Sylvia. Kukil, Karen V (Ed.) *The Unabridged Journals of Sylvia Plath, 1950-1962.* New York: Anchor Books, 2000.

Raab, Diana. *Healing with Words: A Writer's Cancer Journey.* Ann Arbor: Living Healing Press, 2010.

Rainer, Tristine. *Your Life as Story: Discovering the "New Autobiography" and Writing Memoir as Literature.* New York: Jeremy P. Tarcher / Putnam, 1997.

Riehl, Janet Grace. *Sightlines: A Family Love Story in Poetry and Music.* Portland, OR: www.cdbaby.com, 2008

Riehl, Janet Grace. *Sightlines: A Poet's Diary.* Bloomington, IN: iUniverse, 2006.

Roddick, Hawley. *Your Memoirs: Saving the Stories of Your Life and Work.* Lulu.com, 2010.

Sharples, Madeline. *Leaving the Hall Light On: A Mother's Memoir of Living with Her Son's Bipolar and Surviving His Suicide.* Athens, OH: Lucky Press, 2011.

Silverman, Sue William. *Because I Remember Terror, Father, I Remember You.* Athens: University of Georgia Press, 1996.

Taylor, Jill Bolte. *My Stroke of Insight: A Brain Scientist's Personal Journey.* New York: Viking, 2008.

Tiberghien, Susan M. *One Year to a Writing Life: Twelve Lessons to Deepen Every Writer's Art and Craft.* Cambridge: Da Capo Press, 2007.

Thurston, Dawn. *Breath Life into Your Life Story: How to Write a Story People Will Want to Read.* Salt Lake City: Signature Books, 2007.

Ueland, Brenda. *If You Want to Write: A Book about Art, Independence and Spirit.* Saint Paul, MN: Graywolf Press, 1987.

Zinsser, William. *Inventing the Truth: The Art and Craft of Memoir.* New York: Houghton Mifflin, 1987.

Zinsser, William. *On Writing Well, 30th Anniversary Edition: The Classic Guide to Writing Nonfiction.* New York: Harper Perennial, 2006.

Selected Websites on Writing*

Alana Salatz http://alanasaltz.com

Amber Starfire: About Journaling and Memoir
http://www.writingthroughlife.com

Association of Personal Historians: The Life Story People
http://www.personalhistorians.org

Backspace http://www.bksp.org

Blood-Red Pencil: Sharp and Pointed Observations about
Good Writing, The http://bloodredpencil.blogspot.com

Creative Penn, The http://www.thecreativepenn.com

Creative Writing Now http://www.creative-writing-now.com

Dan Curtis, A Professional Personal Historian: Preserving
Memories is an Act of Love http://dancurtis.ca

Evil Editor http://www.evileditor.blogspot.com

Flogging the Quill http://floggingthequill.typepad.com

From the Compost: Kim Pearson's blog about writing, history,
and storytelling http://www.primary-sources.com/blog

Gotham Writers' Workshop http://www.writingclasses.com

Growing Great Characters From the Ground Up, Martha
Engber http://marthaengber.blogspot.com

Heart and Craft of Life Writing, The
http://heartandcraft.blogspot.com

Jane Friedman, Writers' Digest http://janefriedman.com

Jerry Waxler, Memory Writers Network
http://memorywritersnetwork.com/blog

LinkedIn (Join Women's Memoirs group)
http://www.linkedin.com

Literary Mama http://literarymama.com

Memoir Mentor: Helping You Write Your Life Story
http://www.memoirmentor.com/blog

Memoir Writer: Alan Stransman
http://www.memoirwriter.net

Men with Pens http://menwithpens.ca

National Association of Memoir Writers http://namw.org

National Novel Writing Month http://www.nanowrimo.org

Pen American Center http://www.pen.org

Plot Whisperer for Writers and Readers
http://plotwhisperer.blogspot.com

Preditors & Editors http://www.invirtuo.cc/prededitors

Publetariat http://www.publetariat.com

Seth Godin's Blog http://sethgodin.typepad.com/seths_blog

Sheila Bender's Writing It Real http://writingitreal.com

She Writes http://www.shewrites.com

Shirley Hershey Showalter: Discover the Power of Writing
Your Memoir http://www.shirleyshowalter.com

Smith Magazine: Home of the Six-Word Memoir project
http://www.smithmag.net

Soleil Lifestory Network: An Online Memoir Writers
http://turningmemories.wordpress.com

Story Circle Network's Telling HerStories: The Broad View
http://storycirclenetwork.wordpress.com

Story Fix with Larry Brooks http://storyfix.com

Straight From Hel: Writing advice straight from Helen
Ginger http://straightfromhel.blogspot.com

Two Writing Teachers
http://twowritingteachers.wordpress.com

WOW! Women on Writing
http://wow-womenonwriting.com

Women's Memoir Writing http://womensmemoirs.com

Write On! Kay Adams' Blog on the Power of Writing to Heal Body, Psyche, Soul http://journaltherapy.com/writeon

Writer Beware http://www.accrispin.blogspot.com

Writer Unboxed http://writerunboxed.com

Writer's Chatroom, The http://writerschatroom.com

Writer's Digest http://www.writersdigest.com

Write to Done http://writetodone.com

* Readers should be aware that Internet websites listed in this work may have changed or been removed between when this work was written and when it is read. For a current list including updated and new websites, visit:

http://womensmemoirs.com/websites-on-writing

Acknowledgments

Writing Alchemy: How to Write Fast and Deep got its jump start when Susan Wittig Albert invited us to give a pre-conference workshop at Story Circle Network's Stories from the Heart Conference in 2010. We had been working on the concept, teaching students and refining the ideas since 2008, but we hadn't yet gone public with Writing Alchemy as a full-blown writing system. We admire Susan who shows us all what it takes to be an award-winning author who publishes at least four books each year. Somehow, Susan also managed to found and nurture Story Circle Network into a thriving organization focused on helping women tell their stories. We appreciate your confidence in us, Susan.

And while, we're mentioning Story Circle Network, we want to add our thanks to Peggy Moody, SCN's Executive Director, who has always managed to ensure that our presentations, workshops and online classes come off without a hitch.

Our next appreciation is extended to Paula Yost, Events Manager, and Pat McNees, past-president, of the Association of Personal Historians. They have supported our workshop presentations on Writing Alchemy and enabled us to work with an important group of writers—men and women who help record life stories for those who feel unable to do so themselves.

The California Writers Club has been a source of wisdom and inspiration for us as well as giving us the opportunity to speak to members and to present workshops at the East of Eden Writers Conference sponsored by the South Bay California Writers Club. We extend special thanks to Beth Proudfoot, conference director for six years. After her first invitation to moderate the Night Owl Memoir session, we soon found ourselves in the company of a fantastic group of Bay Area writers, including Martha Alderson, Betty Auchard, Martha Engber,

Lori Hope, Becky Levine, Cathleen Rountree, Carmen Richardson Rutlen, Teresa LeYung Ryan, Maralys Wills and many others.

And speaking of authors, we have also learned a great deal from the insightful memoir authors we've interviewed for WomensMemoirs.com—Sue William Silverman, Hope Edelman, Alyse Myers, Jessica Bram, Heather Summerhayes Cariou, Janet Grace Riehl, Leslie Gilbert-Lurie, Nancy Bachrach, Jerramy Fine, Jid Lee, Susan Parker, Judy Mandel, Diana M. Raab, Susan J. Tweit, Tracy Seeley, Shani Raviv, Ingrid Ricks and Terri Spahr Nelson to name a few. Thank you for sharing your stories of writing your memoirs.

We thank our more than 500 students (and counting) because each of you count. You've made Writing Alchemy strong and robust. Each time you looked at us quizzically, we went back and worked on our material. This book would not have been possible without all the work you did applying the system to your writing. Your results gave Writing Alchemy its proof of concept. A few students have been with us from the earliest days of Writing Alchemy and deserve individual acknowledgment—Pat Anderson, Jodi Avery, Barbara Botini, Gale Henshel, Tracy Kauffman-Wood, Kristianne McKee Maas, Rigmor Munkvold, Pat Smith, Michelle Stratton, Lynne Urband, Cindy Wilber.

–Matilda and Kendra

In addition to our joint expressions of gratitude, I have several personal acknowledgements. First is my appreciation of a long personal and professional friendship with Kendra. We've worked together for so many years that we can no longer count that high. Kendra is the ultimate professional and I value her work and her opinions. A friendship that can survive two books is a friendship indeed.

I want to thank my adult children, Ken, Edward, Andy and Will who have always been my cheering section. Your ideas and support are important to me.

And I've reserved for last a special thanks to my life partner, Bill Paisley, who stood ready with ideas, facts and research whenever I needed them, who never dampened an over-enthusiastic train of thought, and who has loved and nurtured our relationship for more than forty years, bringing joy and happiness to each day.

-Matilda

There isn't a day that goes by that I don't wish I could thank my parents, Dovell and Rosemary Bonnett, in person for a lifetime of encouragement that has given me the confidence to tackle any project I've ever chosen. And given that this is a book on writing, I must acknowledge Bayne Kelley, my high school English teacher. On countless afternoons, he spent extra time drumming the finer points of grammar into my head. He'd get a hearty laugh over the fact that I now have a writing craft book to my name.

Thank you to Jim Green for cooking dinner, feeding the kitties and often rescheduling our plans to go fishing, hiking or camping simply because I had to stay focused and write.

And thank you, Matilda, for being first a boss more than 30 years ago and a friend and colleague ever since.

-Kendra

Stimulate Your Creativity with...
StoryMap:
The Neverending Writing Prompt™

Get a town full of storytelling fun with StoryMap.
Our colorful 11x17" map of the fictional town of Five Points, OK,
with its people, places, descriptive detail and story ideas
will get you writing...and keep you writing.

Practice Deconstructing.
Banish Writer's Block.
Enjoy Storytelling Anytime.

"Just received the StoryMap: The Neverending Writing Prompt™ *from
Women's Memoirs. What a great idea for writers' block. I didn't expect any
less from Matilda and Kendra. I'm going to take it to my writing group
Monday night and tell everyone it's a must-buy...Thinking I might have it
laminated and use it as a desk place mat. Thanks to you two great gurus."*
— Judy W.

"StoryMap: The Neverending Writing Prompt™ *is magic. I love it."* —
Jamuna A.

*"Starting a writing session with 10 minutes of StoryMap writing is like
practicing scales before performing on the piano. It limbers me up and
makes my writing time more productive."* — Alice B.

Your story is your legacy...

Share it...Write your memoir.
It's easy when you
**use our [Essential] Women's Memoir Writing
Workshop...with EASY ONLINE VIDEO ACCESS.**

Instant...Unlimited Access!!

Watch and write as you follow the 21 LESSONS
that will take you from planning your memoir...
through research and writing...all the way to publication and marketing.

"For years I wanted to write about my life but never knew where to begin. Then I heard about the Women's Memoir Writing Workshop. Through their tutorials and writing exercises I learned how I could write my story and share it with others...."
-*Rigmor M.*

I feel confident now that I can write my memoir. ...planning and execution steps will guide me in the coming months." -*Jackie F.*

"Your workshop is very motivating and exceeded my expectations." -*Joan E.*

"I loved the step-by-step approach. Your material was well organized and presented with much more detail than I had expected." -*Barbara L.*

CPSIA information can be obtained at www.ICGtesting.com
Printed in the USA
BVOW081247160712

295326BV00004B/2/P